CW01652813

STEP-BY-STEP MASSAGE & AROMATHERAPY

STEP-BY-STEP

MASSAGE
& AROMATHERAPY

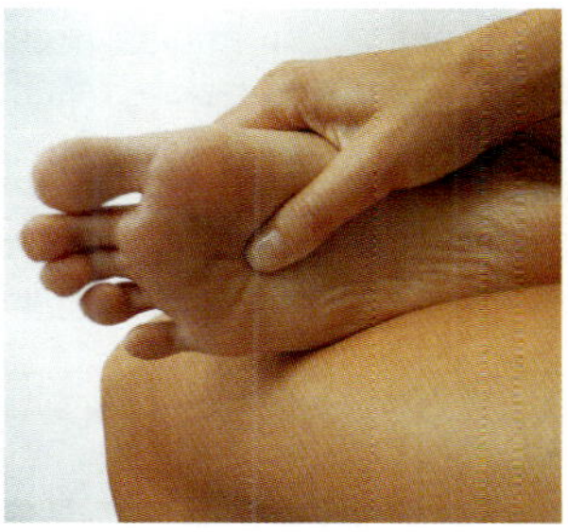

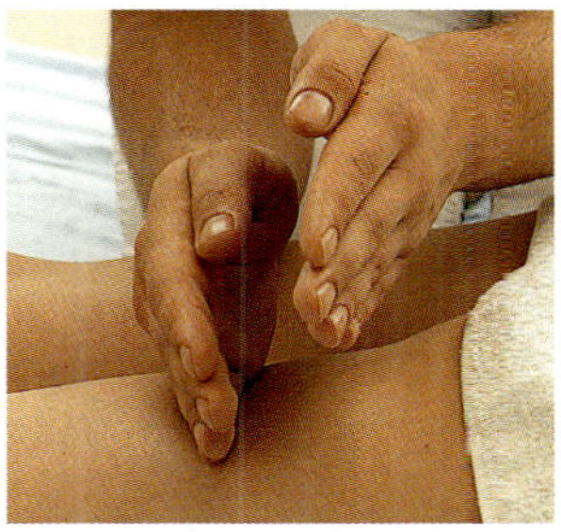

USE THE HEALING POWER OF TOUCH TO SOOTHE, HEAL AND ENERGIZE • EASY TECHNIQUES SHOWN IN 400 PHOTOGRAPHS • INCLUDES SPECIAL FEATURES ON SHIATSU AND REFLEXOLOGY

MARK EVANS, SUZANNE FRANZEN
AND ROSALIND OXENFORD

HERMES HOUSE

This edition is published by Hermes House, an imprint of Anness Publishing Ltd, Hermes House, 88–89 Blackfriars Road, London SE1 8HA; tel. 020 7401 2077; fax 020 7633 9499

www.hermeshouse.com; www.annesspublishing.com

If you like the images in this book and would like to investigate using them for publishing, promotions or advertising, please visit our website www.practicalpictures.com for more information.

Publisher: Joanna Lorenz
Managing Editor: Helen Sudell
Project Editor: Emma Gray
Additional text by: Stephanie Donaldson and Jessica Houdret
Designer: Balley Design Associates
Photographer: Don Last
Illustrator: Giovanna Pierce
Production Controller: Don Campaniello

A CIP catalogue record for this book is available from the British Library.

Previously published as *The Healing Touch*

contents

introduction 6

massage 12

aromatherapy 32

shiatsu 52

reflexology 72

index 96

invigorating healing soothing sensual

introduction

There are many ways of demonstrating the power of touch, from the simple comforting hand on the shoulder to specific techniques such as massage, aromatherapy, shiatsu and reflexology. These different "touch therapies" can help speed recovery from all sorts of ailments, such as colds, poor circulation, menstrual problems and tension, either through direct methods where particular organs are stimulated or energy paths unblocked, or generally, influencing the whole body's healing energy. Whichever therapy you choose, you will find them all enjoyable and effective. Whether you want to treat yourself, a friend or your family, help is at hand, in the following pages.

healing touch

Touch enables us to perceive texture and temperature, and to relate more closely to the person we are with. This book shows how it also lets us convey feelings of calm, confidence and relaxation and how it can also help to relieve the symptoms of various ailments, such as headaches, indigestion, colds and stress. A most primal and vital requirement, touch is sadly neglected by many modern societies, particularly in the West.

All complementary therapies which involve touch are holistic, meaning that the complete person, physically and psychologically, is considered when looking for a cure. Those who practise holistic medicine view the whole body, mind and spirit as being interconnected. Though a symptom may be apparent in just one part, it can best be healed by looking at the whole system, as the causes may be in an unexpected area.

You do not have to be ill to benefit from the healing touch. It is preventative in that it can boost the immune system and so stop you catching infections in the future, and it can act as a general tonic – it improves circulation and can relax or stimulate you, depending upon your need and how it is given. In addition, it can be effective with a wide range of ailments, from high blood pressure, shock, migraines and aching muscles, to menstrual problems, insomnia, reproductive problems and symptoms of the common cold. Touch is also hugely important in counteracting the stress that seems to be an ever-present fact of life in the 21st century. A certain amount of stress is healthy and essential for motivation and personal development. But too much for too long causes the body to take the strain and puts it into what is known as the "fight or flight mode", that is, on constant alert to stand and confront, or to escape. At this point, the body's vital harmony and balance has been lost. It is most beneficial to take steps to recognize and reduce the stresses that

shiatsu

aromatherapy

massage

scented releasing revitalizing

affect you and to use the healing touch remedies so that you can regain inner harmony and so enjoy better health and well-being.

One of the most effective ways of demonstrating the power of touch is through massage. This can be said to start in the womb, when the uterine muscles contract to ease the baby down the birth canal. Babies, children and adults who receive regular massage all benefit from improved emotional and physical development. Ailments can be cured, muscles soothed and moods relaxed, and in addition the human need for bodily contact is fulfilled.

You can use a variety of oils for massage, almost all of which are readily available. Choose from sweet almond, grapeseed, wheatgerm, walnut and olive oil, among others, or you may prefer to blend two or three together. In the chapter on massage, you will find details on the various hand movements – gliding, circling, pressure, kneading – each having a specific effect on the body and each following certain fundamental principles. There are massages that will ease tension in your neck, ones that will relieve headaches and backache, a revitalizing massage for your feet and hands and one to enhance sensuality. All will have a relaxing or stimulating effect on both the giver and receiver but if this is not enough, there are particular massage sequences that are specifically designed to reduce stress.

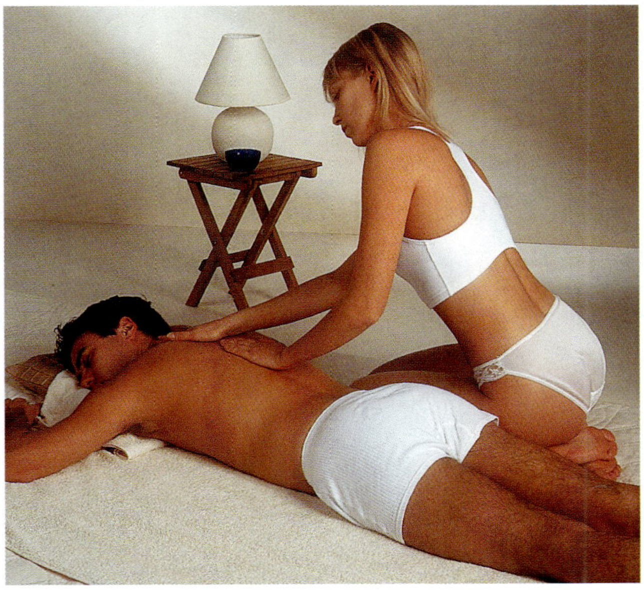

Aromatherapy combines the advantages of massage with the delights of the sense of smell. Everyone has a favourite scent, one that causes an emotional reaction. Aromatic plants, varying from common species that grow in the garden to the exotic found only in tropical regions, have essential oils that can relax, sedate, refresh, stimulate and heal mind and body. They can be used in many ways, in vaporizers to perfume the air, or added to massage base oils to complement the effect of the massage.

Mixing the oils that you have bought for massage with the pure scents of essential oils will help you to create remedies for sleep disturbance, stress, muscular aches and pains, anxiety, colic and menstrual problems. With experience, you will learn to blend the oils to create specific effects and if you are treating others, to tailor them to each particular person. As well as using aromatherapy in massage, you can try it in your bath – a few drops of essential oil poured into the water will have wonderful psychological and physiological effects – or in a steam inhalation, with pot-pourri, an oil burner or simply a scented candle.

The aromatherapy chapter shows you how to mix essential oils with base oils, and also gives recipes to suit different problems, along with ways to apply them. Whether it is through massage or other means, you will soon be able to soothe and relieve aches and pains and other common ailments. The section ends with detailed photographs and descriptions of the plants that are used to make essential oils, together with information about the therapeutic benefits of each herb, seed or flower.

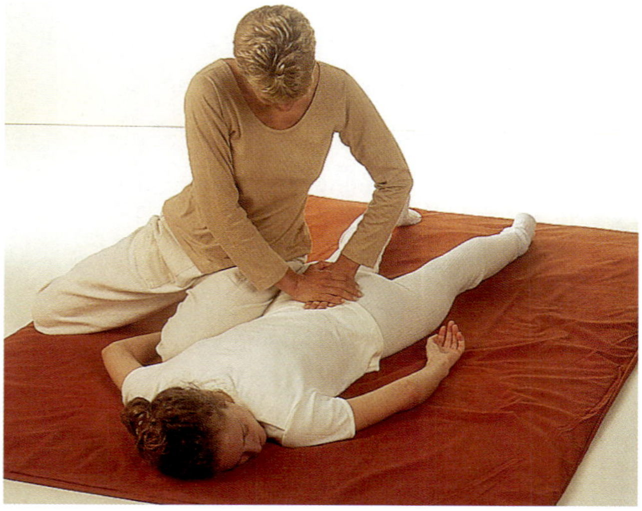

Shiatsu is another example of the healing touch. "Shiatsu" is Japanese for "finger pressure" and like acupuncture, this treatment uses the body's meridians (energy channels) and tsubo (pressure points), but instead of using needles to stimulate the energy flow, it uses pressure from the hands. Its aim is to restore the body's balance and to promote self-healing.

There are twelve meridians, each named according to which vital organ it affects. These vital organs all nurture the body's Chi (energy). Through the application of pressure to specific places, shiatsu can help to improve the flow of chi through the body, wherever

reflexology

massage

shiatsu

sensual relaxing invigorating

it may be blocked. This has a deep effect on the physical, mental and spiritual aspects of your health, enabling you to cope with stress and helping to relieve the symptoms of headaches, backache and digestive disorders amongst others. The shiatsu chapter contains detailed step-by-step instructions on all different kinds of health problems and can be safely used on adults and children.

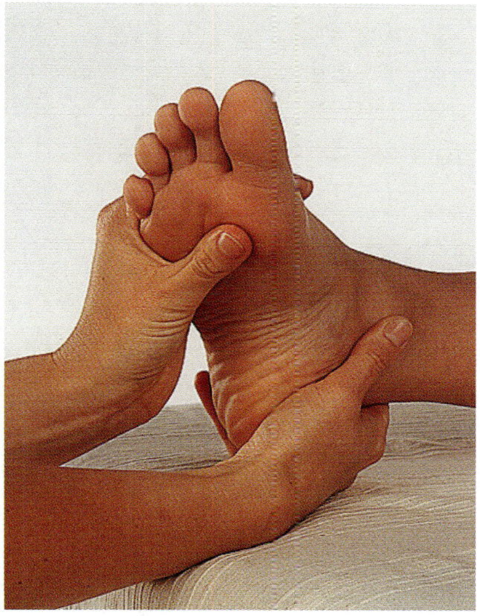

The final chapter in the book focuses on the technique of reflexology. It has been found that certain key points on the body, mostly on the feet, though some are on the hands and a few elsewhere, reflect (hence "reflex"-ology) parts of the body, namely the head and neck, torso and spine, chest, abdomen, pelvis, limbs and vital organs. Reflexology works by massaging and stimulating these key points.

The basic techniques of reflexology are described and are clearly illustrated with photographs, as is the full reflexology routine that must be completed before any specific ailments are tackled. Reflexology has a tremendously relaxing effect, relieves tension and renders the circulatory system more efficient. Detailed information is given on how to combat tension, backache, repetitive strain, stress, cramp, headaches, sleep disorders, reproductive problems and digestive disorders. At the end of the chapter, you will find very useful charts that illustrate the geography of the feet and are your guide to practising reflexology.

The most immediate way to affect another person is to touch them and be with them. The power of touch has long been recognized – think of how people would clamour for the touch of the great healers throughout history. If you follow the recommendations given in the following pages, you will very quickly notice the therapeutic effects of the healing touch – from the alleviation of pain to the restoration of the body's vital harmony and balance. You will also notice just how effectively it calms and relaxes the practitioner as well as the patient. Through the therapies described in this book, you can rekindle the human ability to heal yourself and others with the simple act of touching, and create a wonderful sense of harmony and contentment, inside yourself and for those around you.

massage

Do you come home at the end of the day with your neck and shoulders feeling as if they were set in concrete? Most of us almost unconsciously rub such tense, aching spots to get some instant relief; correctly performed, massage can have a wonderful effect, not just on the muscles themselves but on our whole sense of well-being. Touch is one of the most crucial, and yet often neglected, senses, and the need for human touch remains constant throughout life.

In the last 30 years, many studies have looked at the importance of touch for human development. Dr Saul Schanberg of Duke University in North Carolina, and Dr Tiffany Field from the University of Miami in Florida, have carried out detailed research on premature babies. Those babies who were gently stroked for 45 minutes a day were nearly 50 per cent heavier after 10 days than non-stroked babies, and they were also more active, alert and responsive.

In fact systematic, caring touch through massage has been shown to encourage the release of endorphins – chemicals that affect development in children, as well as emotional and physical well-being in adults. In addition a massage can be an effective treatment for a range of physical problems, and is a wonderfully relaxing experience. Many simple techniques can even be used at home to ease your own and a partner's tensions.

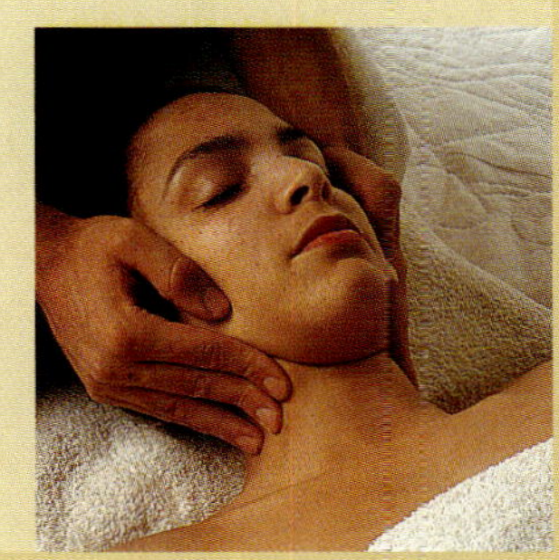

preparing for massage

It is quite possible to give a highly effective, spontaneous massage, but generally it is far better to prepare well in advance. This will certainly give you all the time you need to create the right atmosphere, and to check that you have exactly the right ingredients, everything from towels to oils. A really good massage should be a special occasion, and one that leaves you feeling relaxed, calm, gentle and well.

CREATING THE MOOD

Creating the right environment and space for treatment will definitely help make the massage an even more quietly relaxing and beneficial experience. Before you start, though, make sure that the room is pleasantly warm and that the massage room is sufficiently furnished for your partner to be completely comfortable. Make sure you have plenty of towels or a sheet handy to cover areas not being worked on – remember that if you are working on the floor, draughts can give exposed flesh some very unrelaxing goose-pimples. If you are using oil, place it in a convenient spot where you can reach it easily without the risk of knocking it over.

Preparing yourself is important too; physically this means removing watches and jewellery, trimming nails and wearing loose, comfortable clothing, ideally short-sleeved. Try to do a few stretches and take a few deep breaths to help you to feel calm; if you give a massage when you are tense yourself, this may be transmitted to your massage partner. This can work the other way round too, so feel prepared mentally to let go of any tensions that you feel coming from the other person's body, and avoid absorbing his or her stresses.

When using oil, pour it on to your own hands first to warm it up, never directly on to your partner. Cold oil will be extremely unsettling. The oil may be placed in a bowl, glass bottle or even a squeezy bottle for ease of use. Spread the oil slowly on to the body, and gradually begin.

Gently scented oils have long been a massage favourite.

MASSAGE OILS

The worldwide preference is for locally available oils, usually vegetable oils, to help the hands flow and glide over the skin. Olive oil, goose grease, goat butter and other ingredients have all been used successfully at various times; in parts of Africa a handful of oily dough is actually used to absorb dirt and toxins from the skin as the massage soothes and relaxes the muscles.

Some oils are far more pleasant and versatile than others, and have a beneficial effect on the skin in themselves. Probably the most useful oil, and the one most widely used in professional massage, is that of Sweet Almond. It is light, non-greasy and easily absorbed by the skin. Grapeseed oil seems to suit oily skins quite well; it is reasonably priced and probably more widely available.

Rather thicker, but still useful, is Soya oil. For dry skins a little Wheatgerm oil (but not if the person has a wheat allergy) or Avocado oil may be added. Nut oils such as Walnut are also rich but a bit sticky, and do not smell too good on the skin. Sunflower oil may be used for massage if nothing else is available, though it may give a slight hint of salad dressing! Olive oil can be used though that largely depends on how heavily flavoured it is; it is certainly a traditional favourite in Mediterranean countries. Finally, do not use mineral oils because they sit on the surface of the skin and tend to feel very greasy.

When giving a massage you can choose from a wide range of oils.

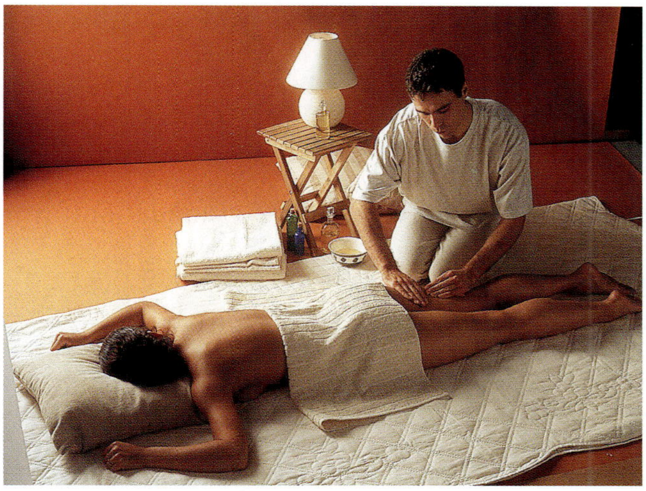

When giving a massage, always stay calm and relaxed because tense vibrations will promptly be picked up by your partner.

Essential Oils

As an alternative, try using essential oils which can be added to these base oils for two reasons – to add fragrance and to give extra therapeutic effects. These oils are highly concentrated and should always be treated with great respect. However, if you are in any doubt whatsoever, do not use them, and if any skin irritation does occur, wash off the offending oil immediately.

Most essential oils are now conveniently sold in dropper bottles, and it is absolutely imperative that they are only used in a diluted form on the skin. A generally safe level is considered to be 1 per cent, which is the equivalent of using just one drop of essential oil to 5ml/1 tsp of base oil. Never be tempted to try and use more than the recommended amount – this is actually counter-productive, doing more harm than good.

Adding essential oils to vegetable oils invariably works well because the latter can contribute their own health-giving properties. The best vegetable oils include Almond, which is high in vitamin D. Borage is an incredibly good source of GLA, and is frequently used to tackle eczema and psoriasis. If you need vitamin E, look no further than Jojoba oil, which has the added benefit of containing anti-bacterial agents which can help cure acne. Peachnut oil is also a good provider of vitamin E, and has the added bonus of toning up the skin, making it more elastic and supple. Try it as a facial massage.

All-purpose vegetable oils that are also worth using include Grapeseed. It suits all skin types, but being refined is best mixed with an enriching agent such as Almond oil. Safflower oil has the twin advantage of being inexpensive to buy and widely available, and it makes a very good base. So too does Sunflower oil, which is rich in vitamins and minerals.

As you get more skilled in the art of mixing oils, you will find that you can blend different essential oils together. When they are blended a particular chemical reaction occurs, creating a new compound. For example, by adding quantities of Lavender to Bergamot you can actually increase the sedative effect. However, if you add Lemon to Bergamot you increase its power to enhance and uplift. Mixing two essential oils in this way to alter effects subtly is known as synergy. It is an extremely useful means of letting you tackle several conditions simultaneously, especially your emotional and physical needs. With a bit of practice you will gradually learn exactly what ratio of oils you need, depending on your mood swings and current condition.

Getting the right scent is equally important. At first it seems quite bewildering. Will Almond oil or Sesame oil alone provide the best results, or should they be mixed, and in what quantities? By following established "recipes", you will gradually learn which oils mix best, and once you are confident at handling them you can start altering the quantities to suit your own specific needs. It is worth noting, though, that essential oils have been divided into three separate sections or "notes" to help you achieve the right balance when creating a scent. The three notes are called the top, middle and base, and theoretically a fine blend will contain one oil from each note.

The top notes are best described as fresh and immediately detectable because the oil evaporates at such a fast rate. The scent is immediately present. The core of the mix, the middle note, provides a deeper scent that wafts through, following the top note, and the base note adds a final, marvellous rich perfume. Be aware that you will need a higher quantity of top notes because the oils do evaporate so quickly. A sensible, general ratio would be 3 (top) – 2 (middle) – 2 (base).

For a generally relaxing massage blend, try essential oils of Lavender and Marjoram in equal amounts in a base vegetable oil. Both of these will help to release those tense, tired, over-stressed muscles, and will induce a general sense of well-being, followed by a warm, relaxed glow. They are highly effective. For a slightly more invigorating, uplifting blend, try essential oils of Bergamot and Geranium in your massage oil. Both have a refreshing effect on the whole system. To release tensions, and also to help increase the libido, try a dilution of an exotic, luxurious blend of essential oils of Rose and Sandalwood.

Use Bergamot oil with care – it can cause sensitivity to sunlight.

basic strokes

There are dozens of kinds of massage movements, each having a specific effect on the body. However, the pattern of each massage invariably follows certain fundamental principles. This crucially always begins with the initial contact; the confident, unhurried, relaxed way that you first touch your massage partner which lays the foundation for a long, soothing experience. It is well worth taking time to make sure you get this right.

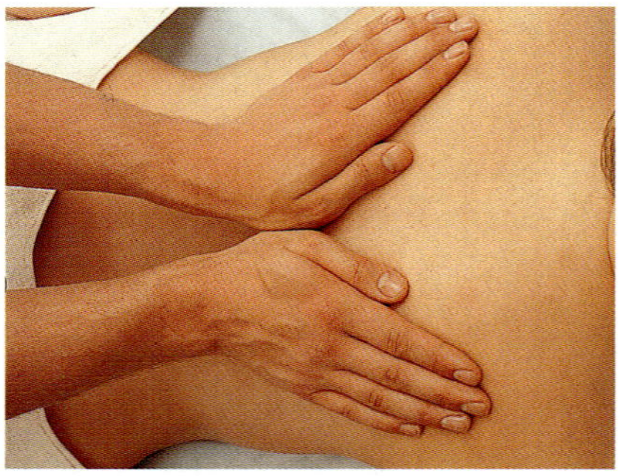

1 Gliding strokes involves the use of the whole hand in smooth movements.

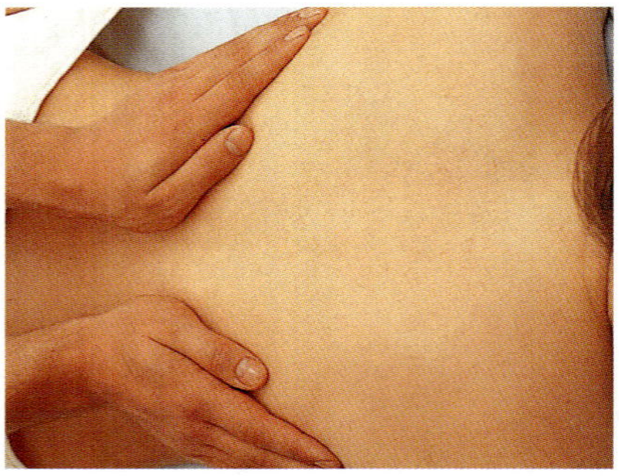

2 Apply even pressure as you move over the skin. Use plenty of oil.

GLIDING

A massage usually starts with slow, broad, relatively superficial movements, leading to deeper and perhaps more specific techniques on smaller areas of spasm or tension. If the person needs invigorating or toning up, then faster movements may be used, and finally more stretching or stroking movements to finish the massage session in a relaxed way. The first and last massage movements often consist of these gliding strokes.

CIRCLING

An allied form of movement is circling, where the hands move over large areas of muscle in a circular motion. Since tension within muscles can produce knotted areas which may need working along or across the length of the fibres, this circular action releases the knots before deeper movements are used.

Circling may be carried out with just one hand, or both hands can be used, one on top of the other, for greater depth and stability of action. Like the gliding motions, circling is essentially a slow, relaxing type of movement and should not be rushed.

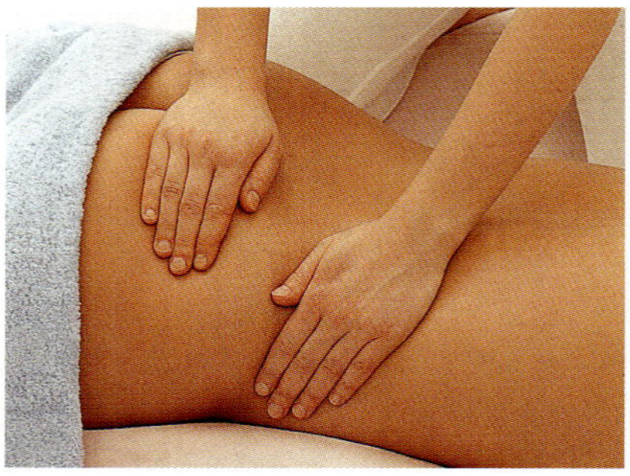

1 A variation on simple circling uses both hands. As with all massage strokes, keep your own body comfortable and avoid tensing your hands or arms.

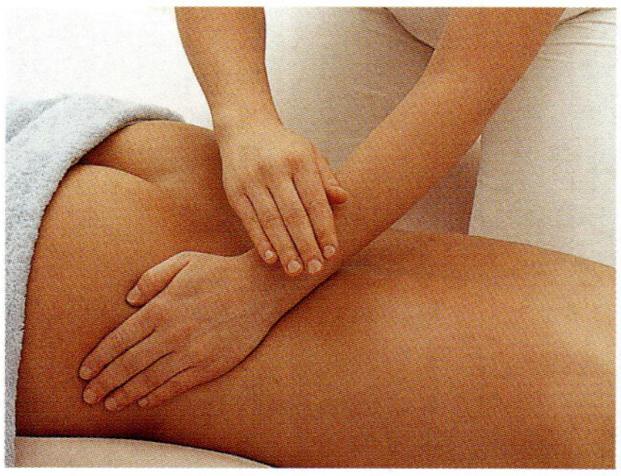

2 Take one hand around in a circle, then the other. This gradually builds up its own momentum and energy, and can be extremely calming and soothing.

Caution

Do not attempt deep work if at all unsure of the effect, or if pain occurs. Underdo rather than overdo massage – effleurage and petrissage movements can make a complete and thoroughly relaxing massage.

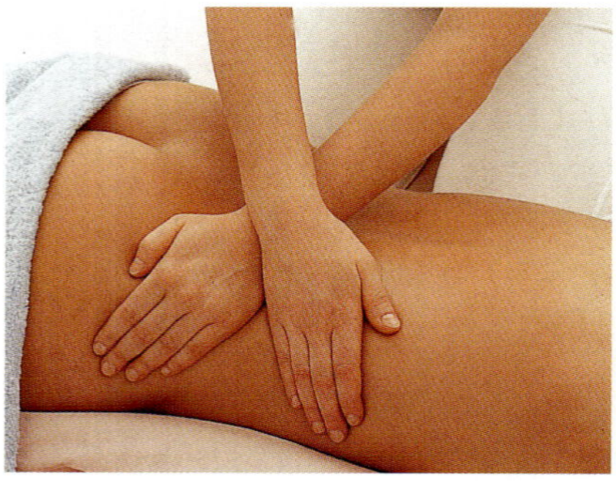

3 The key to success is overlapping the hands so that they follow one another smoothly. Make this action as unforced and flowing as you can.

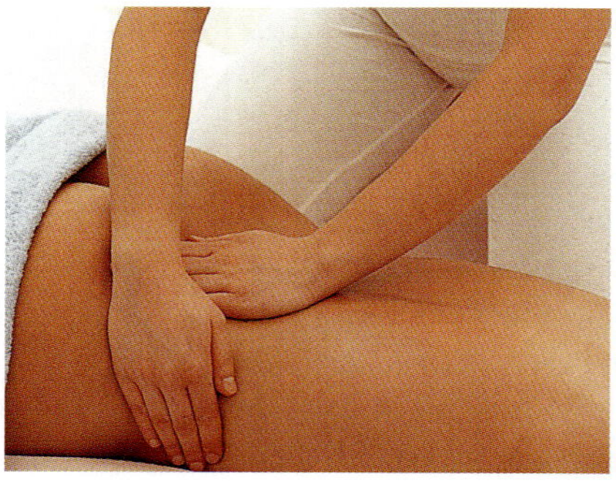

4 Gradually move the small and large circling movements of your hands up and down the back, from the base of the spine to near the neck.

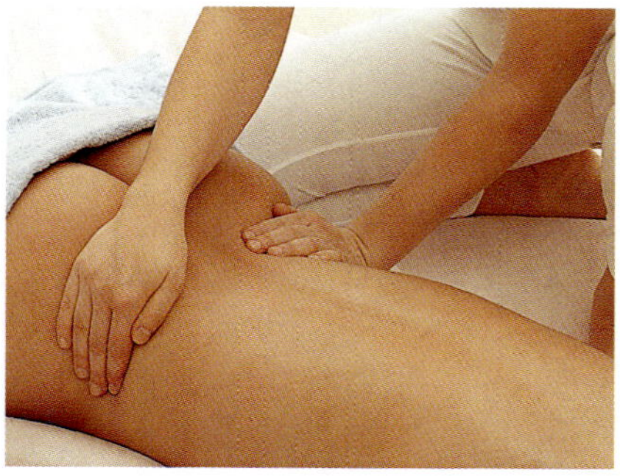

Gradually push one hand against the other in a wringing movement.

WRINGING

Another important type of movement is wringing, where the action of one hand against the other creates a powerful squeezing action. When performed on the back, for example, the person's own spine acts as a kind of block against which the muscles can be wrung. This highly useful technique enables the speedy removal of any waste matter from muscles which are much too stiff and tense.

Do not be at all surprised by the mention of waste matter. All muscular activity actually produces potentially toxic waste materials, notably lactic acid. If the person also gets tense and stiff, these wastes are quickly trapped within the muscles, making them even stiffer with far more aching. Wringing is an extremely effective way of encouraging the removal of lactic acid and any other waste matter, which in turn allows new blood to flood in, bringing oxygen and fresh nutrients to individual cells.

PRESSURE TECHNIQUES

As a massage treatment progresses, general techniques such as gliding and circling often change into more detailed and specific work on smaller areas of spasm. Professional massage therapists may move to even deeper work with firm pressure, using thumbs and fingers. Pressure is achieved by steadily leaning into the movement with the whole body, not by tensing your hands. Thinner people usually need lighter pressure.

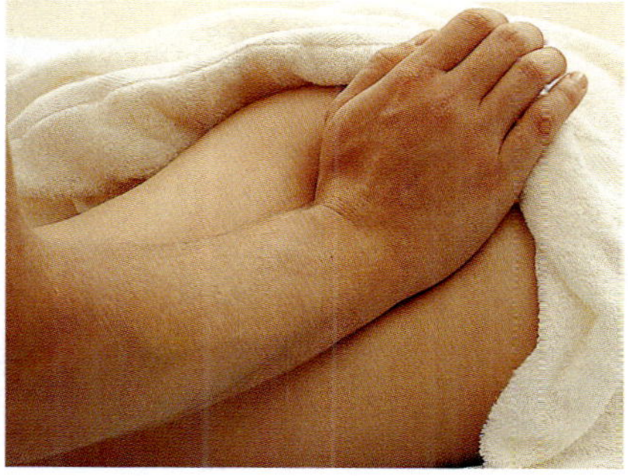

1 The flat heel of the hand gives a broad, firm, no-nonsense effect.

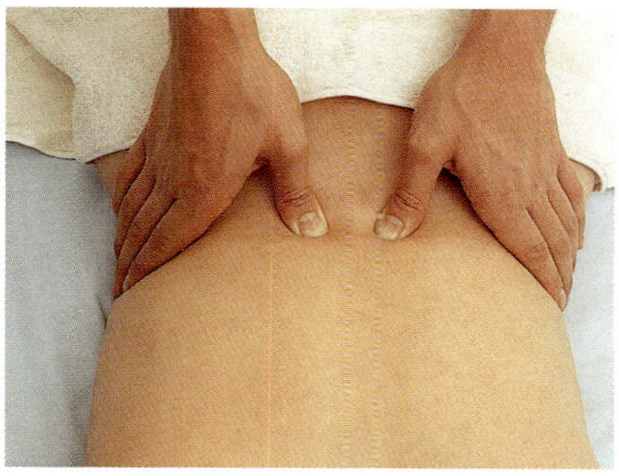

2 The thumbs can be used to exert the most precise kinds of pressure.

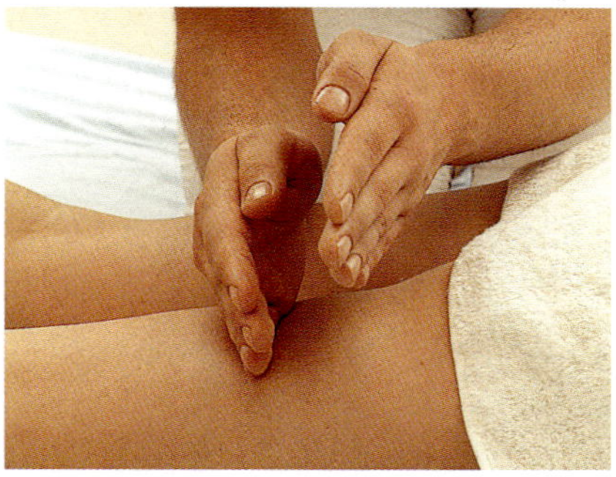

Light hacking movements are excellent for stimulating the circulation.

PERCUSSION

If someone has a generally sluggish system, or needs invigorating, then faster techniques can be useful. The term for these strokes is percussion, or tapotement. Unlike the other strokes that are described here, they need to be performed quickly, to stimulate the circulation under the skin, and to tone the associated muscles (pummelling with loose fists is excellent at toning larger muscles). One of the best known of these movements is hacking, in which the sides of the fingers are used to flick rhythmically up and down to create a slightly stinging sensation. Despite being the movement that most people think typifies a massage, it is not a major part of massage, but does have good results. Cupping is a similar stroke which helps bring blood to the area being massaged. It is used when treating medical conditions such as cystic fibrosis when a lot of thick, sticky mucus can build up in the lungs. Cupping on the back helps loosen this mucus.

KNEADING

After the recipient has been relaxed by steady stroking or gliding movements and any tense muscles start to release, a professional therapist may well begin to use deeper techniques to soften the knotted areas. The general term for many of these movements is petrissage, and they involve a firm, squeezing action to encourage all waste matter to be pumped out of the muscles, so allowing fresh, oxygenated blood to flow in.

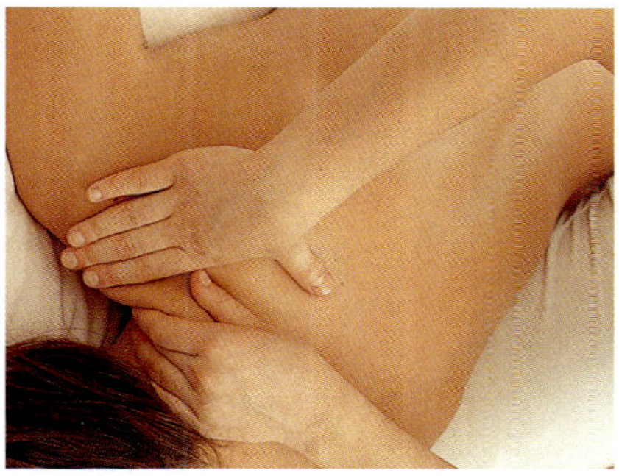

1 Kneading with alternate hands helps to loosen any tense, knotted muscles.

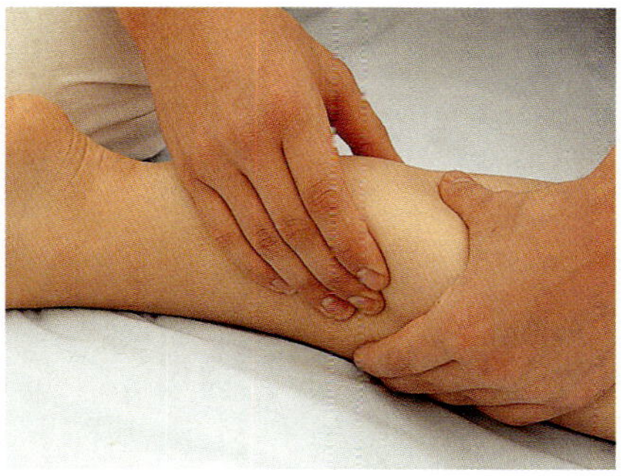

2 On smaller areas like the calves, use less pressure to avoid discomfort.

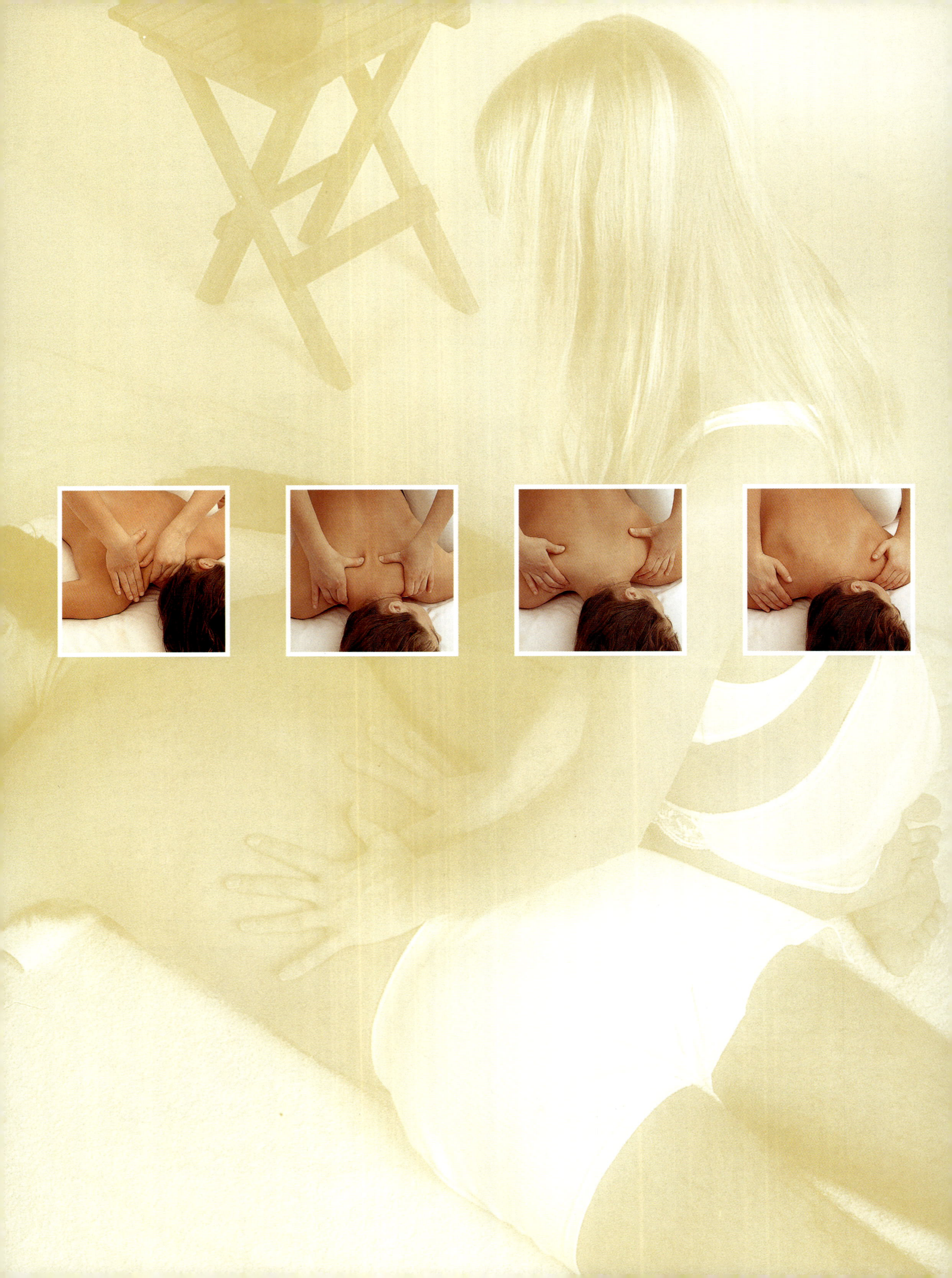

massage sequences
massage sequences

massage sequences

Probably the best way to improve and deepen a relationship is to increase caring physical contact, and massage is an ideal approach. The ability to ease tensions and deeply relax during a massage is very satisfying both for the giver and the receiver.

You can give massage to another person, or just to yourself, but whichever you choose, both are very valable in therapeutic and emotional terms. Massage can help soothe aching and tired muscles, or it can help in releasing anxiety and tension stored in muscles.

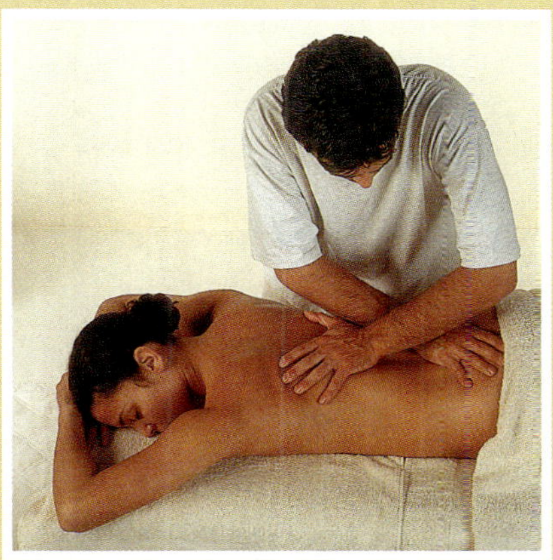

Massage does not have to be limited to yourself or your life partner; there are other members of the family, friends or colleagues who can all be helped in this way, and a better rapport will be developed with them too.

Being massaged by someone else does mean that you can let go of your muscles more completely, than if you are massaging yourself. Being massaged by another person does require a certain amount of trust and if you are massaging a person you do not know too well, do be sensitive to this. Massage practitioners are well aware that they are being given permission to make a deep contact with their clients, which is quite a privilege.

When preparing for a massage, take a few moments to make sure that you have created the right environment. Check that the person is warm and comfortable, and that you have easy access to the part of the body needing massage. You can make a room more comfortable and relaxing by ensuring that no-one can see in from the outside, by darkening the room and by playing some gentle music. When giving a massage, remember to place everything that you might need close at hand, such as oils, talcum powder, cushions and extra towels.

Be aware that what is comfortable pressure for one person may feel like tickling or painful to another. So take care and tailor your massage to each person.

tense neck easer

Aching, tense, tired muscles are undoubtedly most usually experienced in the neck and shoulders. What is more, as you begin to get tired, your posture tends to sag and droop and the rounded shape makes your shoulders ache even more. Although it is actually most relaxing to lie down and have a long, deep massage, a self-massage can easily be done. It is extremely effective, does not take long, and leaves you feeling fine.

1 A simple movement is to shrug your shoulders, exaggerating the movement by lifting them up as far as possible and then letting them drop right down, and relaxing completely. This form of massage does not even involve using your hands.

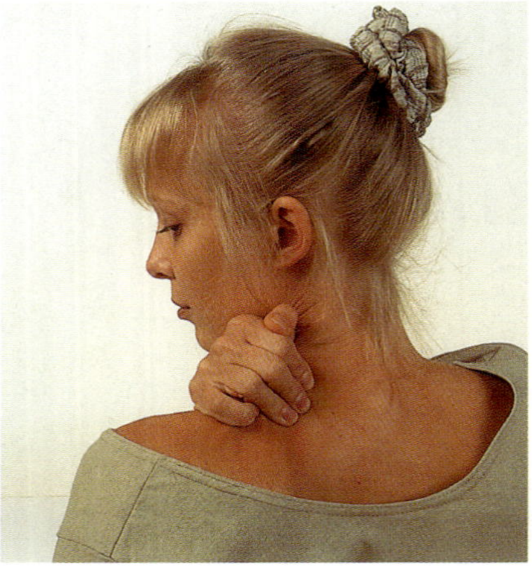

2 One of the best massage techniques for removing any waste matter from tired muscles and getting fresh, oxygenated blood into them, is kneading. You can do this to yourself by firmly gripping your opposite shoulder with your hand and using a squeezing motion.

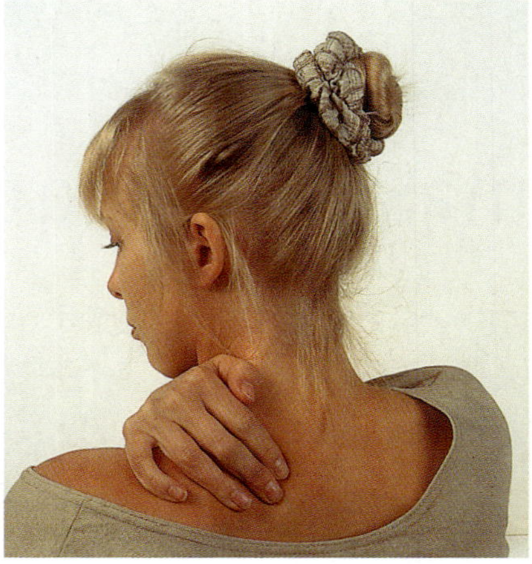

3 Take your time and move your right hand quite slowly along the top and back of the left shoulder, squeezing firmly several times. Now repeat the exercise exactly on the other shoulder, this time using your left hand.

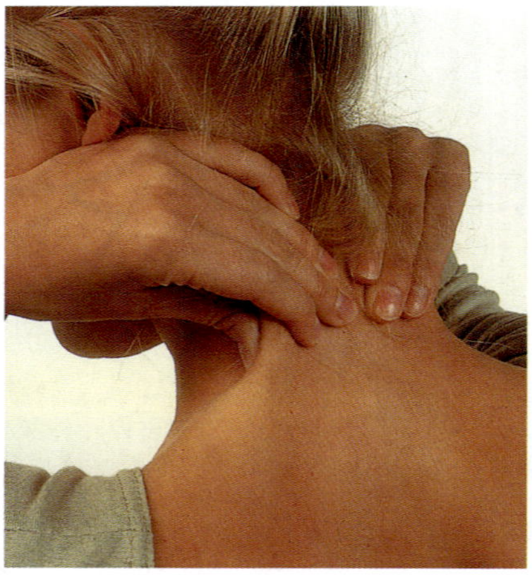

4 Next with the fingers of both hands, grip the back of your neck and squeeze slowly or rapidly in a circular motion. This very helpful technique will help you to relax all those muscles that lead up either side of the neck.

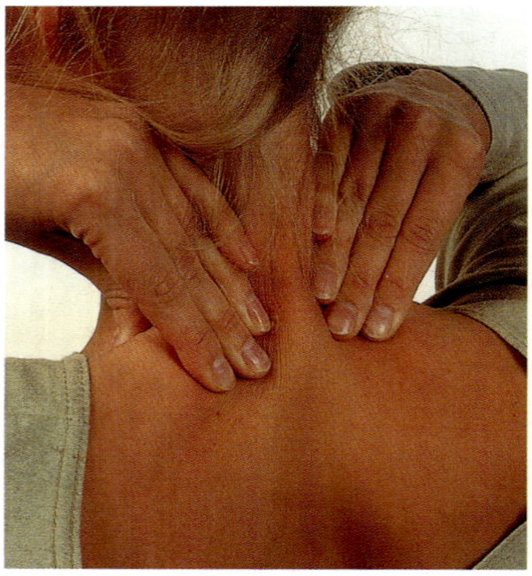

5 Slowly work up as far as the base of the skull, and then work right down again towards the shoulders.

6 To work more deeply into the neck, move the thumbs in a circular movement across the back of the neck, and then right up into the base of the skull. You will soon feel the bone as you start applying quite moderate pressure.

head revitalizer

Almost everyone at some time or another suffers from headaches. They can have a multitude of causes, such as spending too much time in front of a VDU, anxiety, insomnia, fatigue or sinus congestion. However, the most common cause is from tension after periods of stress. Use this simple self-massage sequence to help ease headaches, whatever their cause, and to increase vitality. It will also help you to focus your mind.

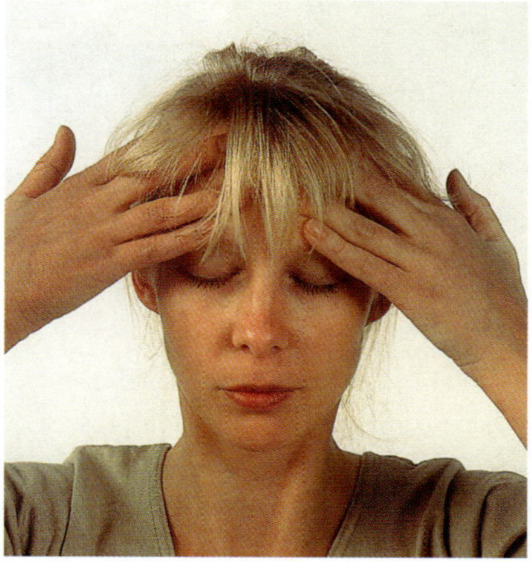

1 Use small, circling movements with the fingers, working steadily down from the forehead, then down around the temples and over your cheeks.

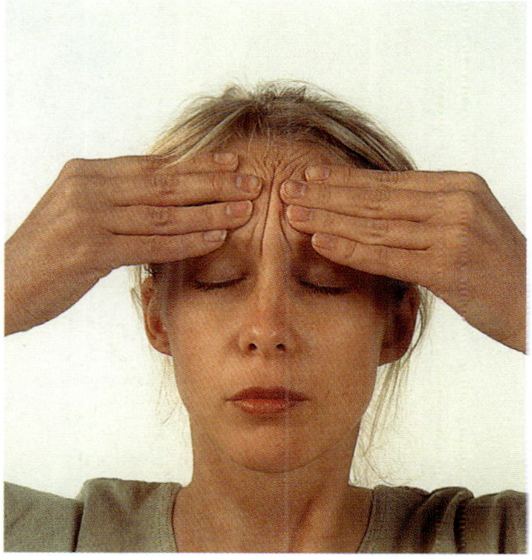

2 Use firm pressure and work slowly to ease tensions out of the facial muscles.

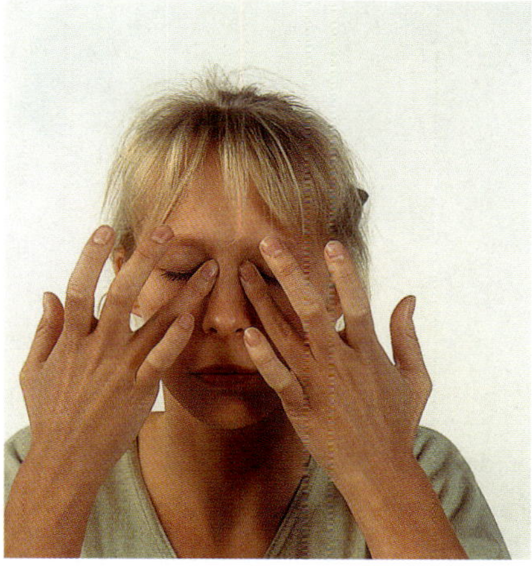

3 You can also use your fingers to gently and firmly press the area just under the eye socket, by your nose. Build up a satisfying regular rhythm.

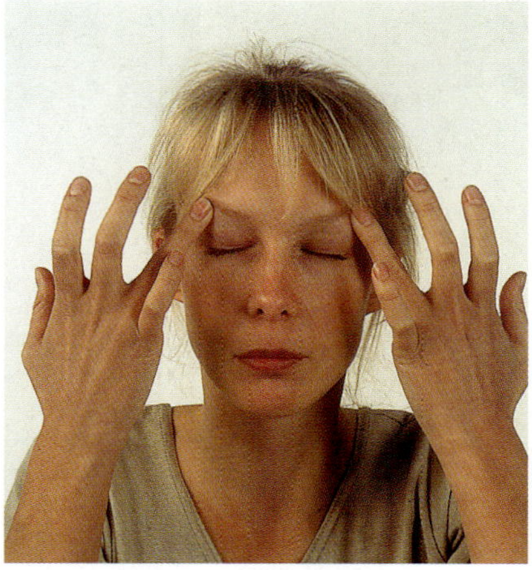

4 Next, smooth firmly and satisfyingly around the arc of your eye socket immediately beneath your brow bone.

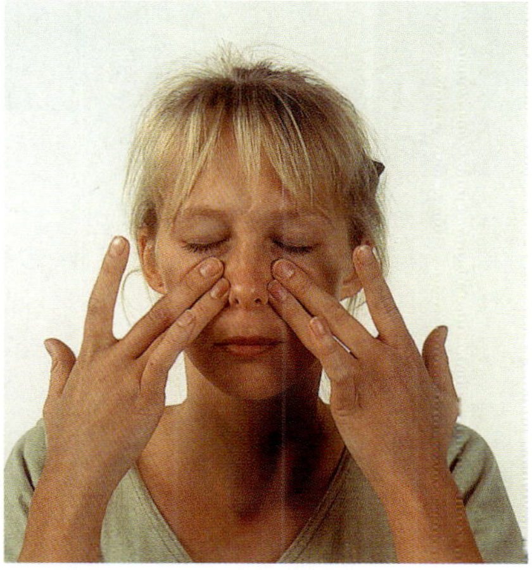

5 Work across the cheeks and along each side of the nose, then move on to the jaw line which is often tense. Try not to pull downwards on the skin. Instead, let the circling movements smooth away the stresses, and gently lift the face as you work. All these techniques can be used at any time of day.

Key Tips

- Headaches are very rarely symptoms of serious disorders. The pain comes from the membranes surrounding the brain, the scalp and the blood vessels.
- There are almost as many types as causes. The causes include a tension-tightening of the muscles from the neck up. This can stay localized or set up a chain reaction, with the pain passing into the head.
- Typical causes include hangovers, bad posture, excessive noise, too much sleep and lack of fresh air. It is also vital to have a regular intake of food.
- Some people might find that certain foods, such as red wine, can trigger attacks. The moment you feel the first signs of a headache, stop what you are doing and relax. The pain is better tackled now than later.

instant revitalizer

Do you find that you always run out of steam by eleven o'clock, or four o'clock? Have you got to be bright and alert for an early morning meeting, a long drive, picking up the kids or going out to a party where you need to impress? At any time of the day your energy can suddenly flag, without any warning. One moment you are fine, the next you are struggling. Give yourself an instant "wake-up" with this effective routine.

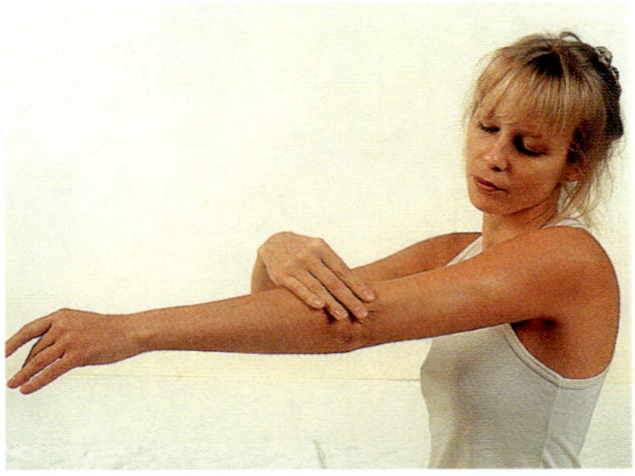

1 Do a kneading action on the arms, from the wrist to the shoulder and back again using a firm squeezing movement.

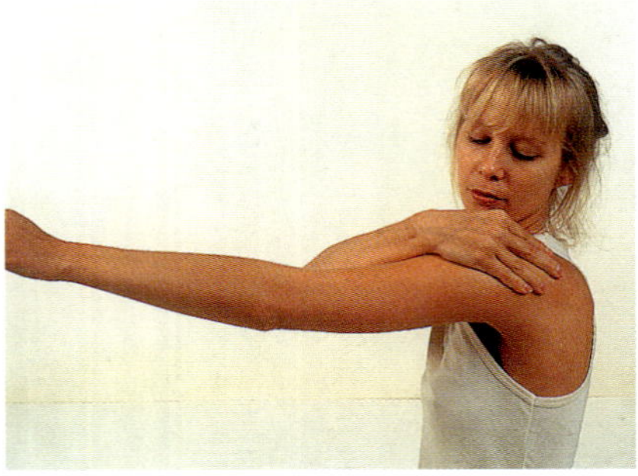

2 Knead more quickly than is normal in a massage. This technique will invigorate each arm and shoulder in turn.

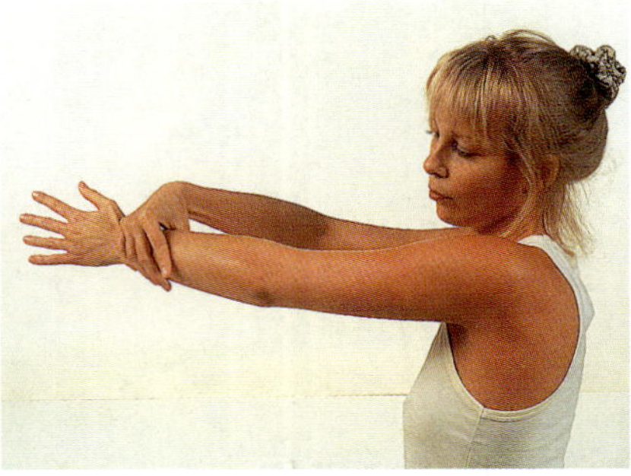

3 Then rub firmly and swiftly up the outside of each arm which will gradually stimulate and improve your circulation.

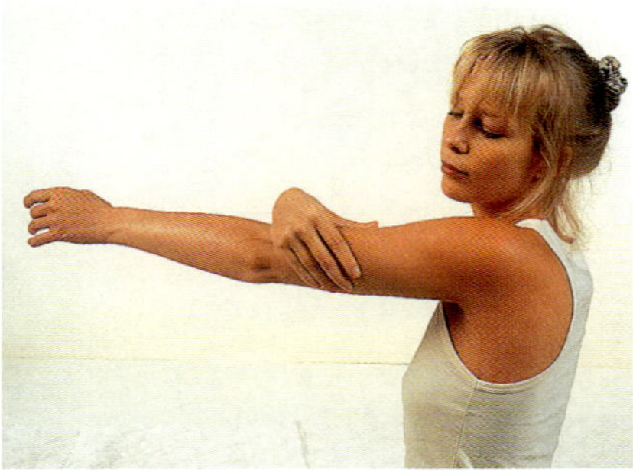

4 Repeat in an upwards direction each time, which is good at encouraging the blood to flow back to the heart.

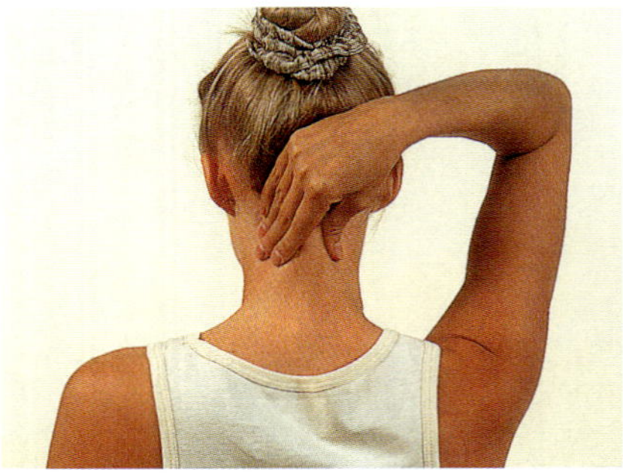

5 With the fingers and thumb of one hand, firmly squeeze the neck muscles using a relaxing, circular motion.

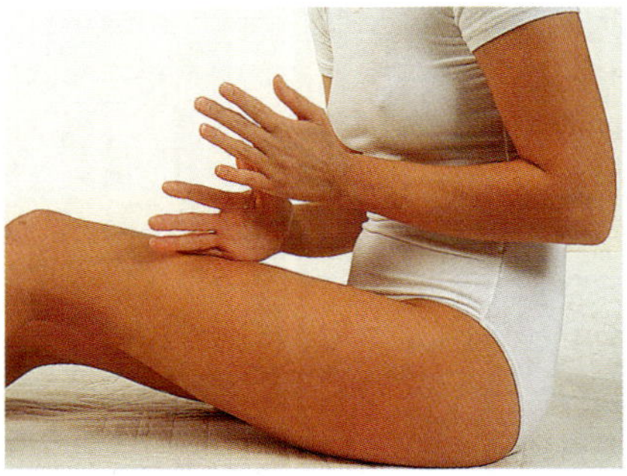

6 With the outside edge of the hands lightly hack on the front of each thigh, using a non-stop, rapid motion.

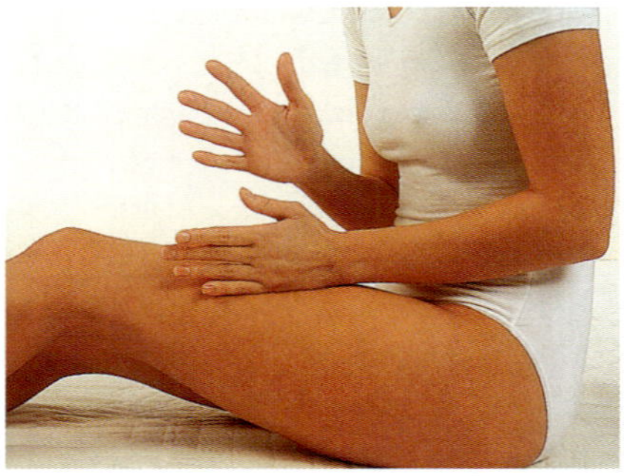

7 Do not try to karate-chop your thighs. Instead, you want the hands to spring up lightly from the muscles.

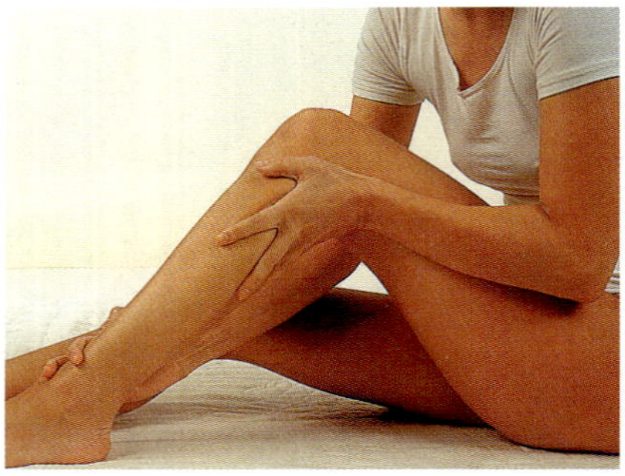

8 Next, rub the calves vigorously to loosen them and to get the blood moving. Do this with the leg bent.

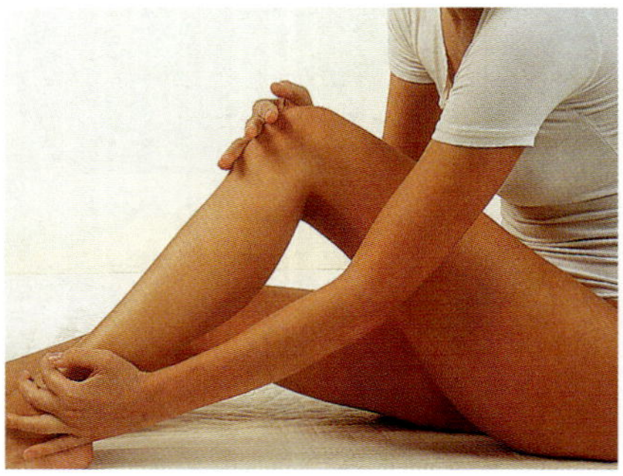

9 Always work from the ankles to the knee, using alternate hands. Finally, stand and shake your whole body.

tonic for aching legs

Many people, such as sales assistants and indeed shoppers, teachers and hotel receptionists, spend far too long each day standing still, or barely moving. Such occupations create real problems for circulation in our legs, which can lead to tired, aching limbs, swollen ankles or even cramp. However, a quick self-massage at the end of the day can help reduce stiffness and sluggish blood flow. It is a wonderful, instant reviver.

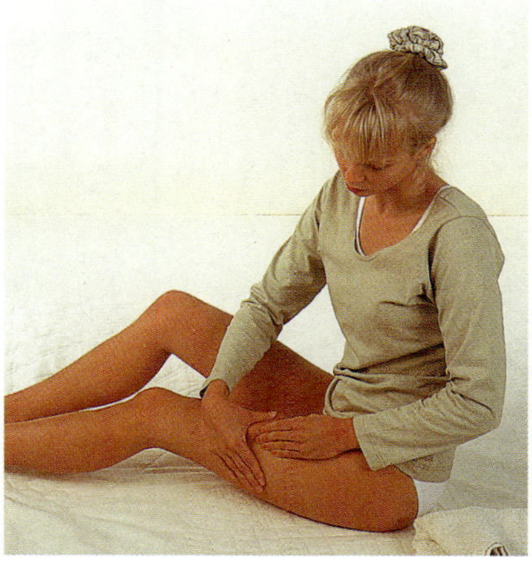

1 Using both hands, knead one thigh at a time by squeezing between the fingers and thumb. Squeeze with each hand alternately for the best effect, working from the knee to the hip and back. Repeat on the other thigh.

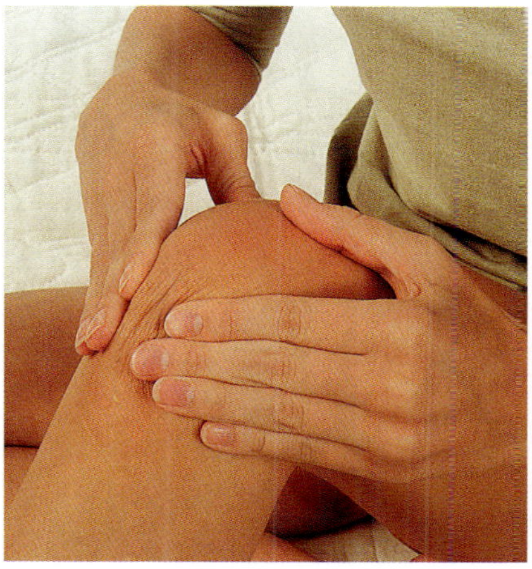

2 Right round the knees commence a similar kind of kneading action, but now use the fingers for a much lighter overall effect. Work in smaller circles.

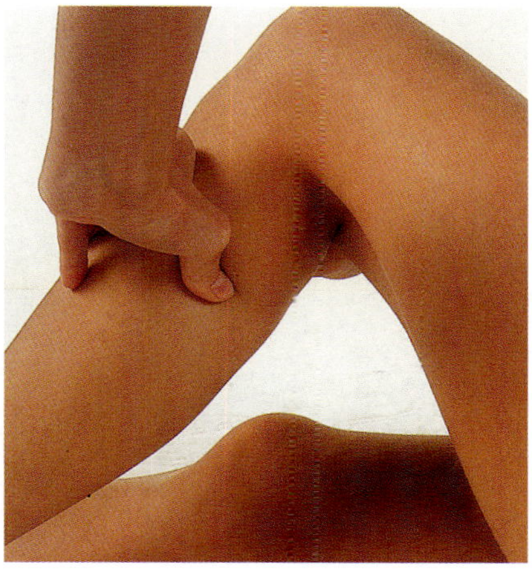

3 Bend your leg, and if possible raise the foot on to a chair or ledge. With your thumbs, work on the back of each calf with a circular, kneading action.

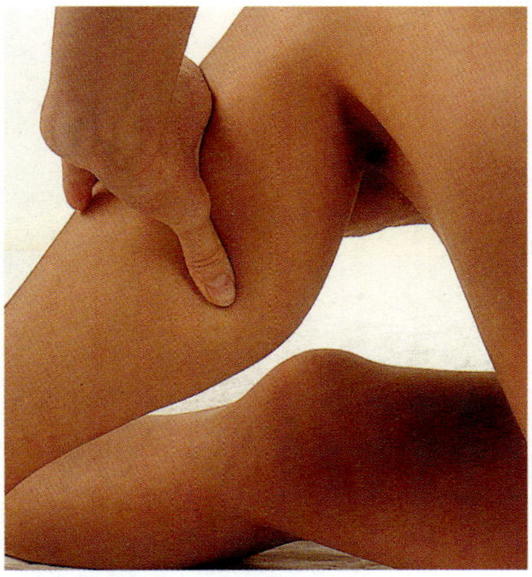

4 Repeat a few times, each time working from the ankle up the leg to the knee.

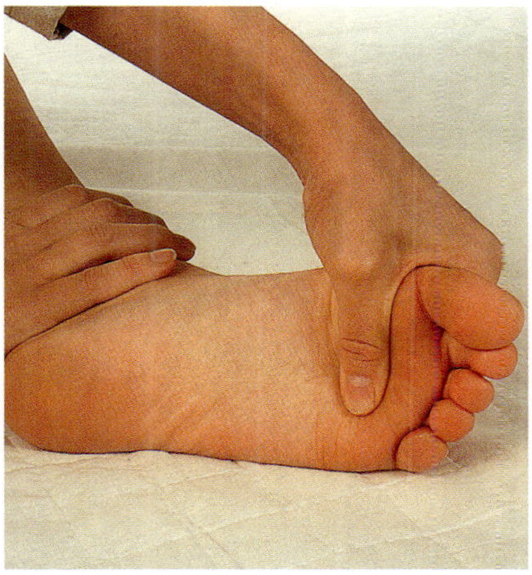

5 Squeeze the foot, loosening the muscles and then gently stretch your arch.

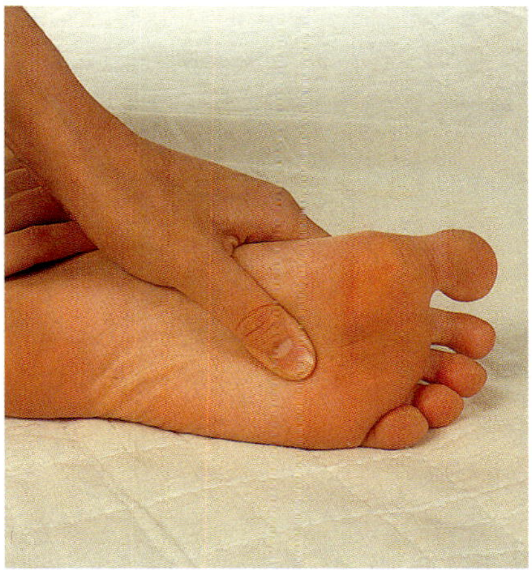

6 Use firm pressure with your thumb to stretch the foot. Repeat on the other foot.

shoulder and neck reliever

The muscle that takes the main brunt of tension in the shoulder is the trapezius; it stands out on either side when you shrug your shoulders, and connects to the neck. Lifting heavy weights, excessive gardening and bending, for example, will tighten it, and when that happens you need help. Gentle kneading is one of the very best ways of relaxing it. This quick, effective massage will soon revive you.

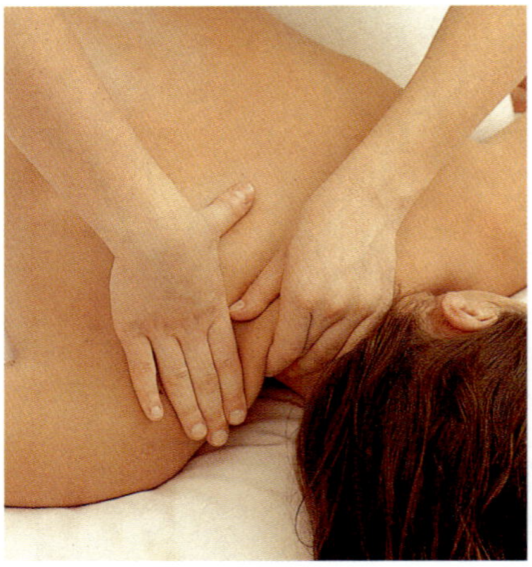

1 This technique takes a little time to master but is well worth the effort. Place both hands on the far shoulder, and with alternate hands squeeze your fingers and thumb together. Do not pinch, but roll the fingers over the thumb. Repeat by moving to the other side, again working on the shoulder away from your body.

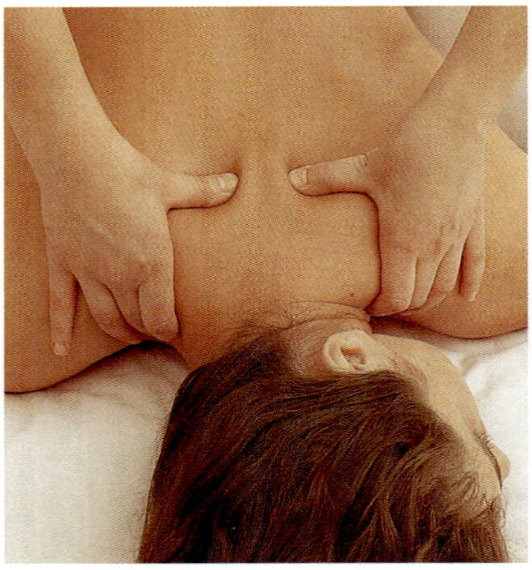

2 Having worked on each shoulder in turn, now work on both together. Place your thumbs on either side of the spine on the upper back, with the rest of each hand over each shoulder. Squeeze your fingers and thumbs together, rolling the flesh between them.

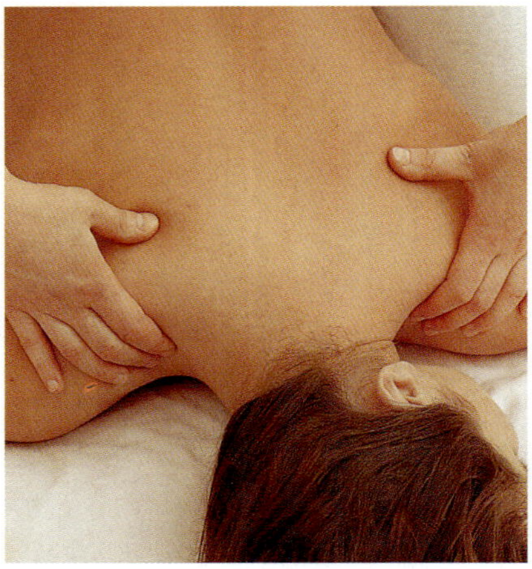

3 Let your thumbs move out smoothly across the shoulder muscles.

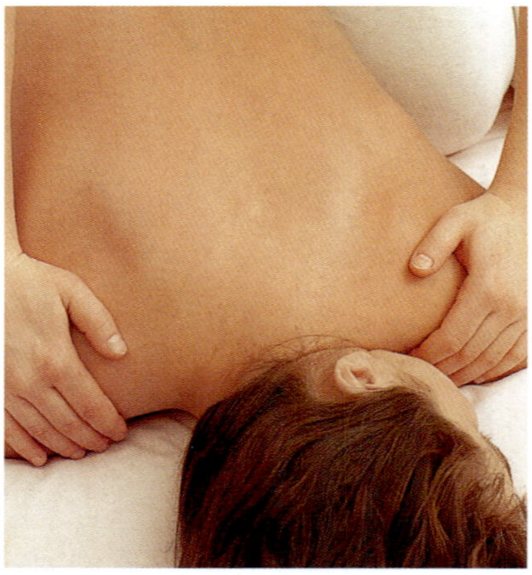

4 Release the pressure of the thumbs, and stretch the blades outwards using both your hands simultaneously.

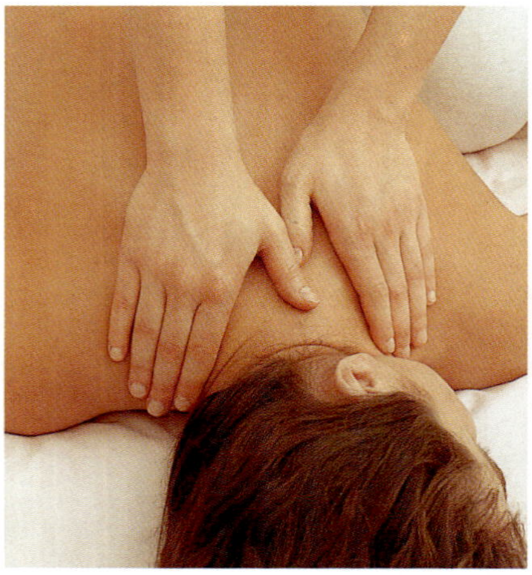

5 Now return both hands to the centre, and get the thumbs well in position to repeat this exercise.

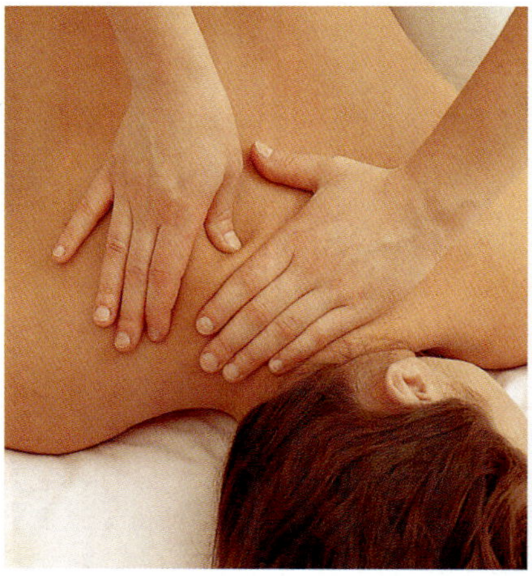

6 If the neck is very stiff, repeat the kneading exercise, applying slightly firmer pressure with the thumbs.

tension and backache reliever

The back is where most of our physical aches and pains are generally located; in fact more days are lost from work each year through back problems than from all other parts of the body combined. That is why it is a good place to massage, using broad, relaxing movements. Make sure that you keep your back in the best possible condition, treating it on a regular basis, not just when things go wrong.

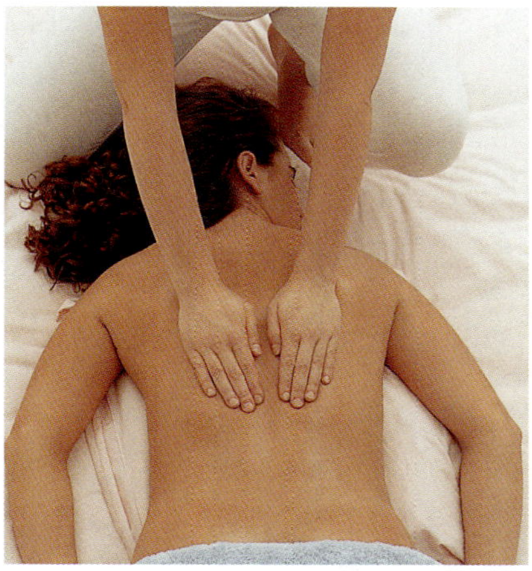

1 The best initial movement is called an effleurage. You begin by either sitting or kneeling at the head end; then place your hands on the back, with the thumbs close to, but not actually on, the spine. It is a comfortable position to find.

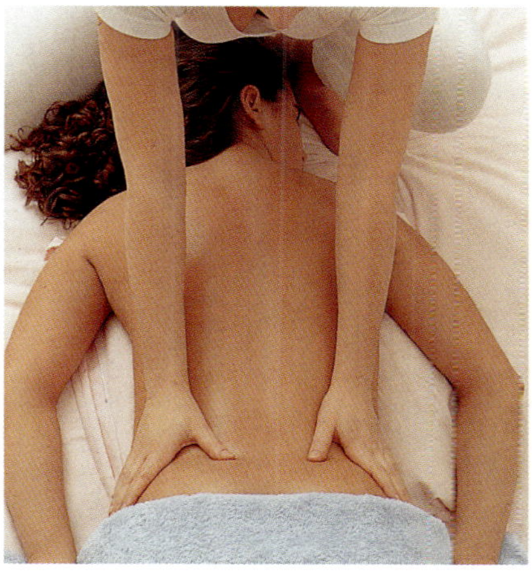

2 Steadily lean forward and glide your hands down the back, keeping a steady pressure all the way down.

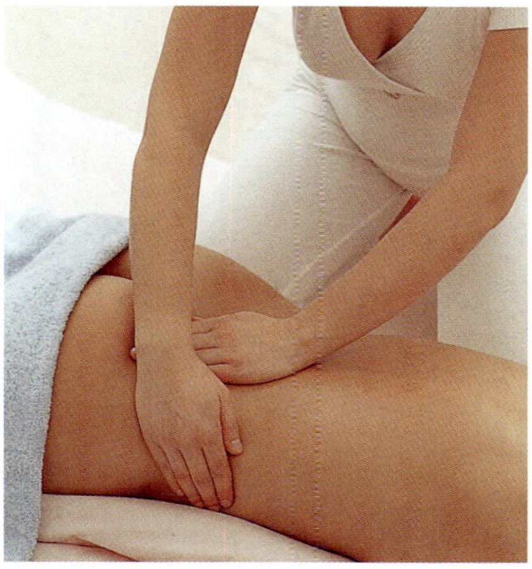

3 Kneeling at the side, place your hands on the other side of the back and move them steadily in a circular motion, using overlapping circles to work up and down the back. Move to the other side and repeat the circling technique.

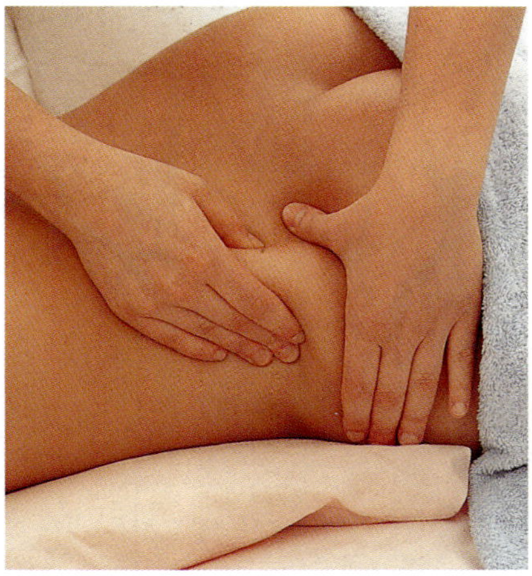

4 Place both hands on the opposite side of the back and use a firm squeezing motion with alternate hands, thereby creating a kneading effect.

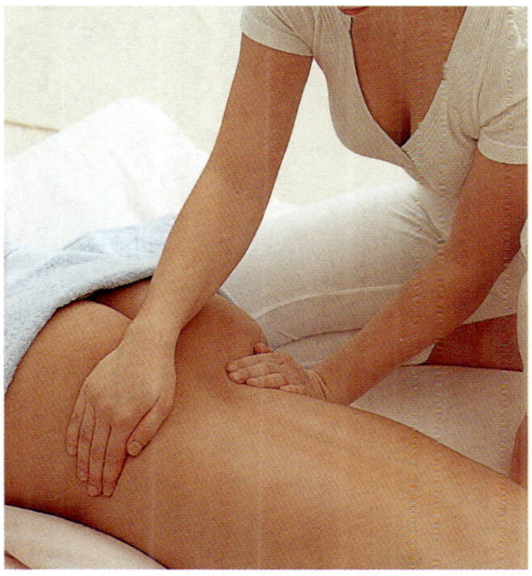

5 With one hand on the side of the back nearest you, and the other hand on the opposite side, push the hands towards and then past each other to reverse their position. Move up and down the back slowly and firmly, repeating this technique.

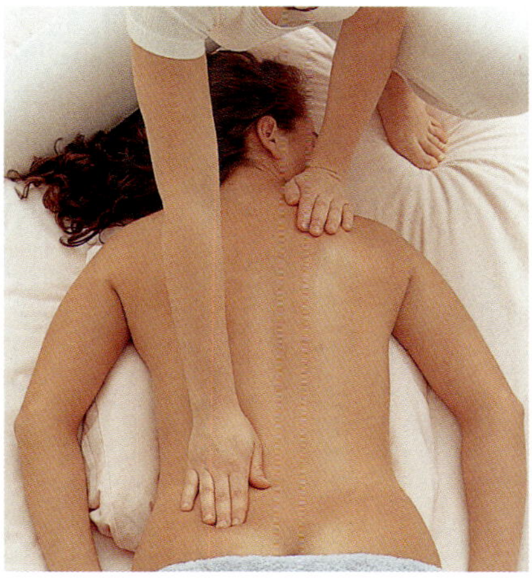

6 Place your hands centrally on the back and then push them away from each other, leaning forward to maintain an even pressure during this stretch.

lower back relaxer

One of the worst possible areas for tension is the lumbar part of the back, where it curves towards the pelvis. Continuous incorrect posture and lifting things without care – you should always bend from the knees and keep your back straight – are some of the causes that can aggravate lower back discomfort. If your partner suffers in any way from such twinges, a massage will stretch and relax the body.

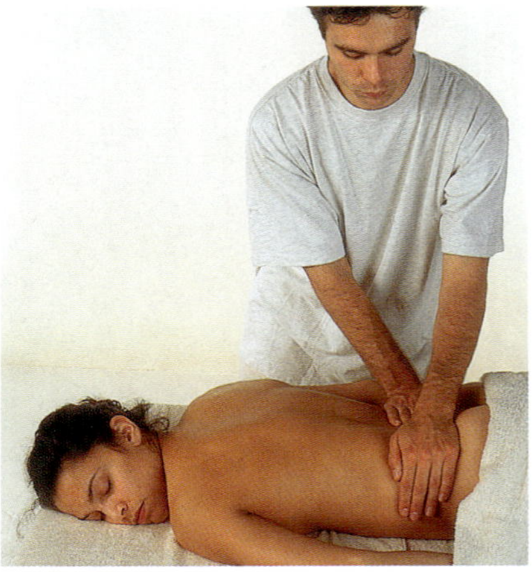

1 Standing or kneeling to the side, place your hands on the opposite side of your partner's back and pull them up towards you firmly; repeat on the other side.

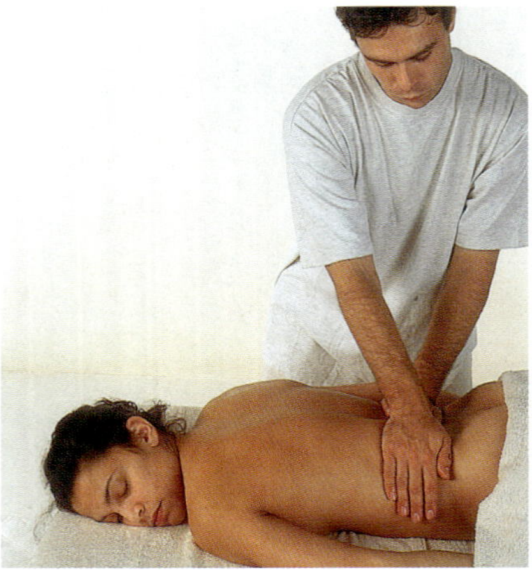

2 Overlap the hands to create an effect like bandaging, but much more soothing.

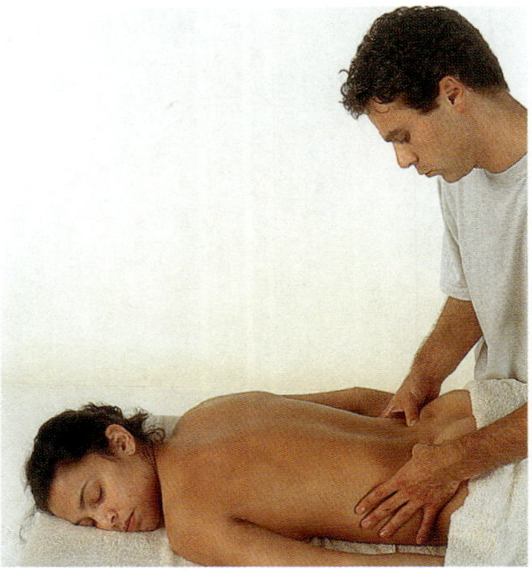

3 Using your thumbs, make circling movements over the lower back. Use a steady, even pressure, leaning with your body, but do not press on the spine.

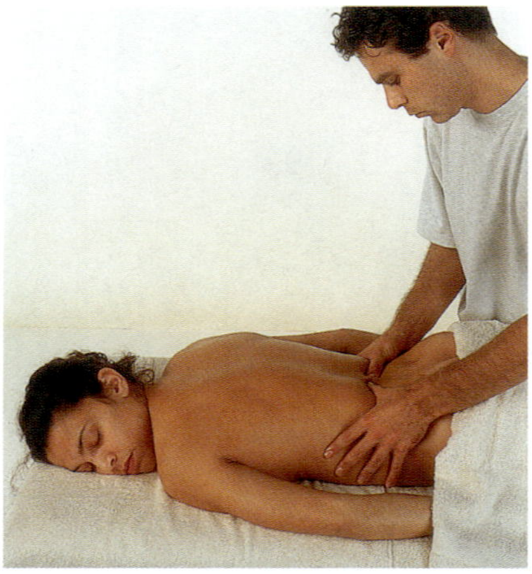

4 Stretch the lower back muscles by gliding the thumbs firmly up either side several times. Press in steadily with both thumbs just to either side of the spine, working gradually up it.

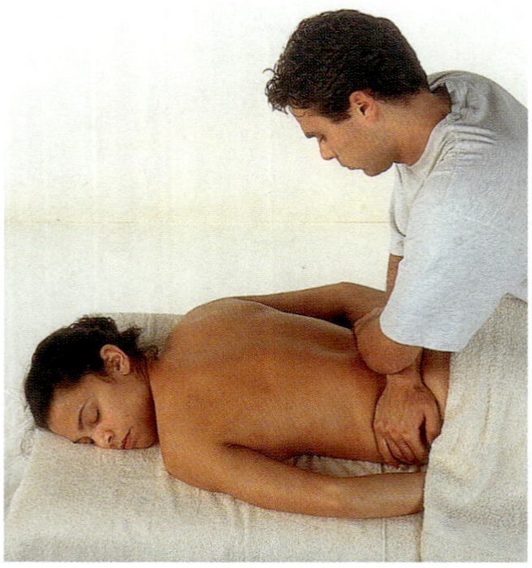

5 Stretch across the lower back with crossed hands moving away from each other to try and ease, and relax, any tense, taut muscles.

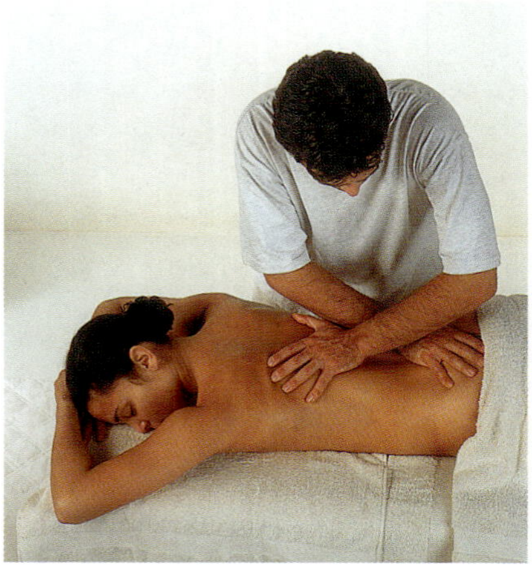

6 Finally, push the hands well apart and stretch the whole back.

Caution

Do not put pressure on the spine, and ease off if it feels at all uncomfortable.

instant foot revitalizer

With really very little complaint, your feet carry you around all day, sometimes for hours on end in the most dreadful heat. When you compare the size of your feet with the rest of you, it is not surprising that they sometimes rebel and feel sore. In fact the best way to relieve tired, aching feet is with a quick, ten-minute massage. It is amazing how quickly it can revive them, letting you get on with your life again.

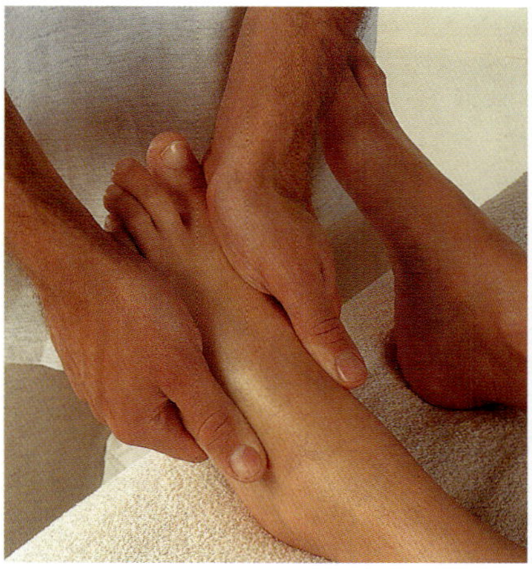

1 Hold the foot in your hands, with your thumbs on top and fingers underneath. Gently stretch across the top of the foot, trying to keep your fingers quite still while you keep moving your thumbs.

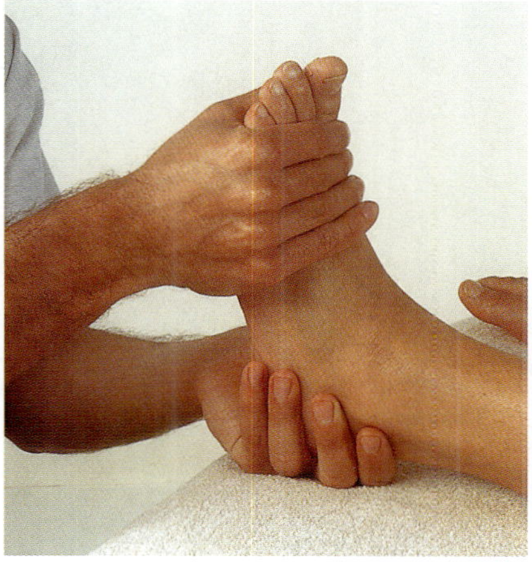

2 Flex the foot, pushing against the resistance to loosen the whole foot and ankle a little. Then gently extend the foot, stretching it as far as is comfortable.

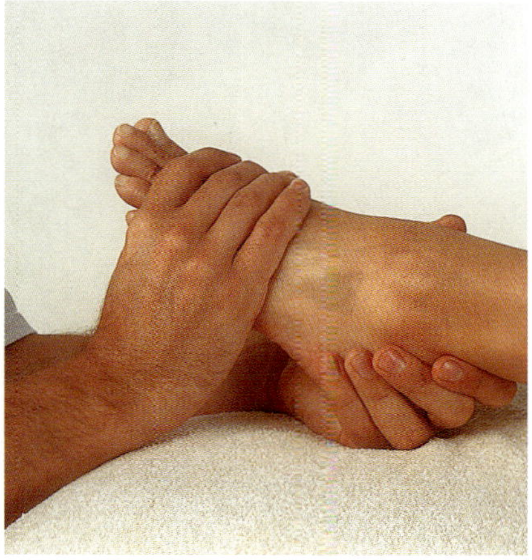

3 Now, twist the foot using a gentle wringing motion in both directions to stretch all the small muscles.

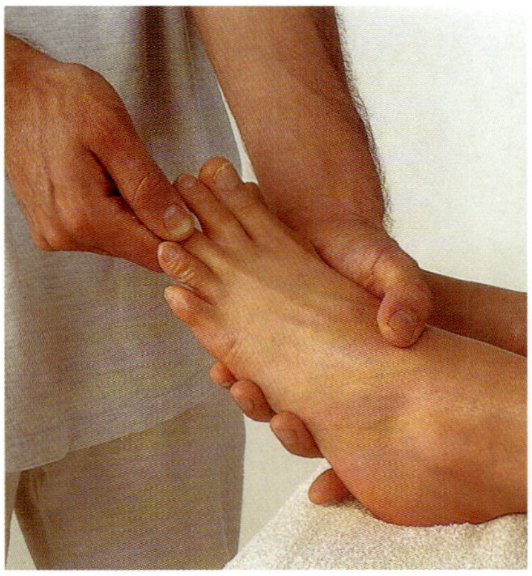

4 Firmly hold one of the toes, and then squeeze and pull it. Now repeat with every single toe.

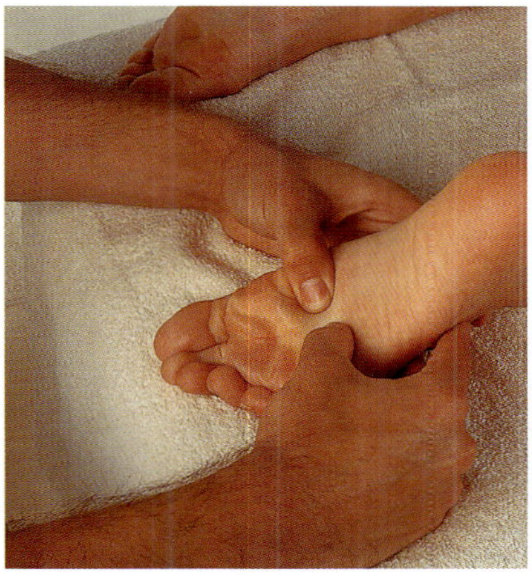

5 Circle over the sole firmly with your fingers, or thumbs if that feels much easier; make sure that you do not end up tickling your partner.

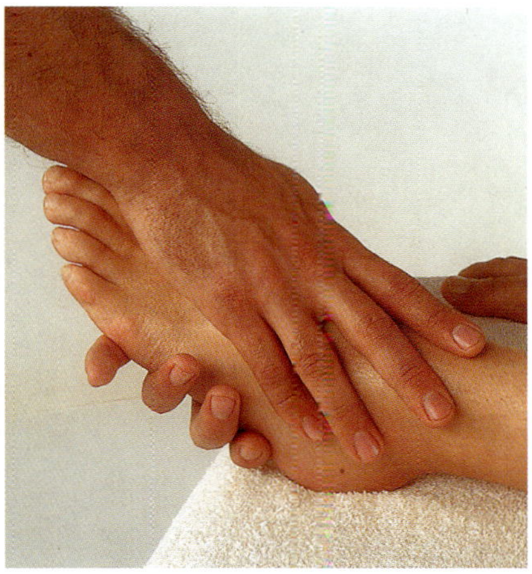

6 Support the foot with one hand, and stroke the upper side with the other hand. Smoothly stroke all the way from the toes up to the ankle. Repeat all the actions on the other foot.

tense abdomen reliever

Tension in the abdomen may reflect a degree of physical discomfort, such as indigestion, constipation or even menstrual cramp. However, the cause is just as likely to be emotional because many people hold their inner fears in this particular area. If you bottle up and cannot release or express your feelings, then abdominal spasms may occur. The following movements should ensure that such tensions soon go away.

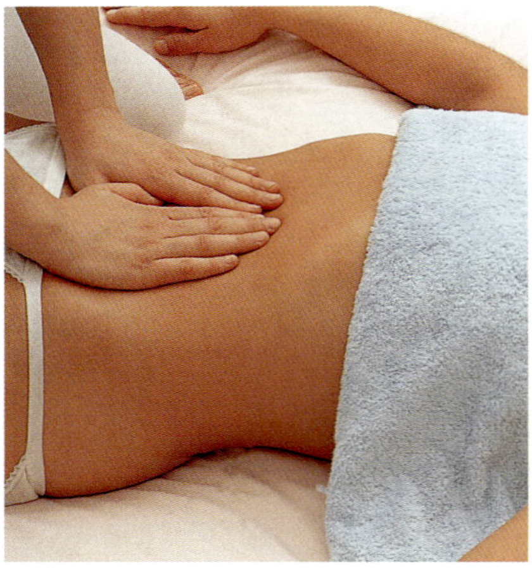

1 Begin by placing your hands gently on the abdomen. At this stage simply focus all your thoughts and energy on trying to pass good vibrations into your partner's body. You will be surprised by the results.

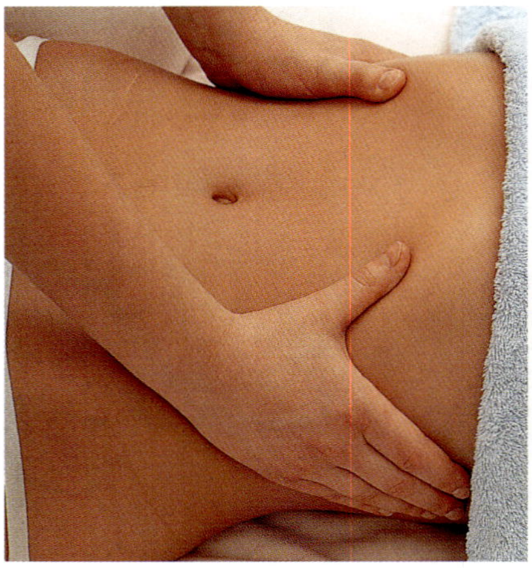

2 Next, spread each hand open, and slowly and gradually move each to the side of the abdomen. Repeat this two or three times, building up a slow, regular, soothing rhythm.

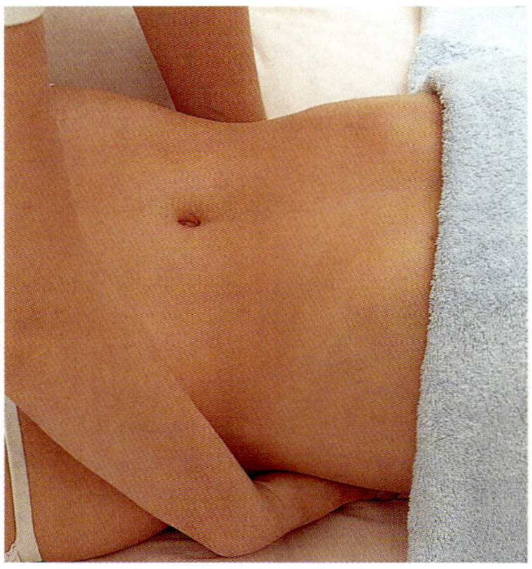

3 Kneeling by the side, now slide your hands under the back to meet at the spine. Lift the body gently to arch and stretch the back before pulling your hands out towards the hips.

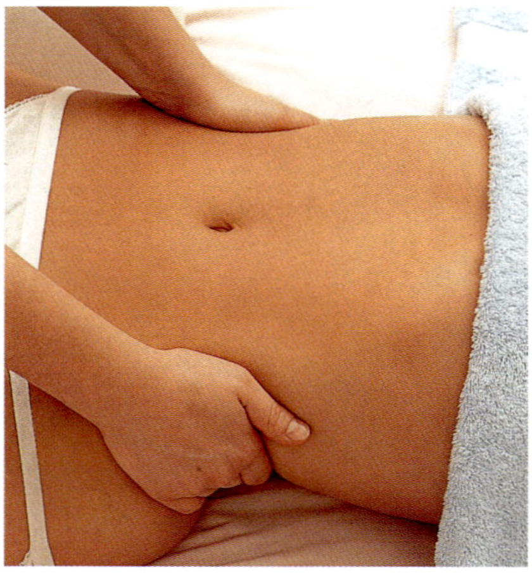

4 Firmly draw your hands out over the waist, and then gently glide them back to their original position to repeat the stroke a few times.

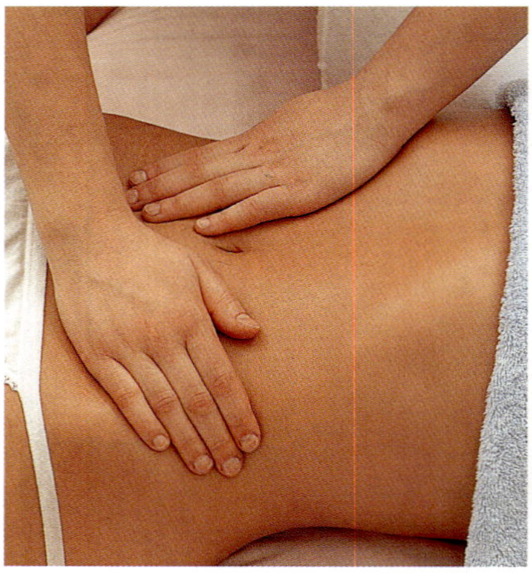

5 Placing your hands on the abdomen, move them around steadily in a clockwise direction (this follows the way in which the colon functions).

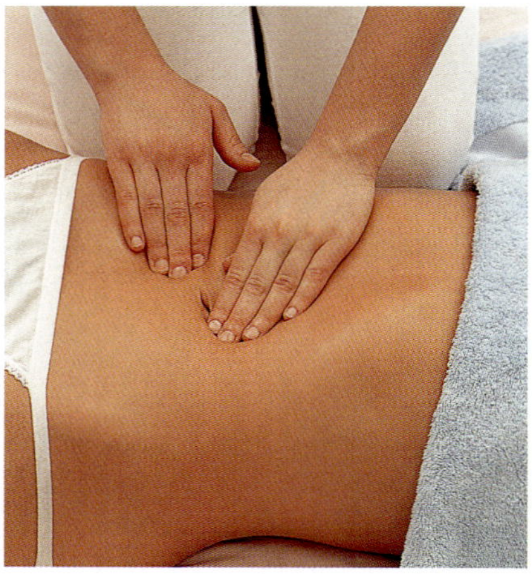

6 Finally, repeat the action, but this time working a little deeper by using your fingers, provided that there are no signs of any discomfort.

de-stress your colleagues

Massage is a highly versatile skill, and can be applied in many different situations, not least the office. How often have you heard one of your work colleagues complain of terrible tense, aching shoulders preventing them from doing any work? Now you can step in and do something about it. A five-minute massage is all it takes. It can be wonderfully effective, revitalizing and refreshing them.

1 Standing behind your seated colleague, place both your hands gently on the shoulders, thumbs towards you and fingers in the front.

2 Using your fingers, knead in small circles up and down the back of the neck. Support the head with your other hand while you are working on the neck.

3 Place your forearms over the shoulders, and then gradually press down with your body weight in order to squeeze and stretch the trapezius.

4 Move the forearms gradually outwards to cover the shoulders, maintaining a firm pressure all the time.

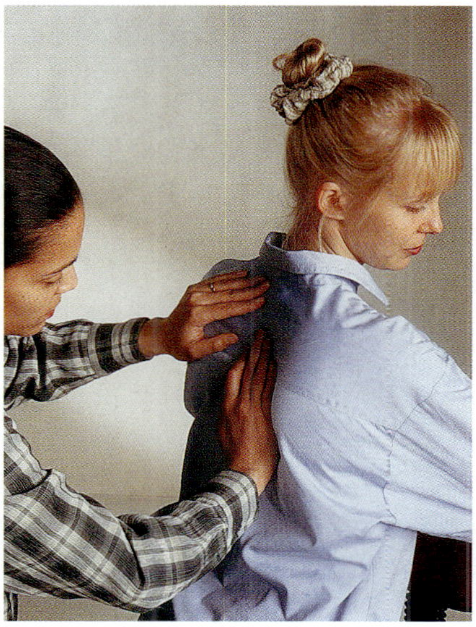

5 Allow your fingers to sink into the muscles around the shoulder blade. Repeat on the other side.

6 Place your hands on your partner's shoulder joints, and press back towards yourself to stretch the upper chest.

sensual massage

As well as releasing stresses and tensions from the muscles, massage is a wonderful way to enhance a relationship by increasing caring, sharing touch. If your relationship seems to have got into a rut, and sexual energy is low, why not revitalize yourselves with deep soothing massage strokes. To make the whole experience a real treat, make the room extra warm, and play some of your favourite, soothing music.

1 Place your hands to either side of the spine and glide them down the back, move out to the side, and then back again. Repeat several times.

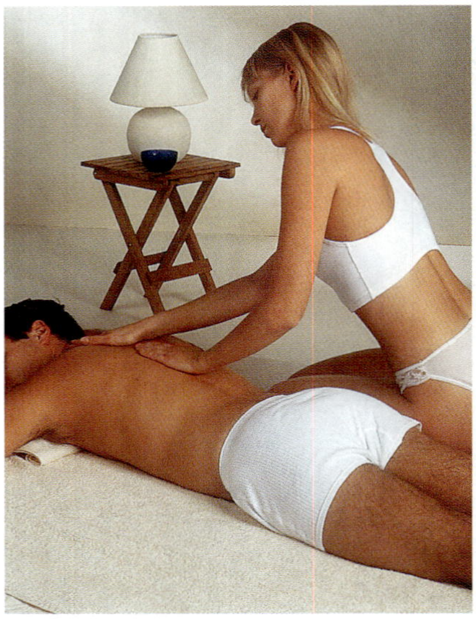

2 With a gentle motion, stroke down the centre of the back with one hand following the other smoothly, as if you were stroking a cat.

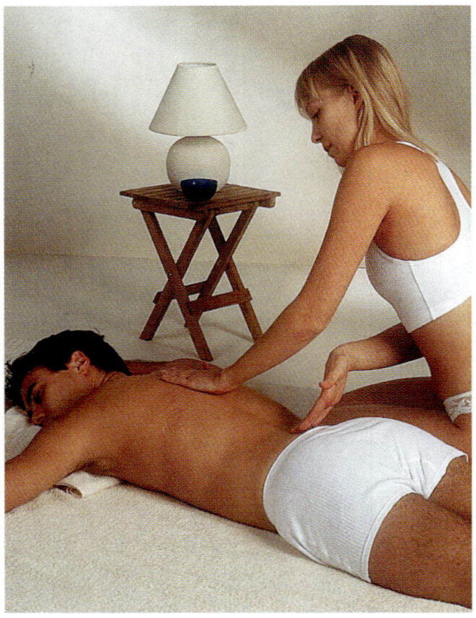

3 As one hand lifts off at the pelvis, start again with the other hand at the neck.

4 Place both your hands on the upper back and stroke outwards in a fan shape.

5 Work down the back, including the buttocks, using a fanning action.

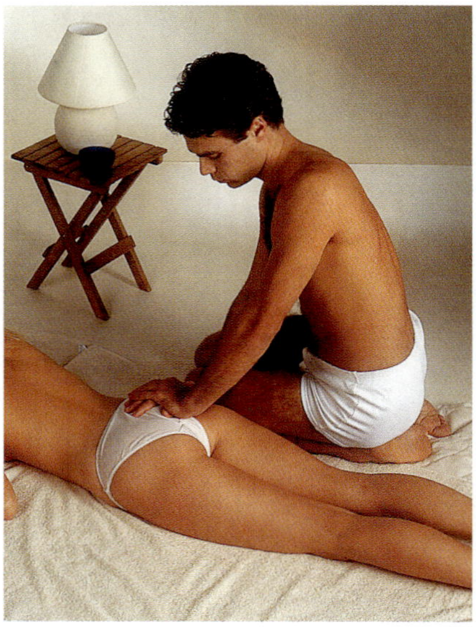

6 Use a firm, steady circling action on the buttocks.

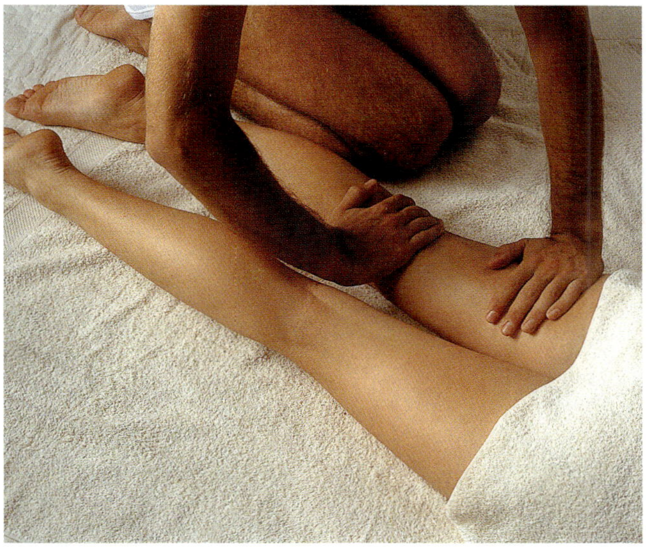

7 Stroke up the back of the legs, with one hand after the other building up a smooth, continuous flowing motion.

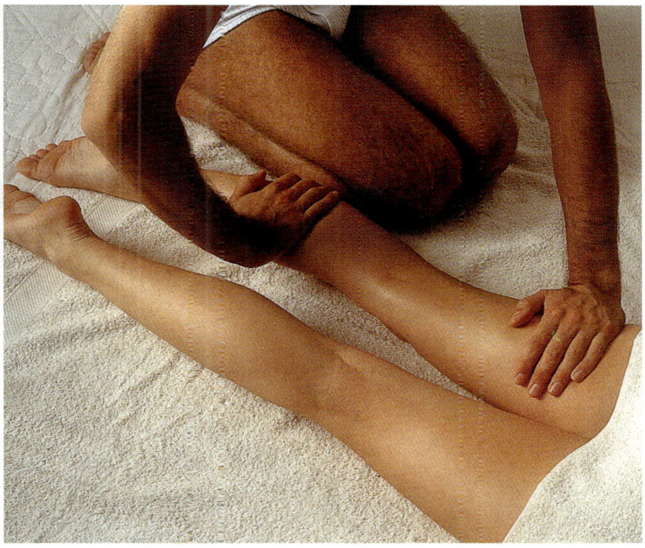

8 As one hand reaches the buttocks, start on the calf with the other hand to keep up that continuous steady rhythm.

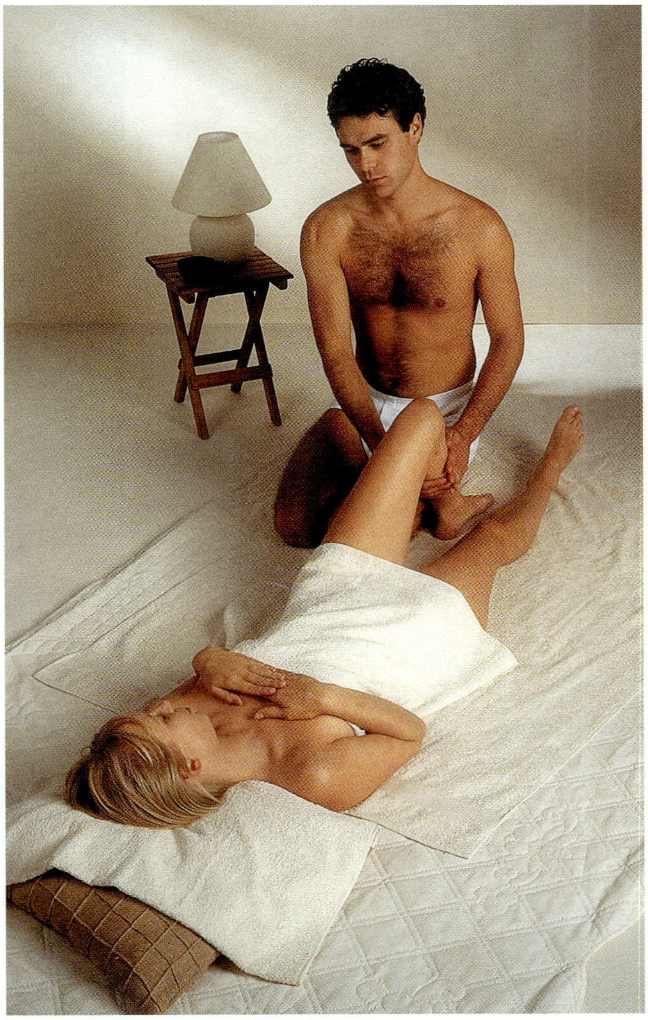

9 Turn your partner over and stroke up the front of the legs; having the leg bent greatly helps the muscles to relax.

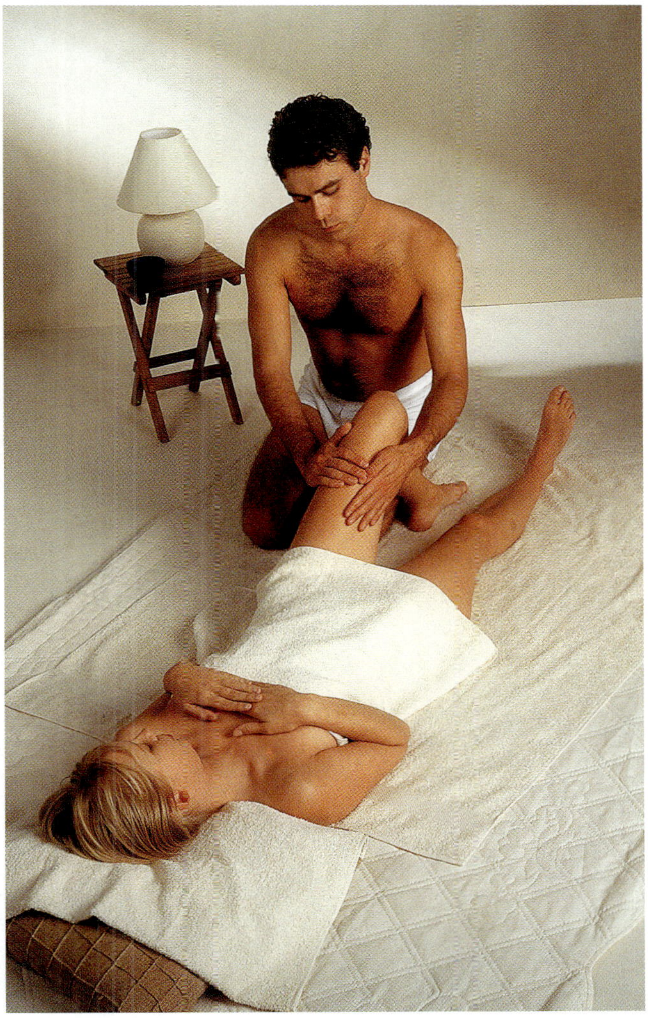

10 Continue the movement, using both hands to make stroking movements from the knees right up the thighs.

aromatherapy

Do you have a favourite scent, one that evokes memories of wonderful times? The power of the sense of smell to arouse an emotional reaction confirms its ability to have an immediate effect on our systems; in fact smell is probably the most underrated of the senses, yet it has the most subtle significance in our lives. But how does it work?

Aromatic plants contain essential oils that have been used for centuries to relax, sedate, refresh and even stimulate. Each aromatic oil has its own individual combination of constituents, and they in turn can interact with your body's chemistry to have specific therapeutic effects.

In the early years of the 20th century, the French chemist René-Maurice Gattefosse was working in the laboratory of his family's perfumery business when he badly burnt his hand and lower arm. He plunged his hand into the nearest liquid, which was a jar of Lavender oil and discovered that this very quickly eased his pain, prevented scarring and promoted rapid healing. Gattefosse then set about investigating the precise therapeutic properties of essential oils, discovering that they were often more effective than isolated or synthetic compounds. He used the term aromatherapy in 1928 to describe the use of aromatic oils for treating physical or emotional problems. In the following pages the art of aromatherapy is mainly used to combat and overcome stress.

using oils

If you have never quite understood the art of aromatherapy, and are afraid that it involves all kinds of strange pieces of equipment, then you could not be more wrong. It actually involves a collection of small, highly attractive bottles that can be quite a feature, and maybe even a candle burner. That is all that it takes to become an aficionado. Once hooked, you will certainly never look back, and those oils will start improving your health.

BUYING AND KEEPING OILS

Aromatic essential oils can be used in various ways to restore good health. However, the oils are in fact concentrated substances, and need to be diluted for safety. A test massage with a weak dose will quickly reveal potential skin reactions. Also, seek medical advice before massaging a pregnant woman.

You will find that many companies now sell essential oils, and when buying them always make sure that they are pure and of a high quality (you get what you pay for in general). If possible, try to smell the sample bottle of the oil that you are buying, and make sure that it has a good, clean, non-synthetic perfume. Since essential oils are liable to deteriorate quite quickly as a direct result of sunlight, they should always be stored in a dark glass jar in a cool, dark place. Keep the lid firmly closed to prevent any evaporation. One good tip is always to buy small quantities, especially of citrus oil which deteriorates quickly.

Aromas are always tempered by an emotional reaction – a lasting memory of them from the past.

Creating Scents

When using essential oils at home, it is very helpful to have some basic equipment. A burner is an excellent way of vaporizing oils into the atmosphere. It consists of a candle in a simple, small, invariably terracotta, open-top container, and a bowl for the oil, which sits on top. When you want to simmer pot-pourri in a bowl, again all you need is a candle. Place it under the bowl and gently warm it until you can detect a delicious scent. This is an an excellent way of making a room much more fragrant. If you want a long-term scent, albeit one that is slightly fainter, use a ready-prepared commercial mix of dry pot-pourri. Place the bowls strategically round the house. They come in different perfumes and strengths.

Rose oil is a favourite for massage as it has such pleasant connotations. It will help even the most tense person relax.

HOW IT ALL BEGAN

When you take up aromatherapy, it is worth noting that it has a highly impressive history. People have been using scented products for thousands of years. Ancient written records dating back 3,000 years, in the case of the Indian Verdic manuscripts, describe in marvellous detail the use of aromatic oils. Egyptian papyri from 1500 BC, and biblical stories of the Jewish exodus from Egypt about 300 years later, also describe the widespread use of aromatic oils. Many were used in religious ceremonies and in rituals, but many were also used when having a massage, taking a bath, and for scenting the body and hair. To that extent, little has changed. Scented products have long been justifiably popular.

A collection of oils quickly becomes an attractive feature.

Aromatic Oils

These oils were probably first made by Arabic physicians in the 10th century AD. That much is definite, though it is now strongly argued by some that they were also used in the Indus valley, in the foothills of the Himalayas 5,000 years ago. Certainly, the Arabic use of concentrated, distilled oils – widely famed in the West as the "perfumes of Arabia" – did lead to a renaissance in the use of aromatic plants.

As distillation was taken up in the West, many more oils were extracted. There was also a gradual separation of the perfume side and more medical applications. Ironically, the former was the one that really provided the impetus for the development of aromatherapy. Today, it is enjoying a worldwide popularity rarely seen before. While aromatherapists now use specific essential oils for their physiological effects, there is no reason why they may not also be used for their relaxing properties. In fact, in today's turbulent, demanding world, that often seems to be their chief attraction. A calming, soothing, marvellously scented way of getting the body and mind back on track. Aromatherapy, with its long history, is guaranteed a long future.

Mixing Essential Oils for Massage

1 Before you begin, wash and dry your hands and make sure that all the utensils are clean and dry. Measure out about 10ml /2 tsp of your chosen vegetable oil. Next, carefully pour the vegetable oil into the blending bowl.

2 Add the essential oil, never rushing things, always with great care, one drop at a time. Mix gently using a clean, dry cocktail stick or perhaps even a toothpick. Make sure that the children are well away before doing this.

how aromatherapy can be used

Aromatherapy is surprisingly varied in its uses. It can help with all kinds of problems, and what can make it such a regular part of your life is that it can also tackle everyday aches and pains. It is also marvellous for coping with poor circulation and headaches, and those long, hard days at work which result in a tired, sore back. Treat oils with respect, and they will soon perk you up.

MASSAGE

Massage is a wonderful way to use essential oils, suitably diluted in a good base oil, for your partner or family. Always try to use soft, thick towels to cover any areas of the body that you are not massaging, and make sure that the room is kept warm, perhaps with an additional portable heater. Do not undermine the effect of the massage by draughty, cold conditions.

Also note that while essential oils are wonderful natural remedies they are highly concentrated and must therefore be used with care and caution. You should consequently only take essential oils internally if they have been professionally prescribed for you, and always use essential oils in a diluted form – normally 1 per cent for massage and just 5 drops in a bath or for a steam inhalation. You should also be extra careful with anyone who has asthma or epilepsy, and if anyone does experience any kind of adverse reaction, use common sense and stop using the oils immediately. A quick test beforehand will usually reveal possible problems.

Gently rubbing the body all over with a loofa greatly increases the effect of an aromatherapy bath.

Hand and Footbaths

The circulation to our extremities can be greatly affected by levels of tension and stress, among other factors, and the warmth of the water quickly helps the blood vessels to dilate. This can be very helpful when treating tension headaches and even painful migraines, when the blood vessels in the head are frequently engorged with blood. When you are using essential oils to make a hand or even a footbath, you should two-thirds fill a large bowl with warm, but not too hot, water and then carefully add and stir in 3–4 drops of your favourite oil.

Excess Heat when Hot and Tired

For hot, aching feet or hands, use a mixture of 2 drops peppermint and 2 drops lemon. To boost your circulation try the following: add 2 drops Lavender and 2 drops Marjoram oils. This is also extremely good for those who suffer from poor circulation and tense, cold extremities.

BATHS

Imagine soaking in a hot bath, enveloped in a delicious scent of exotic flowers, feeling all the day's tensions drop away . . . well, that can easily become a reality with aromatherapy. The oils seem to capture the essence of the plant, and can effortlessly transport you to pine-scented forests, refreshing orange groves or even magical, oriental spice markets.

When using oils in the bath, pour in 5 drops just before you get in. The oils form a thin film on the surface of the water which, aided by the relaxing warmth of the water, will be partly absorbed by your skin as you breathe in the scent, producing an immediate psychological and physiological effect.

Morning and Evening Baths

For a refreshing, uplifting bath in the mornings, try a blend of 3 drops Bergamot and 2 drops Geranium essential oils. To relax and unwind after a long day, make a blend of 3 drops Lavender and 2 drops Ylang Ylang. For tired, tense muscles when you have been overdoing it, have a long soak in a deep, warm bath to which you have added approximately 3 drops Marjoram and 2 drops Chamomile essential oils.

A relaxing bath in the evening promotes enhanced sleep.

STEAM INHALATIONS

Colds and sinus problems may all too easily cause congestion, but we can also feel blocked up and unable to breathe freely as a result of all kinds of tension levels. Using a steam inhalation warms and moistens the membranes, and the use of essential oils also helps to open and relax the airways. Just boil a kettle, pour the water into a bowl, add the oils and inhale deeply. It makes a simple but highly effective cure.

If you suffer from nasal congestion, and have that extremely irritating, stuffed-up feeling, possibly combined with tiredness, do try using 3 drops Eucalyptus and 2 drops Peppermint. Just mix them in a large bowl filled with steaming water; it should make a marvellous remedy. For those who have that tight, tense feeling in their chest which makes breathing rather uncomfortable, try to relax your airways using just 4 drops Lavender, and 3 drops Frankincense.

For respiratory complaints in particular, steam inhalations have long been considered very helpful remedies.

SCENTED ROOMS

Aromatherapy has many applications in the home or office including the creation of an aromatic environment which has wide-ranging beneficial effects.

Pot-pourri

It is possible to scent a room by making a simmering pot-pourri. Place a mixture of scented flowers and leaves (without any fixatives or additives) in a bowl of water and heat gently from below – a candle may well be sufficient. Unlike dry pot-pourri, the simmering variety does not last for long but gives off a much stronger aroma. Try making your own blends; add about 1 cupful of dried material to 1.2 litres/2 pints/5 cups water.

For a sleep-enhancing pot-pourri use ½ cup Lime flowers, ¼ cup Chamomile flowers, 1 tbsp Sweet Marjoram and 1 tbsp Lavender flowers. For a more refreshing, uplifting blend try ½ cup Lemon Verbena leaves, ¼ cup Jasmine flowers, 2 tbsp Lemon peel and 1 tsp Coriander seeds.

A wonderfully fragrant bowl of potpourri.

Essential Oil Burners

Most oils can be used with a burner. The basic principle is very simple: a small dish to hold a few drops of essential oil, with some type of gentle heat underneath, often in the form of a candle. The heat needs to be fairly low in order to allow slow evaporation of the oil and a longer-lasting scent.

If you want to fumigate a room, then try adding 3–4 drops of oils such as Pine, Eucalyptus or Juniper to a burner. In order to help you keep really sharp and alert, a couple of drops of Peppermint or Rosemary may work wonders, while 2–3 drops of Ylang Ylang or Lavender will have the opposite effect and soon help you to wind down at the end of a long, tiring, difficult day.

It is well worth visiting a specialist shop with a wide range of such burners. Chose an attractive one that makes an interesting feature; the Oriental kind often have interesting ornamental styles. They also make good presents – the whole kit, with oils, makes a marvellous surprise Christmas present, one that will get someone quickly hooked on the subject.

Bowl of Hot Water

Adding a couple of drops of an essential oil to a bowl of hot water is a pleasant way to give fragrance to a room or office. Try to use an attractive bowl and make sure that it is placed well out of reach of any children. Use an oil that is a big favourite, as it will release its scent for some time when used in this way. For mornings, Bergamot, Mandarin or Lemon would be uplifting. Later in the day you may wish to use Rose or Jasmine.

Other Scented Products

Essential oils are quite often included in a wide variety of excellent gift items They range from candles to incense sticks and cones. It is quite important, though, that you check the natural essential oil that is being used to scent these products. You may well find that they actually repeat scents that you are already using, which can produce an excessively strong aroma.

therapeutic recipes
therapeutic recipes

therapeutic recipes

One of the great delights of taking up the ancient art of aromatherapy is discovering the many exciting ways in which oils can be blended to create a wide range of enhanced therapeutic effects, with new fragrances to soothe the senses at the same time.

On the following pages you will find scores of all kinds of ideas for using different combinations of oils; they have been specially selected for their healing properties, and also because they provide an array of exquisite aromas. However, since the sense of smell is very individual and highly subjective, do not feel that you have to like certain aromas. Above all, do not feel that the not-so-good has to be enjoyed. It does not. If you find that you dislike a particular combination then feel free to make your own blends, bearing in mind the actions of the oils and the dilution rates that were described earlier.

The key to success is quite simple. Always try to ensure that you buy good quality essential oils, with a pure scent that comes from the natural, unadulterated extract. There are no rules about what you should like. The best way to proceed is by trusting your nose. If something has what might be called the ooh-ah factor, an aroma that is totally arresting rather than subtle almost to the point of not being present, but without being fiercely competitive and dominating your senses, then feel free to enjoy it.

For each of the blends suggested in this section, the number of drops of oils given should be diluted for massage purposes in 20ml/4 tsp of a base vegetable oil such as sweet Almond oil. When creating a steam inhalation, use the number of drops given in a large bowl holding about 1 litre/1¾ pints/4 cups hot water, and for a compress add the specified number of oil drops to a bowl holding 250ml/8fl oz/1 cup hot water. Also remember that when creating a mix about which you are slightly unsure, make a tiny dose to check that it is what you want. It is prudent to proceed by caution.

stress soothers

Sadly, stress is now playing far too large a part in all our lives, and while we cannot always avoid the causes, we can at least dispel its effects on us. All you need to do is set aside just a few minutes at the end of the day when you can be quiet and relax. Then, using a variety of soothing, relaxing therapeutic measures, such as a marvellous, long, slow rhythmic massage, you will end up feeling totally invigorated and refreshed.

STRESS RELIEVERS

Stress, or rather our inability to cope with an excess amount of it, is one of the biggest health problems today. Lifestyles seem to include so many varied and often conflicting demands that it is not surprising that most of us feel stressed at times, sometimes constantly. We all react to excess stress in different ways, perhaps through anxiety, depression or exhaustion, but we can all certainly benefit from the wonderfully balancing and stress-calming effects provided by aromatic oils.

Our bodies are geared to cope with a stressful situation by producing various hormones that trigger off a series of physiological actions in the body; they are known collectively as the "fight or flight" syndrome, and serve to place the body in a state of alert in a potentially dangerous situation. Extra blood is shunted to the muscles, and the heart rate speeds up while the digestion slows down. These responses are appropriate when we are faced with a physical threat, but can nowadays be triggered by quite different kinds of stress and end up placing a strain on our bodies without fulfilling any useful need.

In order to help reduce the impact of stress on the whole system, it is necessary to find ways both to avoid getting over-stressed in the first instance, and of letting go of the changes that occur internally under stress. Aromatherapy can be a great help in each case, especially during and immediately after a long relaxing massage, because the oils will help to keep you calm.

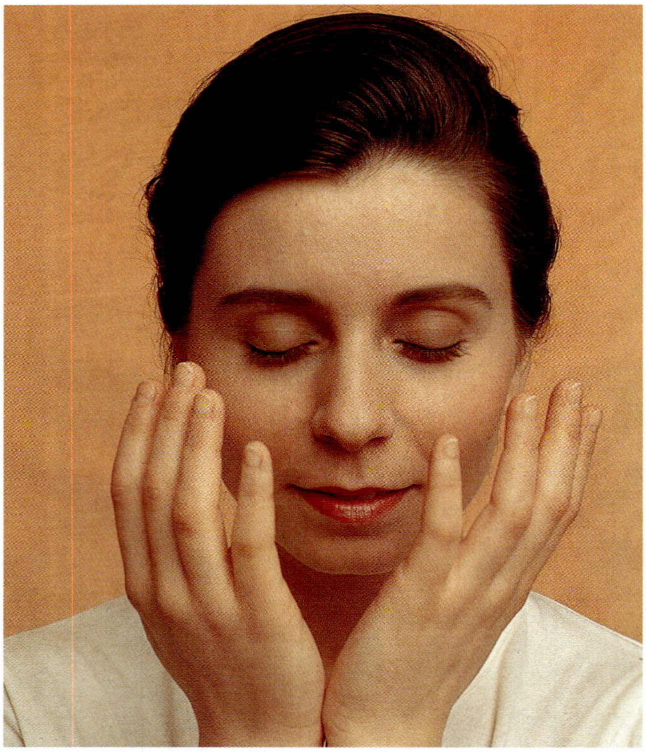

It should not take you long to discover which particular essential oils work best for you as an individual.

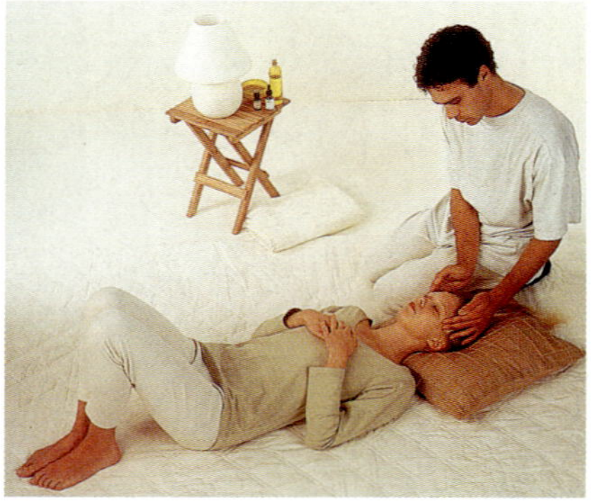

1 Ideally have the person lying down with the head in your lap or on a cushion. With your fingertips, gently begin smoothing the essential oil into the face.

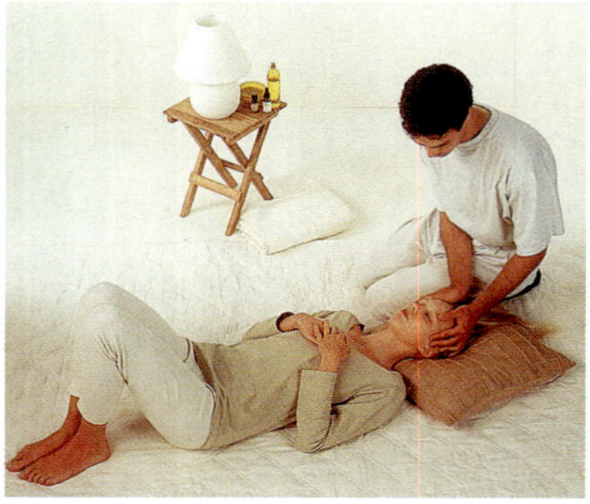

2 Using your thumbs, one after the other, stroke tension gently and carefully away from the centre of the forehead.

ANXIETY CALMERS

When people are described as being "uptight", that is often exactly what they are: tense muscles in the face and neck are a sure sign of anxiety. You can release that tension with a face massage, using gentle, soothing strokes on the temples and forehead especially. This is very good as an evening treat, calming away the day's cares and worries.

Use just a few drops of oil because most people do not like having a greasy feeling on the face. Make up a blend of 4 drops Lavender and 2 drops Ylang Ylang in a light oil such as Sweet Almond.

MUSCULAR ACHES

When you are under any kind of difficult stress for any length of time, your body promptly reacts by becoming and staying permanently tense. Clearly this is not good for you. It can make quite specific muscles, or indeed all of your muscles, ache and feel overwhelmingly tired and sluggish, leaden and heavy.

In order to relieve this all too familiar list of thoroughly unwanted symptoms, and also to start releasing the underlying tension, use essential oils in what is called a massage blend.

As the massage movements begin to work on the aching muscles at surface and deeper levels, the oils begin to be absorbed. In time they too get to work and start tackling the inner tension. Such treatment is in itself quite refreshing.

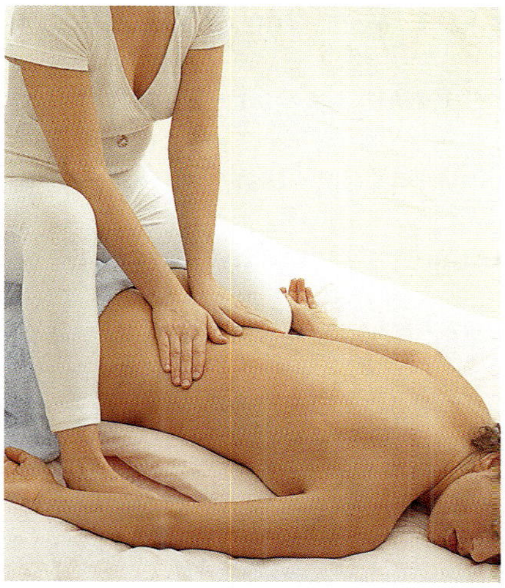

1 Rest your hands on the lower back to either side of the spine. Lean your weight into your hands and stroke up the back towards the head. Mould your hands to the body as they glide firmly along.

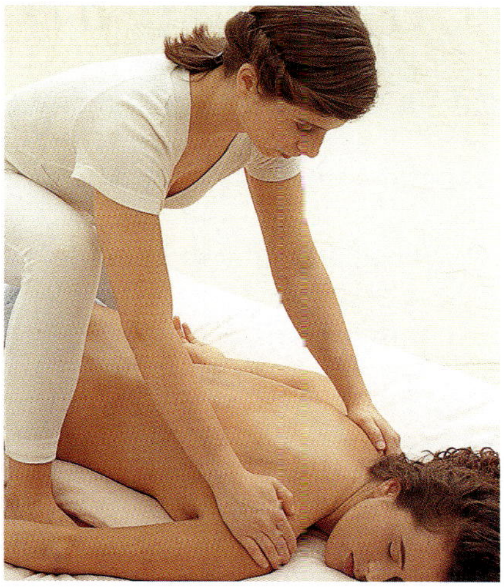

2 As your hands reach the top of the back, fan them out towards the shoulders in a long, smooth, flowing, ceaseless motion.

BLOOD PRESSURE

It should be emphasized that anyone with very high blood pressure should first seek expert medical (or professional) treatment. You should not even think about trying to tackle such a condition yourself without accurate guidance. However in much milder, far less dangerous or acute cases, which are almost entirely related to anxiety and tension, you can help get temporary relief by using essential oils.

Begin by giving yourself or your partner a special treat – a marvellous soothing footbath. For such a bath you should fill a large bowl three-quarters full with hot water. Then carefully add 2 drops Rose, 2 drops Ylang Ylang and 3 drops Lavender. Using a clean, new wooden kitchen spoon, specially reserved for the job, mix everything in, and let stand for a couple of minutes. Then let the feet sink into the water and soak for at least five well-earned, relaxing minutes.

COLIC

Colic is the term that is used to describe spasmodic bouts of cramping pain, building up in intensity until it finally reaches a peak, before abating and returning a short while later.

The causes can range from an obstructing stone, for which professional medical treatment is required, to intestinal gas. The latter is extremely common in babies, and it may strike adults as a result of high tension levels. Fortunately, you can easily aid the adult condition by having a short gentle massage that will also leave you feeling calm and gently relaxed. It only takes about ten minutes.

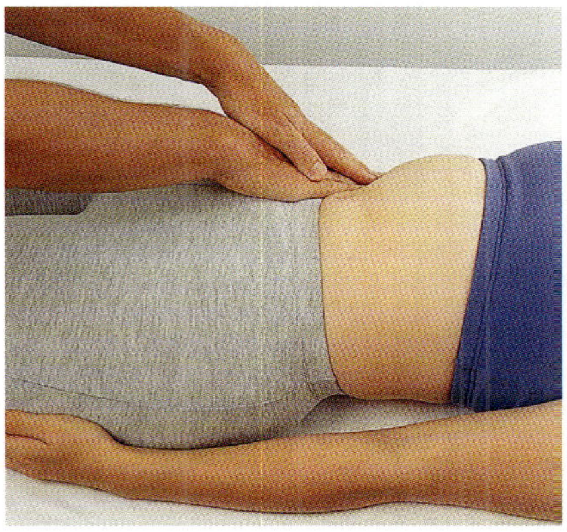

1 Starting in the lower right-hand corner, steadily and firmly press in using both your hands, but taking care not to cause any discomfort.

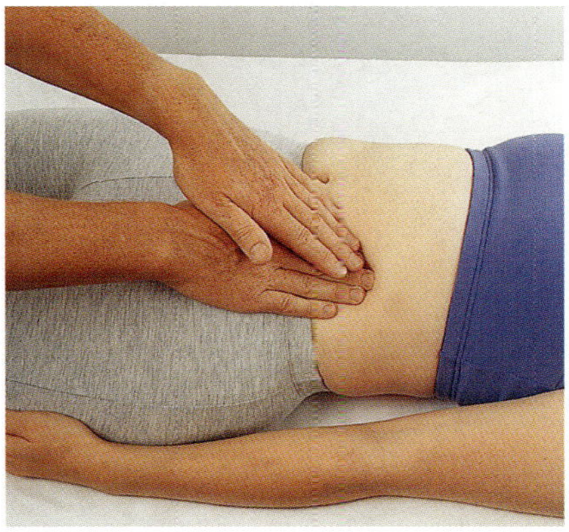

2 Slowly move the hands in a clockwise direction around the abdomen. Keep making continuous small circles to massage the colon.

reducing anxiety

One of the worst problems of anxiety is that it can end up causing headaches. To some people they are but a mild inconvenience, others might find that they slow them down, but in severe cases they can be totally debilitating. The sooner you act, especially if you tend to have major attacks, the more likely you are to be fine. One of the best remedies is a soothing head massage – it can work wonders in reducing the pain.

HEADACHE EASERS

Tension headaches are quite a common feature in most people's lives. In fact they are often completely unavoidable, caused by anything from long tedious slavish hours on a computer to bringing up unruly small children.

Whatever the cause, try and stop what you are doing at the first available opportunity, and take a break. Impractical though it sounds, it is the only way to stop the massive build-up of a nasty headache.

Try to draw the curtains, and to create a deep, dark relaxing astmosphere shut off from the outside world. Besides the massage described on the right, see if you can find time to make yourself a wonderful warm compress. If the head feels at all hot, then try using an oil infused with 4 drops of Peppermint. Another option is 4 drops of Chamomile.

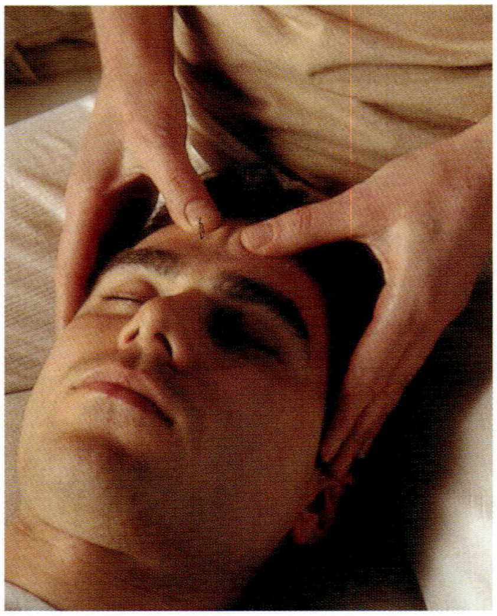

1 Ease tension headaches by massaging oils gently into the forehead. With your thumbs, use steady but gentle pressure to stroke the forehead. Repeat this technique for several minutes.

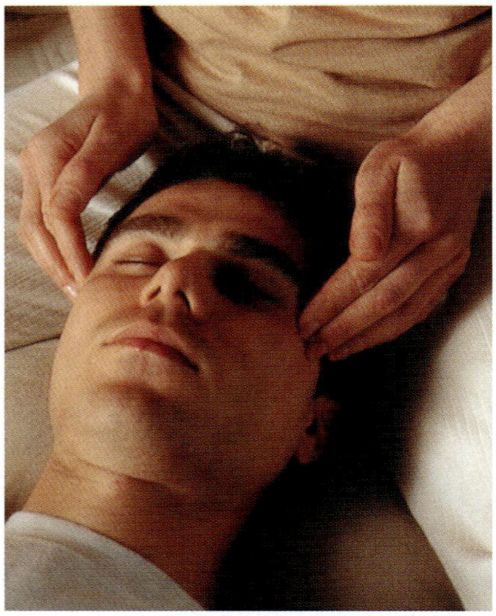

2 Gently massage the temples with the fingers to release tension and stress.

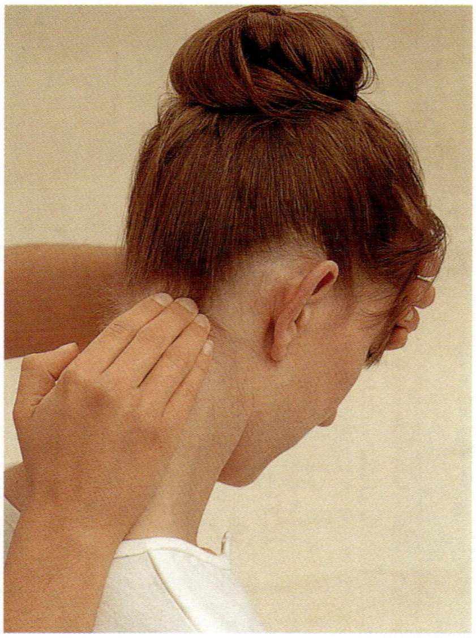

1 Use small circling movements just under the bony edge of the skull.

2 Now gently squeeze the neck muscles in a slow, rhythmic way.

MIGRAINE EASERS

One of the most complex of health problems, migraines are nature's way of shutting us down when life has been too demanding. The triggers that spark off a migraine attack are highly individual, and professional treatment is really needed to try to understand the causes for each person. Since many migraine sufferers have a heightened sense of smell at the onset of the attack they may find any aroma intolerable, so do use oils sparingly and sensitively.

At the earliest stage of a migraine attack, try using a blend of 2 drops Rosemary, 1 drop Marjoram and 1 drop Clary Sage, diluted in a massage oil and very gently massaged into the temples and forehead.

BREATHING ENHANCERS

"Breathe" . . . how often have we said this to ourselves when we are tense and stressed? Although breathing occurs without our conscious control, it can be affected to quite a considerable extent as we start to tense up, with a tightening of the chest muscles, which restricts any lung expansion.

The tightening feeling in the chest can be extremely uncomfortable, and you should most certainly seek expert medical advice at the first onset if it appears on the left-hand side of the body. Assuming that it is nothing too serious, though, your first consideration is to make sure that you start to relax, and begin breathing deeply and regularly. Take your time, and do not rush this. It is important that you regulate your controlled breathing sensibly.

Once you are happy that you have taken every step to calm down, shutting out whatever the cause might be, you can try the following steam inhalation. The key to success is making an aromatic blend. This is best done by taking a bowl of steaming water and adding 3 drops Benzoin, 2 drops Marjoram and 2 drops Eucalyptus. Mix them all together, leave to stand for a couple of minutes, and then with a covering towel placed over your head, begin inhaling deeply. You will soon notice the beneficial effects.

As the oils vaporize, inhale the steam deeply. If you hold a towel over your head this will slow down the evaporation.

MILD SHOCK SOOTHERS

You bump your head, trip over the cat, fall down the stairs, or stand on the upturned end of a garden rake so that it suddenly smacks you viciously on the head. In fact garden injuries are among the commonest, and most dangerous kind. As in the case of the rake, they can leave you absolutely taken aback, shocked and stunned. You might well feel a little weak and giddy, and need to sit down for a few minutes. At these times, essential oils can be a remarkably useful first-aid help, quickly bringing us right back to our senses.

The quickest, and by far the simplest way to benefit from aromatherapy in instances of mild shock, is to put an open bottle of either Lavender or Clary Sage oil under the injured person's nose and let them sniff the aroma directly. Of course you cannot always have such an oil on the spot, and it is therefore well worth having the pre-made "Rescue Remedy" ready to hand for such an occasion. Another extremely good remedy involves putting a couple of oil drops on a tissue, holding it under the nose and inhaling deeply for just a few minutes.

If, however, you suspect that the injured person is in severe shock, then do not try to treat them at home. Seek medical advice immediately. Such shock is caused by a sudden reduction in blood flow which, in extreme cases, can lead to collapse. The symptoms to look out for include fast, shallow intakes of breath, cold damp skin, a weak pulse, dizziness and even fainting.

tummy problems

Stomach problems might sound slight and comical, but they certainly are not when you are the sufferer. They can be completely debilitating, easily ruin a night out, make a long journey impossible, or disrupt that highly crucial meeting at work. Knowing how to deal with them promptly, however, can quickly revolutionize your life. Take any of the measures described and explained below, and you will find that you never look back.

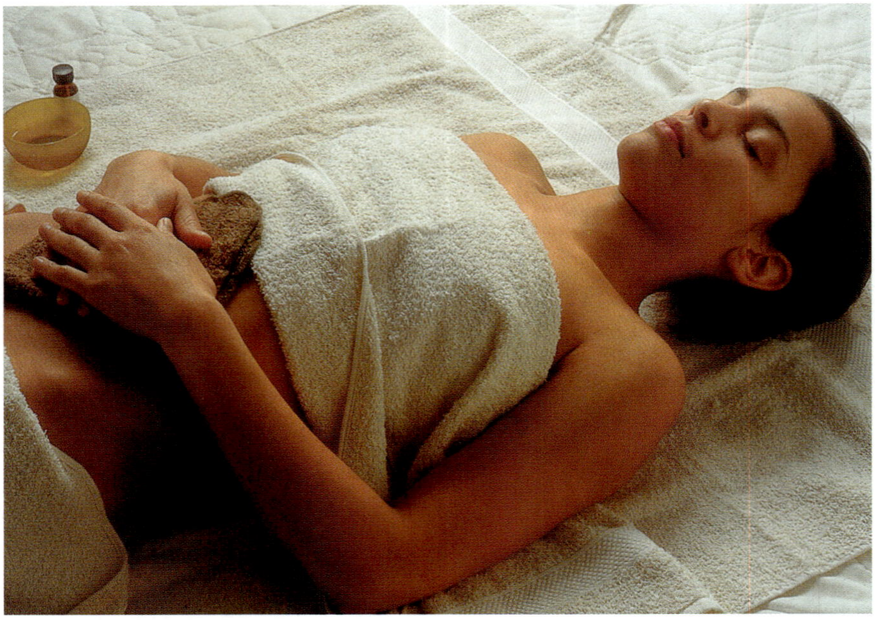

DIGESTIVE SETTLERS

Nervousness often shows itself in an upset stomach, or abdominal spasm. It has been said that our digestive organs also digest stress, and too often they end up storing emotions, causing all manner of discomfort and indigestion.

The key is to teach our bodies to let go of any such worries, and aromatherapy can help a great deal. One of the easiest ways to use oils in this context is to make a hot compress and then place it over the abdomen, keeping the area warm for about ten minutes. Begin by filling a bowl of hot water with either 2 drops Orange and 3 drops Peppermint, or 3 drops Chamomile and 2 drops Orange. Then soak a flannel in the hot water. Place the compress over the abdomen and relax.

TRAVEL CALMERS

They say that travel broadens the mind; unfortunately, for some people it does quite the opposite. It contracts the mind and condenses it into a compact series of dark, inescapable worries – will the car break down? Is this plane safe? Will I be sick? Will I come though this in one piece, and alive? Once you are on the conveyer belt of anxiety and possible problems, it simply does not stop.

If you are indeed such a poor traveller, try using one of the following essential oils to calm the mind and stomach. They will let you enjoy the delights of new horizons freely without being stressed by how to reach them. The simplest way to use essential oils is to put a couple of drops on to a tissue or handkerchief, and smell them frequently. Useful oils are Peppermint, Mandarin or Neroli.

1 Put a couple of drops of essential oil on a tissue, and keep it freely available so that you can reach for it when you wish.

2 To use, hold the tissue under the nose and lean the head slightly forward. Inhale two or three times.

women's health

While for many it used to be a case of grin and bear any problems, and suffer in silence, widespread help is fortunately now available. In extreme cases you should, of course, always consult your doctor, but for more minor conditions there are all kinds of different, soothing massages you can have. They should certainly reduce the impact of too much discomfort, and make sure that normal life is not too greatly disrupted.

PMT SOOTHERS

For many women the days leading up to a period can be fraught with mood swings, irritability and other symptoms. Sometimes they feel guilty that they are snapping, and this adds to the general sense of irritability. One feeds upon the other. While in particularly difficult cases professional help can be sought, in more low level cases there is much that you can do to help yourelf.

Try this satisfying blend of oils using 3 drops Rose, 3 drops Jasmine and 2 drops Clary Sage to a bath. Then get in and lie back, allowing the tension to soak away. Alternatively use this mixture to make a massage oil, and rub it gently into the abdomen for a relaxing, soothing, long-lasting effect. In fact you may find this so comforting it becomes a habit.

1 Slowly and firmly massage the abdomen with your hands. Rub in increasing and then decreasing circles, so that you can actually feel the discomfort slowly diminish and then vanish.

2 You can try moving your hands first in a clockwise, then anti-clockwise direction. It may be more beneficial if your partner helps give the massage This should help make him more understanding.

MENSTRUAL PAIN RELIEVERS

Painful periods can be due to a number of reasons, but tension will certainly add to muscle spasm and cramping pains. There is nothing more infuriating and frustrating than having a gnawing, cramping painful period just when you have reached a crucially important stage at work, or are planning a major day out.

If there is no organic or structural cause of the discomfort, try using essential oils as part of your routine. They can be applied in one of two key ways, either as a hot compress over the lower abdomen, or while having a deliciously long and soothing bath. Some oils actually have a reputation for improving the menstrual cycle in other ways; seek advice from a professional aromatherapist if you would like to find out more about such long-term treatments.

To make a compress, use 1 drop of Rose, Geranium and Clary Sage oils. Alternatively a fairly hot bath with 3 drops Rose, 3 drops Geranium and 2 drops Clary Sage will relax cramped muscles.

A long bath with a few drops of oil will help you to relax and soon soothe away any discomfort.

mood changing recipes

It is all too easy to get dragged down by the ever-increasing, remorseless demands made on you. There never seems to be a moment when you can be quiet and alone, and recharge your batteries. Everything seems stacked against you. But just take a little time out with these oils and you can quickly change your mood, getting rid of the blues and giving yourself a wonderful, refreshing pick-me-up.

UPLIFTING OILS

There are unfortunately times in all our lives when we get depressed to some extent, whether due to a specific event or an accumulation of chronic tiredness. As part of a programme of recuperation and restoring your vitality, aromatherapy can certainly be very effective in lifting the mood and giving a boost to your overall energy levels.

For a strong, but relatively short-lived effect, try 4 drops Bergamot and 2 drops Neroli in the bath, ideally first thing in the morning when you are still feeling quite well and relaxed. Do not leave it until too late in the day when the effects of tiredness and stress have taken a strong hold. Aromatherapy stands a far better chance right now of working, and what is more, when it does work it will set you up for the day, giving you renewed confidence. Incidentally, after the bath, gently pat the skin with a soft towel. Do not rub yourself too vigorously.

A gentler effect, which should also pervade the atmosphere all day long, involves using Bergamot or Neroli oils in an essential oil burner. You will probably only need just one drop of each oil at a time, repeating the process as many times as you like.

REVITALIZING OILS

In today's high pressure world, "high pressure" is exactly what it is all about. We are all expected to pack two lifestyles into one. Mother and worker, father and possibly chief provider. Nobody gets the right amount of time to themselves to boost their energy levels, or become quietly absorbed in reading or listening to music, etc. The end result of trying to juggle too many demands is that nearly all of us reach a state of "brain fag", when mental fatigue and exhaustion grind us to a halt.

Rather than reach for the coffee, or worse still alcohol, which far from being a relaxant is actually well known for depressing the central nervous system, try using these revitalizing oils. They will give you an instant, revitalizing pick-me-up and make you feel wonderfully more alert.

You can use 1–2 drops of Rosemary or Peppermint oil in a burner. Alternatively, add 3 drops Rosemary and 2 drops Peppermint to a bowl of steaming water, or use 4 drops of either oils on their own. Give the oils plenty of time to evaporate into the room, and breathe freely. Make sure you then spend some time quietly relaxing, taking in the full benefits of these oils.

INVIGORATING OILS

Chronic tension all too often leads to a feeling of inescapable exhaustion, when we just totally run out of steam. At these demoralizing, difficult times we need a sudden boost, and many oils have a tremendous tonic effect, restoring vitality but without in any way over-stimulating. As a group, the citrus oils are excellent for this purpose, ranging from the more soothing Mandarin to the highly refreshing Lemon oil.

Have a warm, but not too hot bath, with 4 drops Mandarin and 2 drops Orange or 4 drops Neroli and 2 drops Lemon. Alternatively, just add a couple of drops of any of these oils to a bowl full of steaming water. Then sit down calmly, and gently begin inhaling. This will soon help you clear away the tiredness and lift your spirits again.

This kind of steam inhalation is a valuable and simple way to receive the benefits of essential oils when either time or circumstance prevents a massage or indeed a bath.

SENSUAL OILS

Tension, anxiety, worry, depression, and loss of confidence and self-belief – these are just some of the many factors that can adversely affect your sexual energy and performance. Sometimes this leads into a no-escape negative spiral of anxiety about sex, leading to less enjoyment, and so on.

The best answer is not to get dragged down, feeling ever more anxious and depressed, until the problem becomes seemingly insurmountable, but to take a little time out of your hectic life. Be together with your partner and have fun; add to your sensual pleasure with an intimate massage session, using one of these excellent blends to release tensions and allow your natural sexual energy to respond freely.

Use whichever of these blends – 5 drops Rose and 5 drops Sandalwood or 4 drops Jasmine and 4 drops Ylang Ylang – appeals to you both, and include in a massage oil. Use gentle, stroking movements all over the back, buttocks, legs and front.

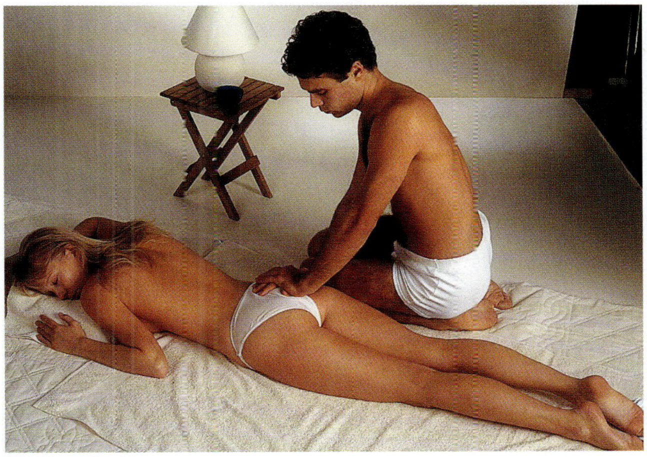

Massage gently all over the body with a light, caring touch. The secret is taking your time, getting the atmosphere right and making sure you choose the right moment.

SLEEP ENHANCERS

Worries can go round and round inside our heads, usually just as we are trying to get to sleep. Worse, they strike in the middle of the night and get blown out of all proportion. The resulting disturbed and restless night leaves us more prone to stress and anxiety, and a vicious cycle can be created. Help break into this cycle with a pleasantly hot and relaxing evening bath. Many oils can be useful – just having a fragrance that you enjoy will help you to unwind after a long day.

Add oils to an evening bath to aid relaxation and sleep. A couple of blends that relax without over-sedating are 4 drops Rose and 3 drops Sandalwood or 5 drops Lavender and 3 drops Ylang Ylang. Incorporate aromatherapy preparations into your daily bathing routine.

the oils

The more you study and learn about oils, the better you will be at making up your own mixtures or recipes to tackle your own highly individual needs. It is not as difficult and demanding as you might think. Just take your time and quietly browse through the following descriptions, and you will quickly see how oils are capable of overcoming a wide range of problems. They will make a wonderful addition to your lifestyle.

THE KEY PLANTS

Essential oils may be extracted from exotic plants such as Sandalwood or Ylang Ylang, or from the more common plants such as Lavender and Chamomile, but each one has its own characteristics and properties. Try to get used to a few oils at first, understand their different effects, and enjoy their fragrance!

Essential oils are in fact concentrated substances; while the skin of citrus fruits such as Lemon or Orange may yield a fair amount of oil, flowers such as roses only contain tiny amounts of the precious essence – about 5,000 roses may be needed to obtain 5ml/1 tsp of what is called a pure essential oil. Such a concentration really emphasizes the importance of only using drop doses of the oils in a suitable dilution, because a little goes a long way.

Oils are extracted from many different plant parts. Each contains powerful healing properties. Nature provides an abundance of therapeutic compounds to help us regain our health.

SANDALWOOD

(Santalum album)

Probably the oldest perfume in history, known to have been used for over 4,000 years. Sandalwood has a heavy scent, and often appeals to men as much as to women. It has a relaxing, antidepressant effect on the nervous system, and where depression causes sexual inhibitions and problems, Sandalwood can be the answer – a genuine aphrodisiac.

CHAMOMILE

(Matricaria recutita [German] or Chamaemelum nobile [Roman])

Roman and German Chamomile are both used to obtain essential oils with very similar properties. Chamomile is relaxing and antispasmodic, helping to relieve tension headaches, nervous digestive problems or insomnia, for instance.

BENZOIN

(Styrax benzoin)

This Asiatic tree produces a gum which is usually dissolved in a solvent to produce the "oil". It has a wonderful fragrance of vanilla, and is widely used in various kinds of inhalation mixtures. It is good at relaxing the airways, and it can be used whenever tension levels lead to an uncomfortable tight chest or cause restricted breathing.

GERANIUM

(Pelargonium graveolens)

The Rose-scented Geranium has very useful properties, not least being its ability to bring a blend together, to make a more harmonious scent. Geranium has a refreshing, antidepressant quality, good for nervous tension and exhaustion.

YLANG YLANG

(Cananga odorata var. genuina)

This tropical tree, native to Indonesia, produces an intensely sweet essential oil that has a sedative yet antidepressant action. It is very good for a range of symptoms such as excessive tension, insomnia, panic attacks, anxiety and depression. It also has a good reputation as an aphrodisiac, through its ability to reduce stress levels.

PEPPERMINT

(Mentha piperita)

This oil is another classic ingredient in inhalations for relieving catarrh, although commercial menthol (a major part of the oil) may be used with good results. Peppermint's many known analgesic and antispasmodic effects make it very useful for rubbing on the temples in order to ease any tension headaches; ideally dilute a drop in a little base cream or oil before you begin applying.

JASMINE

(Jasminum officinale)

One of the most wonderful aromas, Jasmine has a relaxing, euphoric effect, and can greatly lift the mood when there is debility, depression and listlessness. Use in the bath or in massage oils, or use Jasmine flower water for oily skin.

EUCALYPTUS

(Eucalyptus globulus)

One of the finest oils for respiratory complaints, found in most commercial inhalants. Well diluted (never use more than 1 per cent) in a base vegetable oil, it can be applied to the forehead to help relieve a hot, tense headache.

LAVENDER

(Lavandula angustifolia)

One of the most well-known scents, Lavender has been used for centuries to refresh and add fragrance to the home, and as a remedy for many stress-related ailments. It is especially useful for helping to relieve tension headaches, or for nervous digestive upsets; use in a massage oil or in the bath for a deeply relaxing and calming experience. The finest oil is produced from the true Lavender (Lavandula angustifolia), and is one of the most versatile of all oils. Its uses range from first-aid treatment of burns, to stress reduction.

ROSEMARY

(Rosmarinus officinalis)

With its highly penetrating, stimulating aroma, Rosemary has been used for many centuries to help relieve nervous exhaustion, various tension headaches and migraines. It is also known to improve the circulation to the brain, and is an excellent oil for overcoming mental fatigue and debility. **Caution** Do not use in pregnancy without seeking professional advice.

MARJORAM

(Origanum marjorana)

Marjoram has a calming and warming effect, and is good for both cold, tight muscles and for cold, tense people who might suffer from headaches, migraines and insomnia. Use in massage blends for rubbing into tired and aching muscles, or in the bath, especially in the evening to help obtain a good night's sleep. **Caution** Do not use in pregnancy without seeking professional advice.

PINE

(Pinus sylvestris)

There are a few species of Pine that produce oils, notably the American Long-leaf Pine which is a commercial source of oil of turpentine. However, the Pine oil used in aromatherapy generally comes from the Scots Pine. It helps to clear the air passages when used as an inhalation, and is also good for relieving fatigue. Tired, aching muscles can be eased with massage using diluted Pine oil.

CLARY SAGE

(Salvia sclarea)

This oil gives a definite euphoric uplift to the brain; do not use too much, however, as you can be left feeling very spacey! Like Ylang Ylang and Jasmine, its antidepressant and relaxing qualities have contributed to its reputation as an aphrodisiac. **Caution** Do not use in pregnancy without seeking professional advice.

ROSE

(Rosa x damascena, centifolia)

Rose is probably the most famous of all oils. There is probably more symbolism attached to roses than any other flower. Several kinds have been used to extract the oil, notably the Damask Rose and the Cabbage Rose. Each one is slightly different, but the overall actions are sedating, calming and anti-inflammatory. Not surprisingly, Rose oil has a wide reputation as an aphrodisiac, and where anxiety is a factor, it may be very beneficial. Use in the bath for a sensual, unwinding experience, or add to a base massage oil to soothe muscular and nervous tension.

BERGAMOT

(Citrus bergamia)

The peel of the ripe fruit yields an oil that is mild and gentle. It is the most effective antidepressant oil of all, best used at the start of the day. Its leaves give the distinctive aroma and flavour to Earl Grey tea. The oil can be used on a burner for generally lifting the atmosphere. Do not use on the skin in bright sunlight, as it increases photosensitivity.

LEMON

(Citrus limon)

Possibly the most cleansing and antiseptic of the citrus oils, useful for boosting the immune system and in skin care. It is also very good at helping to refresh and clarify the thinking process.

GRAPEFRUIT

(Citrus x paradisi)

Oil of Grapefruit is very helpful in the digestion of fatty foods and helps to combat cellulite and congested pores. It has an uplifting effect and will soothe headaches and nervous exhaustion.

shiatsu

Touch is the essence of shiatsu. We all need to be touched in some form, and shiatsu gives you a wonderful opportunity to fulfil this need in a loving and caring way. The nurturing touch of shiatsu helps trigger the vital self-healing process within each of us.

Shiatsu is a physical therapy aimed at treating your condition through the application of touch, as well as helping you to learn how to heal yourself. The treatment approach and philosophy is similar to acupuncture in its usage of the meridians (energy channels) and tsubo (pressure points) but shiatsu does not call for needles.

"Shiatsu" is a Japanese word meaning finger pressure. The application of pressure is the underlying principle of shiatsu. Different stretching techniques and corrective exercises may also be part of the treatment with the intention of creating balance in the body, both physically and energetically.

It is easy to learn the basic principles of shiatsu; it is also enjoyable and makes you feel good. You are taking responsibility for your own health, and taking care of yourself which is very important because it empowers you to create changes when required. In shiatsu we take a holistic approach and look at the whole person – body, mind and spirit – in trying to find out where the imbalances and causes of stress actually lie.

meridian health

It is always very exciting to hear and learn about radically different interpretations of how the body and mind work. While you may not agree with every last precise detail, they do, as in the case of shiatsu, provide a large number of marvellous insights into how we can manage and regulate our lives. One really beneficial result is knowing how to eliminate stress, enabling you to stay young, vibrant and healthy.

COPING WITH STRESS

Stress upsets both your mental and physical well-being, and every one of us has felt its grasp at one time or another. Stress is well known to all shiatsu practitioners and is recognized as one of the major factors affecting health in our modern society. It is a normal part of life; in fact, a certain level of stress is actually considered quite good for us. Some people seem to be able to thrive on it, yet for others the same degree of pressure can quite simply be too much.

A well-balanced diet, with plenty of daily fruit and vegetables, is essential for excellent health.

The increasing, cumulative impact of events sometimes means that, eventually, we can not cope. The pressure becomes overpowering and we begin to react to the stress in different ways. These reactions will affect our health and well-being and may interfere with our jobs and social lives in a significant, negative way. The body reacts to a stressor with first a diminished, then an increased, level of resistance. This is usually called the "fight or flight" reaction, which means that the body is instinctively ready to stand and confront, or escape. But stress, with all its different symptoms, is a sure sign that we have lost the wonderful sense of balance in our lives. Human beings have a marvellous natural system for maintaining balance, and the body is always striving to achieve this state of inner harmony. It is this balancing adaptive energy that is tested by stress, and which is constantly under challenge.

Coping with stress can be made easier by asking for help and support from family and friends. Talking to someone helps you to see a problem more clearly. It puts it into a sharper, wider perspective. Far better than just talking, however, having someone give you a long and gentle shiatsu treatment will relax your body and mind, and bring back a marvellous sense of general well-being. It is the ultimate experience when it comes to winding down.

A BALANCED LIFESTYLE

You can improve your general health and well-being, and your battery of defences, by understanding exactly what causes you stress, and by learning how to avoid it or even how to adapt to it. There are basically two key aspects to stress reduction: lifestyle modification and relaxation.

Lifestyle modification could mean changing your job and reassessing your goals in life, or simply adapting a more open attitude to what you are doing. Having a sense of control over events lessens their stressful impact. There is no point in trying to over-reach yourself. Ambition is good, but not when it leaves you constantly floundering with a marked sense of failure and desperation. Give yourself a chance.

Daily relaxation represents the most important element of maintaining health and vitality. Deep relaxation is not the same as sleep, and to gain full benefit from it, it is important not to fall asleep while you are relaxing. Giving or receiving a shiatsu treatment will relax your whole body and mind, and you will feel totally refreshed and energized afterwards.

The back-up treatment involves eating a well-balanced diet rich in fibres, grains and fresh vegetables. Cut down on sugar and salt as well as coffee, tea and carbonated soft drinks. Water and quality fruit juice are so much better for you. A certain amount of physical exercise is also necessary if you want to maintain your health and vitality. A pleasant, brisk 20-minute walk in the fresh air every day will stimulate and balance the energy within. Never attempt any kind of exercise that is too difficult or demanding.

Fight or Flight Response

- The brain registers danger and sends messages along the nerves to different muscles and organs to react accordingly (nervous/muscular system).
- The heart beats faster, pumping out blood to muscles and areas in need and you start to sweat (circulatory system).
- The breathing rhythm changes; you start to breathe faster due to more air being drawn in through the bronchial tubes as they expand (respiratory system).
- The digestion slows down (digestive system).
- Increased production of certain hormones, such as adrenaline and noradrenaline (hormonal system).

Organs - Meridians

The balanced functioning of our body is controlled by 12 vital internal organs. In Oriental medicine the organs have a wider meaning than in the West, based on their physiological and energetic function. Each has a different quality of energetic movement and responsibility and is linked to a meridian, or energy channel, named according to the internal organ it affects. The meridians run in pairs either side of the body, and they ensure the successful nurturing of energy, known as Chi.

Tsubo – Pressure Points

Along each meridian are a varying number of tsubo, or pressure points. They are points along the meridian where the energy is thought to be flowing near the surface of the body and therefore more accessible for treatment. There are more than 700 tsubo in your body, and they are numbered in sequence according to which meridian they are on. The first point on the kidney meridian, for example, will be Kidney 1 (KID 1). The points reflect the internal functioning of the body.

Lungs (LU):

- Take in air and vital Chi during respiration to refine and distribute it around the body. A fundamental process for building up resistance against external intrusions.
- Elimination of gases through exhalation.
- Openness, emotional stability, enthusiasm and a fulsome positive approach.

Large Intestine (LI):

- Helps the function of the lungs. Processes food substances and eliminates what is unnecessary.
- The ability to "let go". Elimination.

Spleen (SP):

- Corresponds to the function of the pancreas in Western terms and governs all organs secreting digestive enzymes. It also relates to reproductive glands in women and is a controlling factor in the immune system.
- Maintains the health of the flesh, the connective soft tissue and the muscle tissue.
- Self-image is strongly affected by the spleen function, as is the desire to help others. Self-confidence.

Stomach (ST):

- It is responsible for "receiving and ripening" ingested food and all fluids.
- Information for mental and physical nourishment.
- Groundedness, centredness, self-confidence and reliability.

Heart (HT):

- It governs blood and blood vessels as well as the circulatory system.
- Houses the mind and our emotions.
- Joy, calmness and communication.

Small Intestine (SI):

- The quality of the blood and tissue reflects the condition of the small intestine, and anxiety, emotional excitement or nervous shock can adversely affect the small intestine energy.
- Emotional stability and calmness.

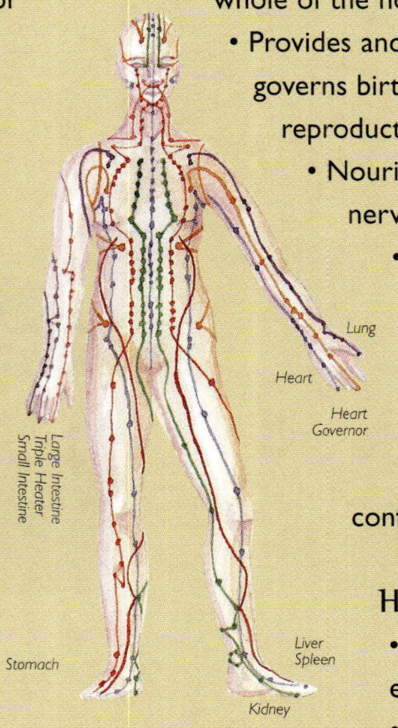

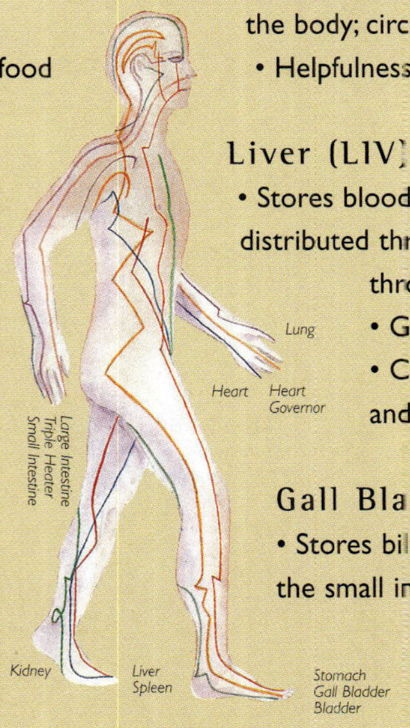

Kidneys (KID):

- The kidneys include the function of the adrenals, controlling the whole of the hormonal system.
- Provides and stores essential Chi for all other organs and governs birth, growth, reproduction and development; the reproductive system.
- Nourishes the spine, bones and the brain; the nervous system.
- Vitality, direction, courage and will power.

Bladder (BL):

- Purification and regulation.
- Nourishes the spine.
- Courage and the ability to move forward confidently in life.

Heart Governor (HG):

- Protector of the heart and closely related to emotional responses.
- Related to central circulation.
- Relationships with others; protection of others.

Triple Heater (TH):

- Transports energy, blood and heat to the peripheral parts of the body; circulatory system.
- Helpfulness and emotional interaction.

Liver (LIV):

- Stores blood and nutrients which are subsequently distributed throughout the body. Ensures free flow of Chi throughout the body.
- Governs the muscular and digestive systems.
- Creativity and ideas; good planning and organization.

Gall Bladder (GB):

- Stores bile produced by the liver and distributes it in the small intestine; digestive system.
- Practical application of ideas and decision-making.

treatments
treatments

treatments

Giving and receiving shiatsu is both extremely enjoyable and relaxing, and a wonderful way of spending time with another person. Before you begin, however, you must consider a few key points. First, consider your own health and condition. How are you feeling? Never try to give a shiatsu treatment if you are feeling in any way tired or depressed, or even intoxicated, have a contagious disease, or for any reason do not feel quite up to the task in hand. You must be fully alert, and able to concentrate. Your partner will quickly pick up the fact that your heart is not in it.

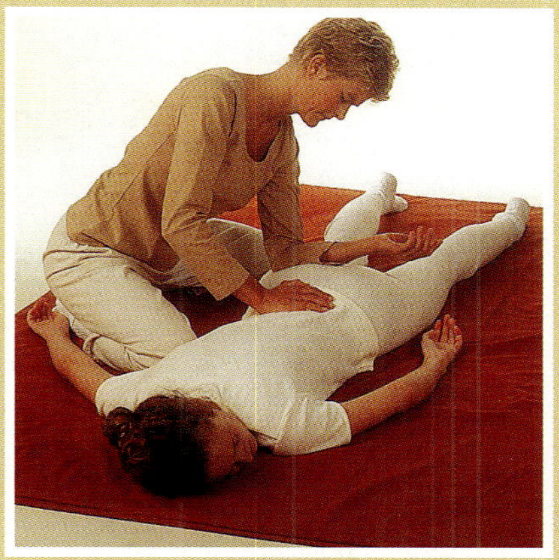

Before giving treatment you must also check that the environment is clean, warm and totally comforting. In fact it is well worth spending quite a bit of time getting this side of the treatment right. You do not want the excellent effects of shiatsu being undermined by the likes of a small, hot, airless room with the radio playing pop music. What you do want is calm, relaxing music, perhaps even a tape of bird song or early morning church bells, and soft muted lighting instead of a fierce glare. As for clothes, wear a loose fitting, airy, comfortable garment, possibly one made of cotton, and avoid eating any heavy meals for two hours before giving the treatment. Such detailed consideration is essential for a good session.

The next crucial step involves taking just a few moments to prepare yourself and your partner. Sitting in the Seiza position (that is, on your knees), to your partner's right-hand side, place your hand on the sacrum, as shown. Sit quietly, gradually begin to regulate your breathing, empty your mind until you feel totally quiet and at one with your partner, and focus on how they feel right now. Shiatsu practitioners always have excellent empathy.

The final point to note is that when giving treatment, sometimes your touch needs to be very light, and at other times it should be firm for deep tissue work. Try using your hands as an extension of your heart, and remember to be sensitive to your partner's needs at all times.

doin exercises

The term "Doin" literally means self-massage, and involves a combination of different techniques to improve the circulation and flow of Chi throughout the whole body. The following exercises can be used not only to revitalize your tired muscles and low spirits, but also to relieve a stiff, tense body and a stressed mind. Starting your day with a Doin session will quickly awaken your body and mind. You will soon notice the benefits.

THE PREPARATION

Prepare yourself by gently shaking all your limbs, and body. Shake your arms and hands to help release any tension in your upper body. Now gently shake your legs and feet as well. Place your feet shoulder-width apart and unlock your knees. Straighten your back to allow a better energy flow, relax your shoulders and then close your eyes. Take a minute to focus internally, and get in touch with how you and your body are feeling before starting the Doin routine.

Note that when doing this exercise it is vitally important that you become aware of any areas that might be in any discomfort, and that you try completely to empty your mind of any disturbing or distracting thoughts. It takes time to learn how to do the latter, and you will eventually succeed. What counts in the end is that you do not let tension ruin the effects of the Doin.

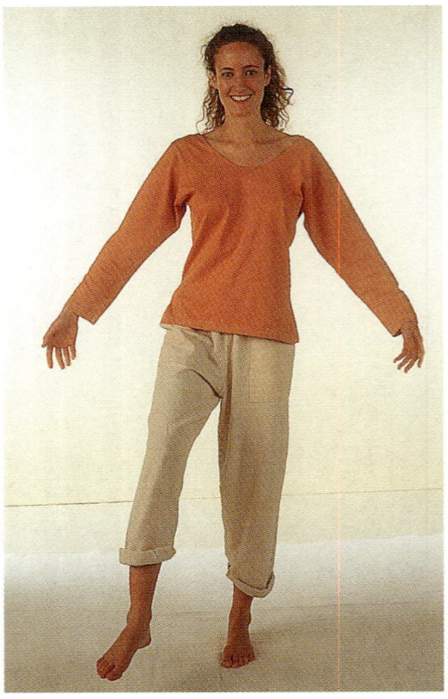

The Best Way to Complete

After having worked through your whole body as described in the following pages, stand up and gently shake out again. Now place your feet shoulder-width apart and bend your knees slightly. Imagine a string passing through your spine, from the tail bone to the top of your head. Stretch the string and feel your spine straighten up to allow for better Chi flow. Close your eyes for a moment and see how you feel after your Doin session. Try to remember how you felt at the beginning and compare that with the sensation you have now. Open your eyes again and to complete your session, practise breathing deeply.

You can do this Doin exercise as often as time permits. Ideally it should become a part of your daily routine, being practised early in the morning and again perhaps later in the evening. You will quickly notice and appreciate the benefits.

NECK

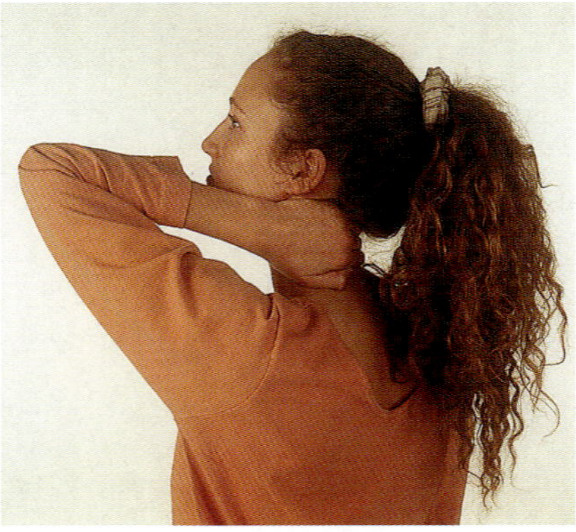

1 Using one hand, place the palm across the back of your neck and firmly massage in a squeezing motion. This will increase the flow of blood and Chi to the area, release stagnation, and remove waste products such as lactic acid.

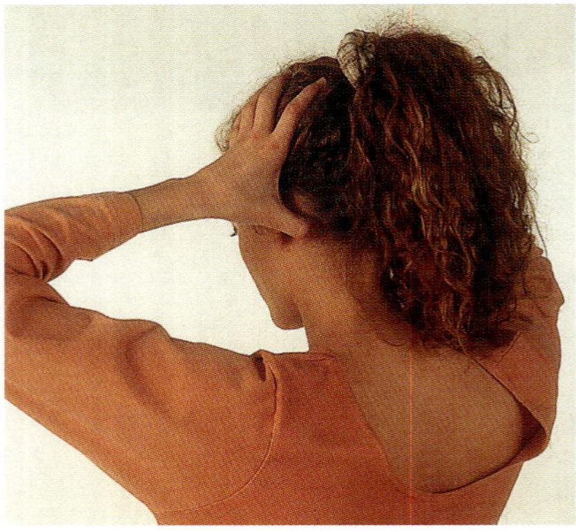

2 With your thumbs, gently apply pressure to the point at the base of the skull, directing the pressure upwards against the skull.

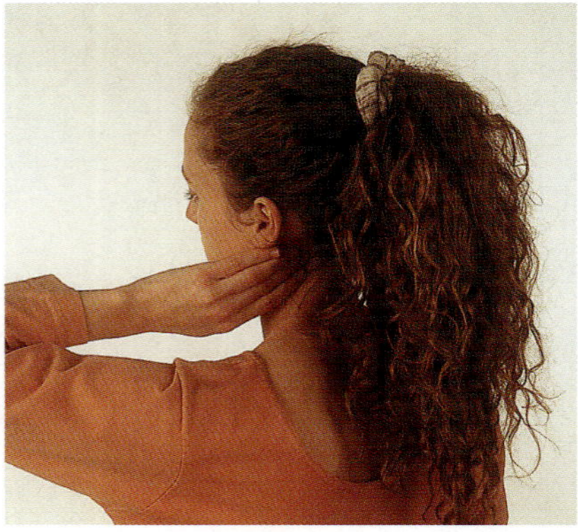

3 Use your fingers and rub across the muscle fibres at the base of the skull. This technique will release the muscles and tendons in the area, and also help to relieve headaches and any level of pain in the shoulder.

HEAD AND FACE

1 Open your eyes and make a loose fist with both hands. Keep your wrists relaxed and tap the top of your head.

2 Slowly work your way all around the head, covering the sides, front and back. This exercise will wake up your brain and stimulate blood circulation.

3 Pull your fingers through your hair, stimulating the bladder and gall bladder meridians on the top and side.

4 Place your fingers on your forehead, and apply a little pressure and stroke out from the centre to the temples.

5 Bring your fingers up to your temples. Drop your elbows, and massage your temples, using circular movements.

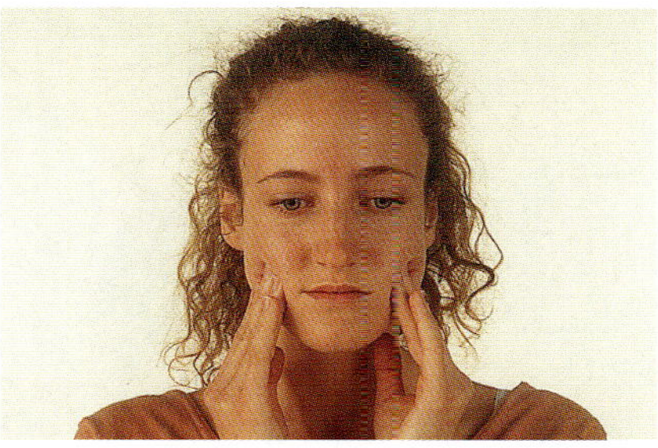

6 Massage down the sides of your face until you reach your jaw.

7 Squeeze along the jawbone, working outwards from the centre. This is a very good technique for trying to relax.

8 Using your index finger and thumb, squeeze your eyebrows starting from the centre line and move slowly and laterally.

9 Bring your thumbs to the inside of the eyebrows (point BL2). Allow the weight of your head to rest on your thumbs.

10 With your index finger and thumb, pinch the bridge of your nose and the corners of your eyes.

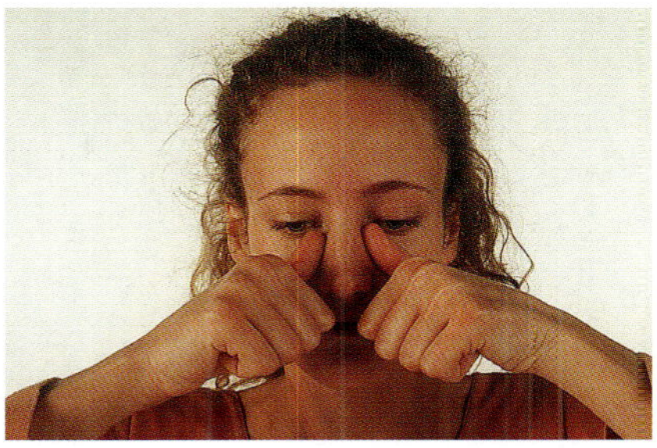

11 Apply your thumbs to the sides of your nose. Breathe in as you stroke down the side of your nose.

Key Tips

The above routine is particularly good if you feel a cold coming on, or have one already. Although Doin exercises are specifically designed for self-help, they can just as easily be carried out by another person, particularly if you are feeling too lethargic to do it yourself. The above routine will ease discomfort and speed recovery.

SHOULDERS, ARMS AND HANDS

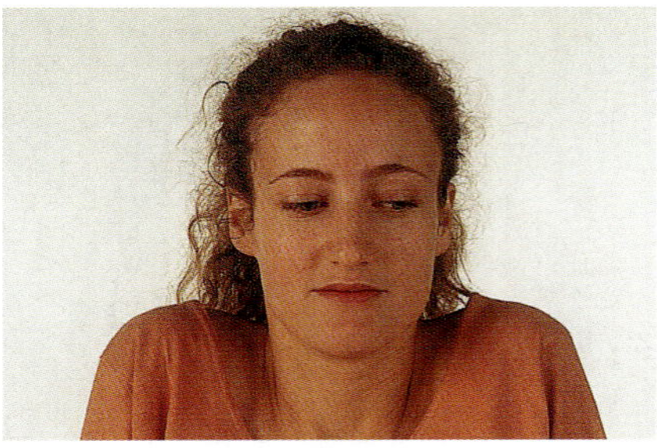

1 Lift up your shoulders up and breathe in. Breathe out, letting your shoulders drop and relax. Repeat.

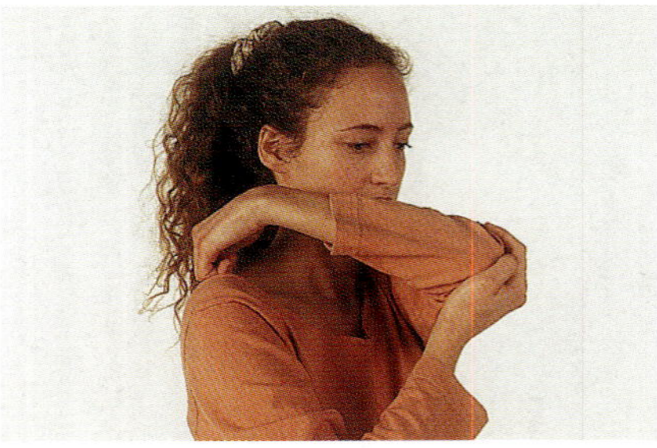

2 Support your left elbow and with a loose fist you can begin tapping across your shoulder.

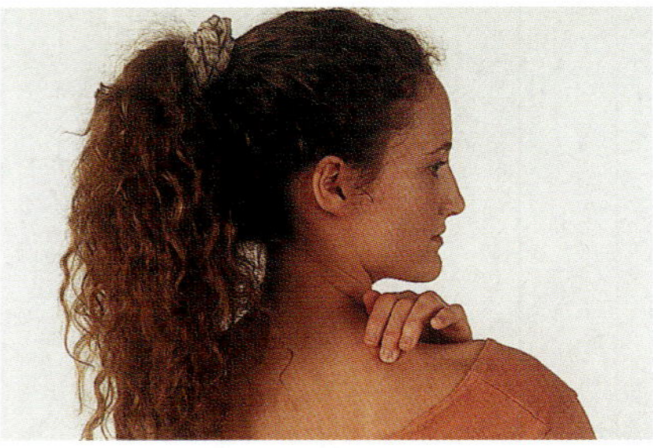

3 Press your middle finger into the shoulder's highest point, known as point GBL21, the "Shoulder Well". **Caution** Sometimes used in childbirth to speed up labour; do not use during pregnancy.

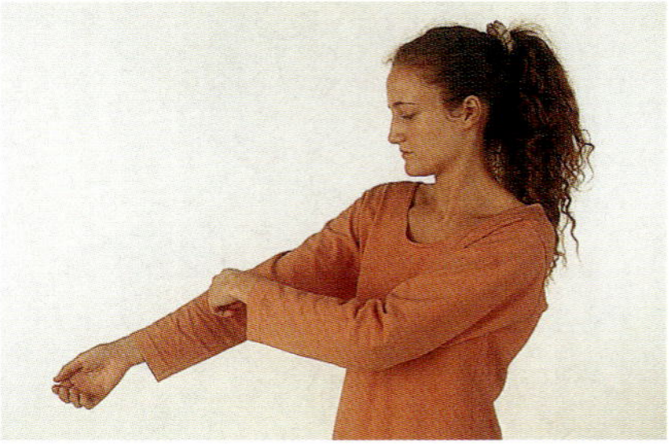

4 Straighten your arm, open your palm and tap down the inside of your arm from the shoulder to the open hand. Good for the heart meridians.

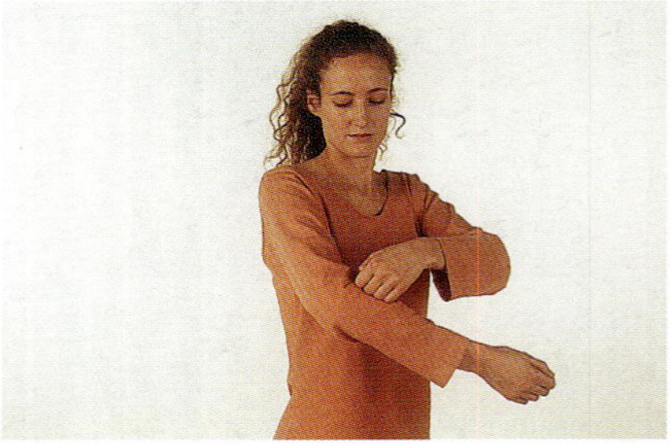

5 Turn your arm over and tap up the back of your arm, from the hand to the shoulders. This technique stimulates the meridians for the intestines. Repeat three times.

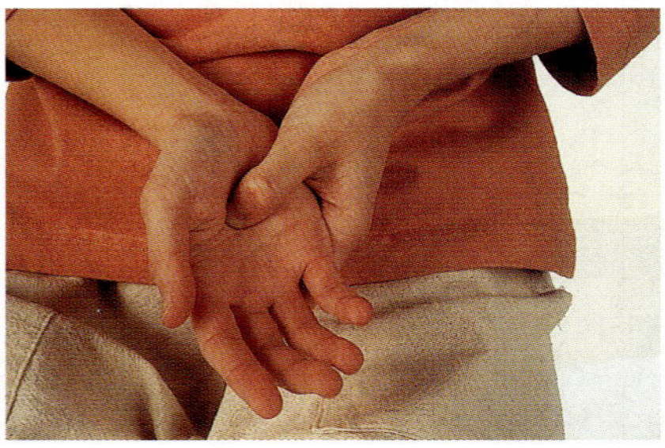

6 Use your left thumb to work through your right hand, gently massaging the centre of your palm to relieve general tension and revitalize you spiritually.

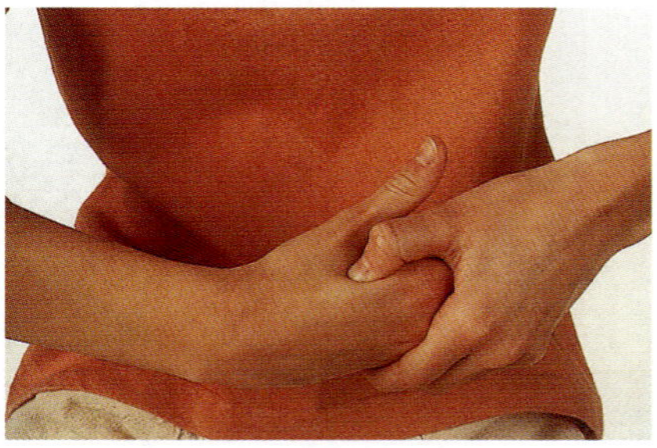

7 Stimulate the "Great Eliminator" on the large intestine meridian, in the web between the index finger and the thumb. **Caution** Sometimes used in childbirth to speed up labour; do not use during pregnancy.

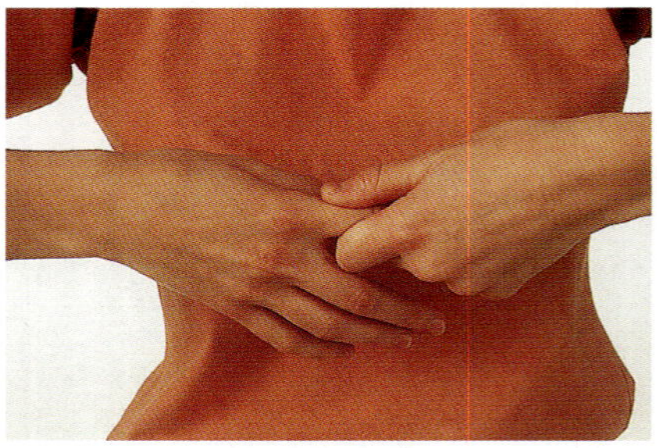

8 Carefully squeeze and massage the joints of each finger using your index finger and thumb. Repeat as often as you find it necessary.

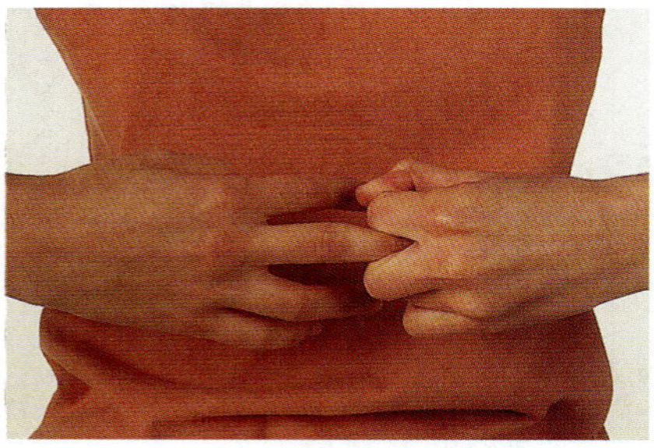

9 Pulling out the fingers will stimulate the starting and end points of all the meridians. This is a great way to release any stress and tension in your hands.

CHEST, ABDOMEN AND LOWER BACK

1 Open up your chest, and using either a loose fist or flat hands for comfort, tap across your chest, above and around the breasts. This will stimulate your lungs and strengthen your respiratory system.

2 Take a deep breath in as you open your chest again; then on the out breath tap your chest and make a deep resounding "Ahhh…" sound.

3 Proceed down towards your abdomen, and with open hands tap round your abdomen, clockwise, for about a minute.

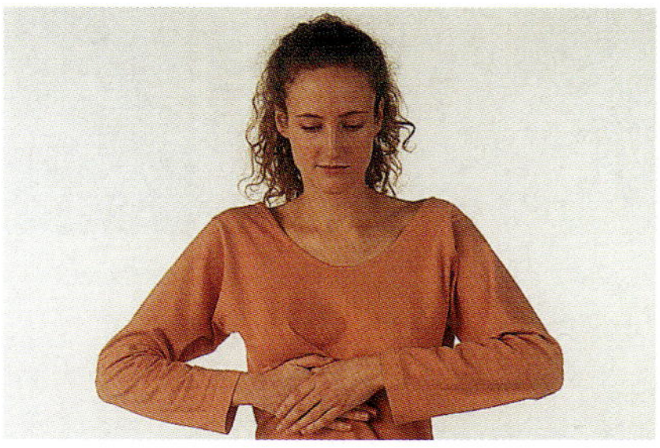

4 Place one hand on top of the other, and then make exactly the same circular motion around your abdomen for about another minute.

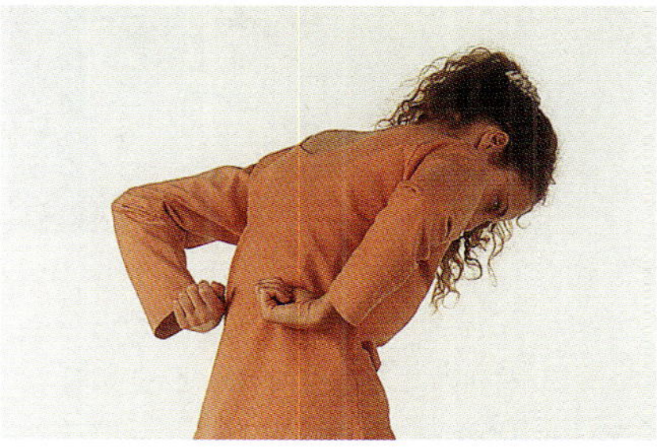

5 Place your hands on your back, just below your ribcage. Start to rub the area until you feel some warmth. This will stimulate your kidney energy.

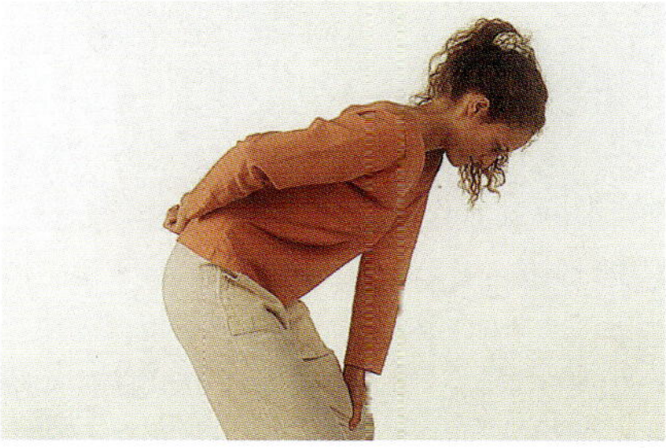

6 Place one hand on your knee. Using the back of your other hand, tap across your sacrum bone at the base of the spine. It activates the nervous system.

LEGS AND FEET

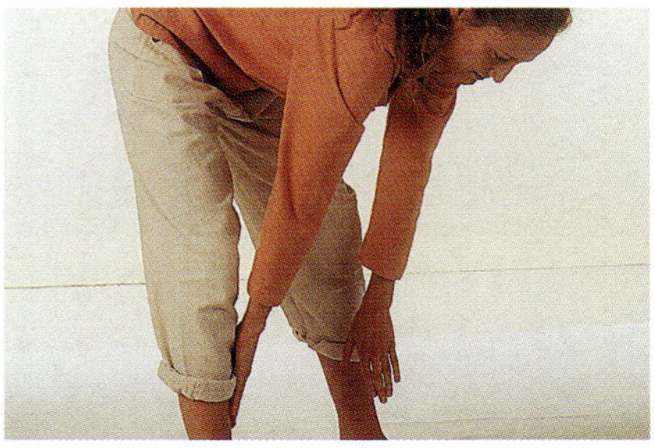

1 Tap down the backs of your legs from your buttocks to your heels, following the flow of energy. Tap up the inside of your legs, stimulating your liver.

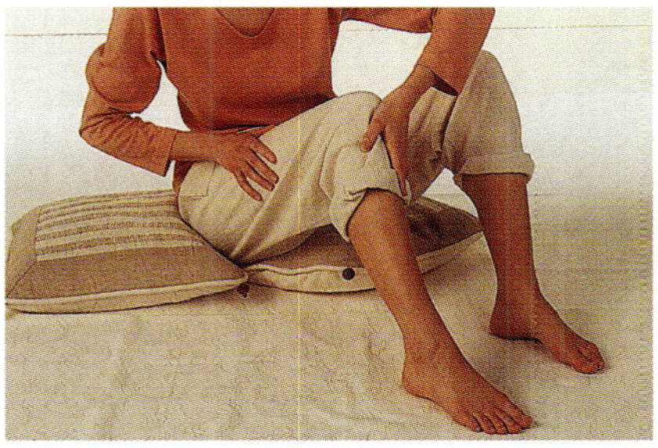

2 Sit down on the floor, and measure four finger widths down from the knee-cap on the outside of your leg. Place your thumb on the point ST36 and press. Good for tired legs.

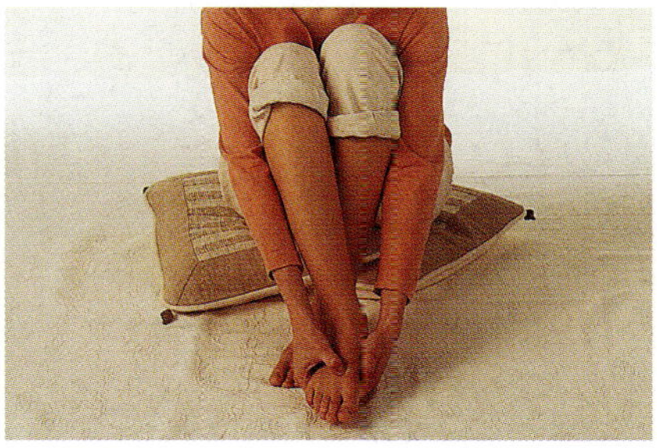

3 On the dorsal part of your foot, between the big toe and the second toe is LIV3, "Big Rush". Good against cramp. **Caution** Do not use this particular point during pregnancy.

system calmers with a partner

If you notice that your partner looks listless, is feeling at all tired and stressed, is experiencing any tension in the upper body, or suffers from shallow, rapid breathing, the following treatment will be very beneficial. It will aid relaxation and promote much deeper breathing, facilitating a more efficient energy distribution to all parts of the body. The treatment is quickly and easily given.

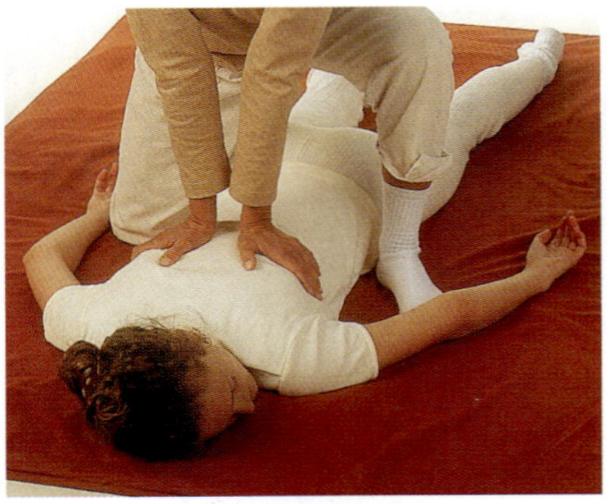

1 To prepare for treatment, kneel by your partner's side and place your hand at the base of the spine. Concentrate on how your partner feels. Then place your palms on either side of your partner's spine. Crouch down if it feels easier.

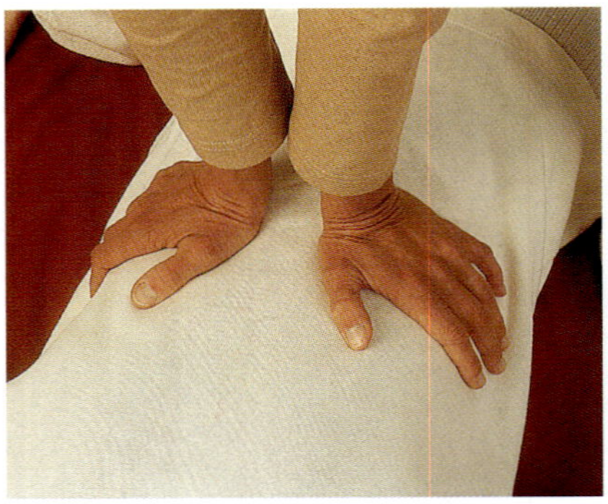

2 Ask your partner to breathe in; on the out-breath lean into your hands and apply pressure to your partner's back. Ease the pressure to allow your partner to breathe in again. Move your hands down and press on the next exhalation.

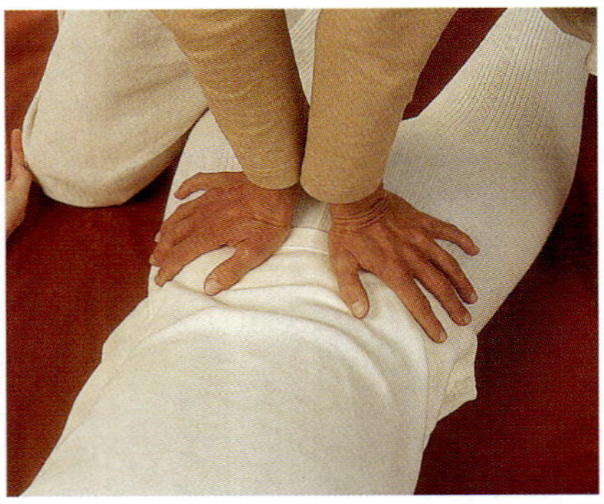

3 Start at the top of the back between the shoulder blades. Work your way down towards the sacrum. Repeat three times. Always keep your elbows straight, and use your body weight as you work.

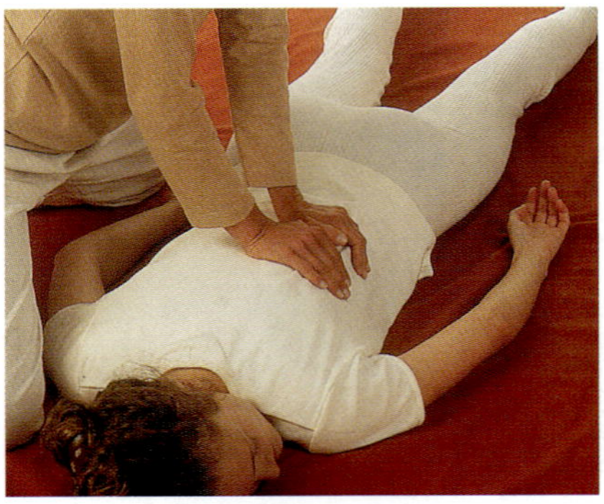

4 Kneel at 90 degrees to your partner, place your palms in the valley (on the opposite side of the spine) formed by the spinous processes (spinal bumps) and the broad muscles running on either side of the spine. Rock the body with the heels of your hands. As you rock, you can move your hands down the back, one following the other. The rocking should be continuous and rhythmic. Repeat three times. Do both sides, working from the opposite side of the body.

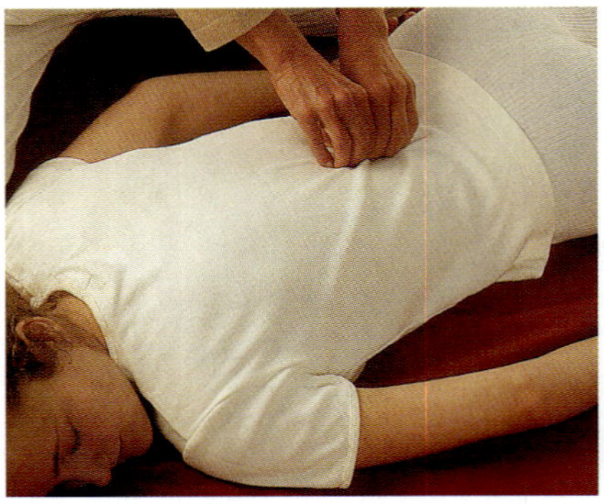

5 This technique allows you to focus specifically upon the spinal column. You still need to rock; however, this time the spinous processes are gripped between the fingers and the thumbs. Applying a positive (firm) contact, gradually work the hands along the full length of the spine, moving it from side to side. This action is good for loosening the muscles and stimulating the nervous system.

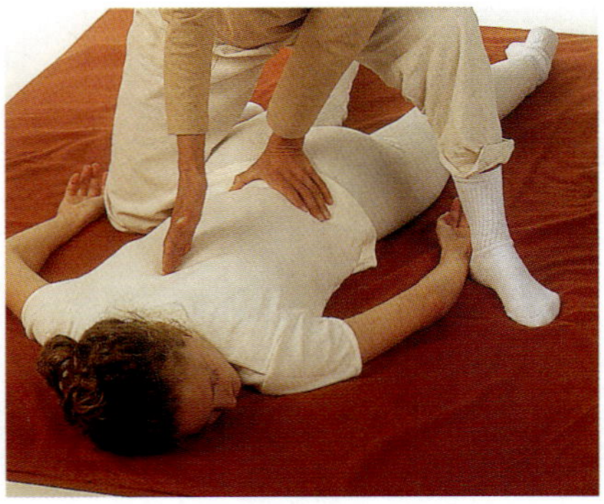

6 Place your left hand on your partner's sacrum. Using the edge of your right hand like a knife, perform a sawing action down either side of the spine. Work both sides alternately, repeating the sequence three times.

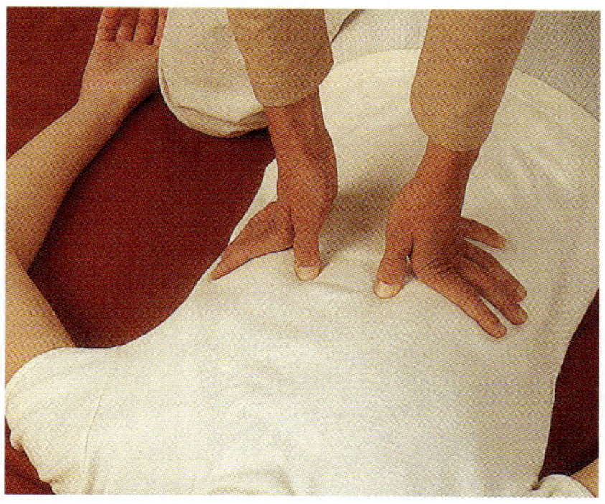

7 Run your hands along the spine to feel the undulations of the spinous processes. Bring your thumbs sideways, two fingers' breadth from the dip between the two spinous processes. Apply perpendicular pressure.

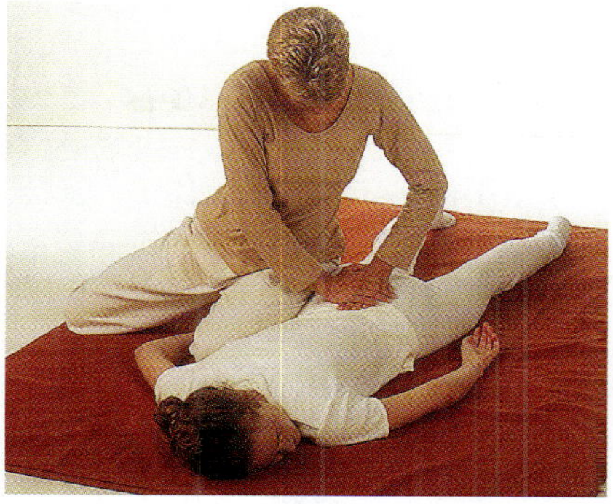

8 Put one hand on top of the other and place your hands on your partner's sacrum. Apply pressure to the sacrum, focusing all your energy into the base of the spine.

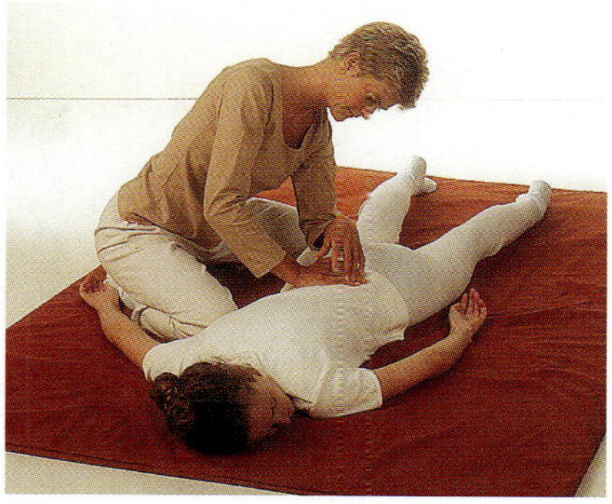

9 Turn around to face your partner, spread your knees and, using the fleshy part of your forearm in a penetrating and rolling action, apply pressure across the buttocks. Stay on the same side to work both buttocks.

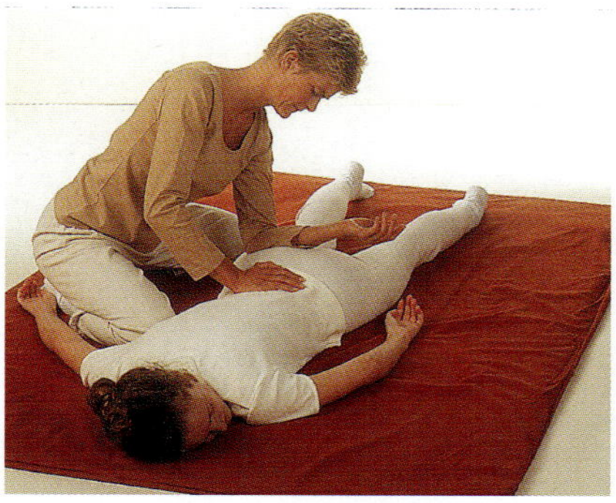

10 Note the position of the "mother hand", and keep the hands relaxed as you roll your forearm right across the surface of the buttocks.

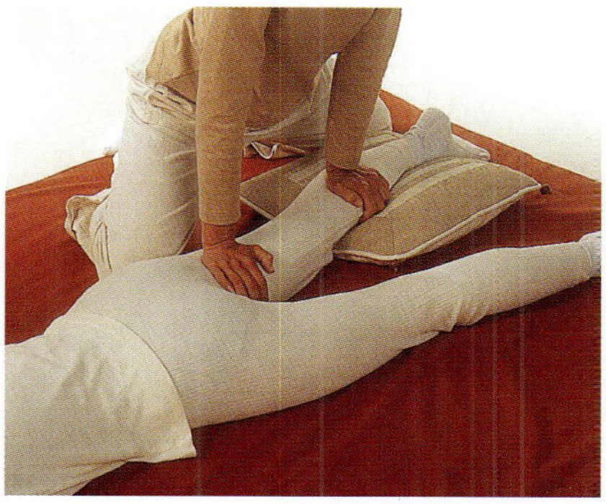

11 Adjust your position so that you can move down the leg. One hand remains on the sacrum or is placed on the back of the thigh. Starting from the back of the thigh, gradually work down the leg, applying pressure with your thumb. Support your partner's lower leg with a cushion beneath the shin.

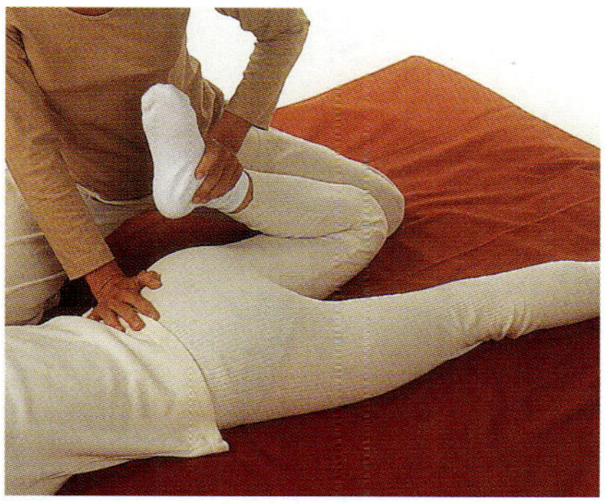

12 Take hold of your partner's ankle and bend the leg towards the buttock. Adjust your position to allow you to use your body weight to achieve the stretch. Now move yourself all the way down to the feet. With both hands, take a firm hold of the ankle, lean back and stretch out the leg to its full length.

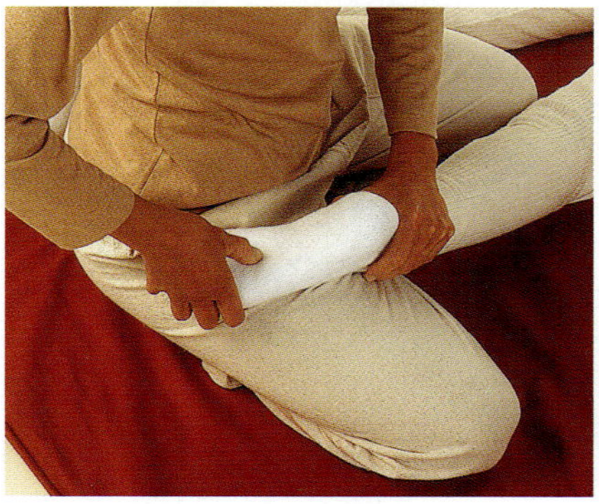

13 Place your partner's foot in your lap and using your thumb apply pressure to Kid 1, "Gushing Spring", one-third of the distance from the base of the second toe to the base of the heel.

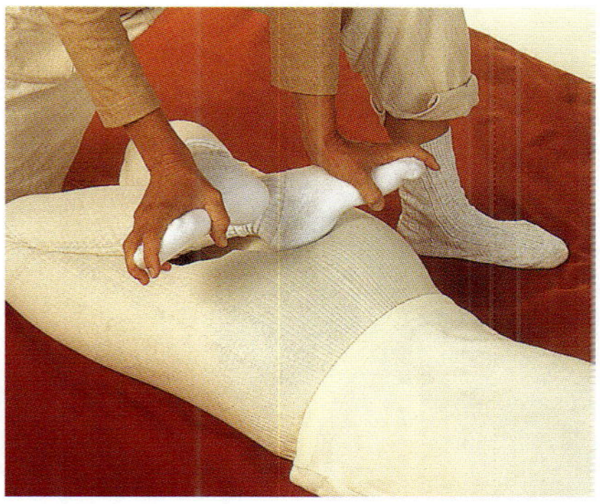

14 Cross your partner's ankles and bring them slowly towards the buttocks. Do this stretch twice, the first time placing the more flexible leg in front (nearest to the buttocks), then reverse the position.

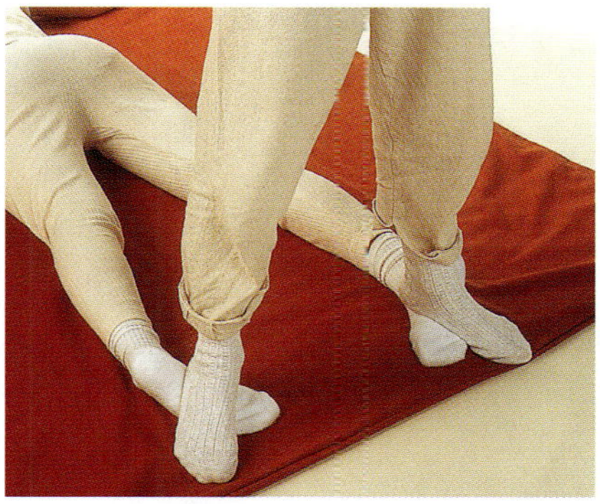

15 Stand up and walk on the soles of your partner's feet using your heels. Have the feet turned inwards and apply pressure to the soles but with no weight at all on the toes.

nervous system calmers: self-help

Stress can have quite a significant and dramatic effect on the nervous system, and badly affect a wide range of functions, including breathing. One excellent way to get you back on track is to balance the energy in the bladder channel through the following exercises and the shiatsu treatment of the back. Both techniques are tailor-made to calm your nervous system.

1 Stand with your feet shoulder-width apart and knees bent. Keep your back straight. Let your arms hang loose at your sides. Swing them from side to side.

2 Swinging your arms will create a twist in your spine, gradually loosening up the joints between the lumbar vertebrae and allowing for better flexible movement.

3 Bring your arms a bit higher up so that you now feel the twist in the middle part of your back. This will loosen up the thoracic vertebrae and the diaphragm.

4 With your feet wider than shoulder-width apart place your hands on your legs, above your knees, and straighten your back. Sway back and look up.

5 Bend your arms and slowly bring your upper body down towards the floor. Keep looking at the ceiling until you no longer see it. Relax the head downwards.

6 Pull your abdominal muscles in and slowly roll up your spine allowing the head to come up last. Lift your head and straighten your spine. Return to the sway back and repeat the whole movement about ten times.

7 Stay in the same position as for the last step of the previous sequence.

8 Breathe in and, on the exhalation, drop the left shoulder down as shown. Keep your elbows gently locked and look up to the ceiling over your right shoulder. Feel the twist in your spine.

9 Take another deep breath in, return to the starting position and drop your right shoulder down as you exhale. Repeat another three or four times on each side. Finish by coming back to the starting position. Relax your upper body forward. Move your feet closer together and slowly roll up your spine, until you come to a relaxed standing position.

10 To treat your back further in case of pain and tension, or whenever you feel in need of general relaxation, try using tennis balls as extra help. Put two tennis balls into a sock and knot the top. Lower yourself on to the tennis balls, which should be placed on either side of the spine. This is where your bladder meridian is located. Start from the area between your shoulders, or anywhere where you feel any pain and discomfort.

11 Breathe deeply and allow your back to sink on to the balls. The balls will mould themselves to the contours of your back and stimulate your bladder energy. Keep the balls in one place until you feel the muscles relax and then slowly roll the balls to the next area "in need". Work this area in the same way, using your breath to enhance the relaxation. Give yourself 10–15 minutes, working down the whole spine. Afterwards your spine will feel open and relaxed against the floor. You will have a sensation of warmth down your back.

12 When you have finished these spinal exercises it is good to lie down on the floor and relax with your lower legs resting on a chair. This relaxes the lumbar area of your back and realigns the whole spine. Close your eyes, allow your breathing to slow down and feel the energy moving from the top of your spine down to the sacrum like a wave. Stay in this position for 10–15 minutes.

This relaxation exercise works directly on the nervous system, calming it down, and you can use the exercise at any time when you feel stressed.

breathing enhancers with partner

Correct breathing is the first, fundamental technique that keeps us going. Surprisingly, when things get stressful we do not always breathe as we should. Deep, relaxing inhaling is replaced by short shallow gasps for air, and the whole body quickly suffers. The following techniques are aimed at the upper part of the body, helping you feel calm, relaxed and well in control again.

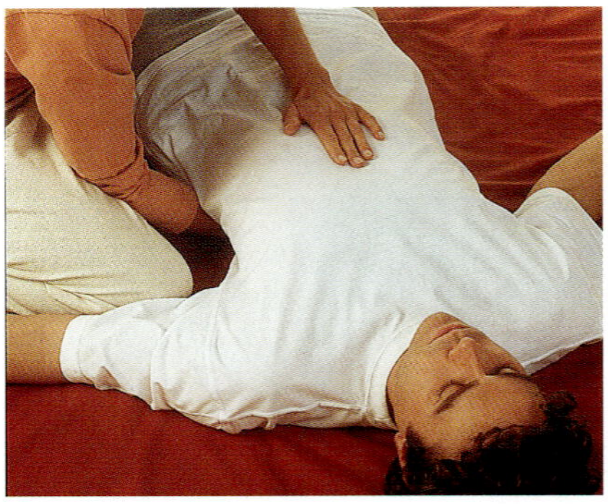

1 Place one hand underneath your partner's back in the area opposite the solar plexus and the other hand on top covering the area just below the sternum (breastbone). Focus into the area between your hands and encourage your partner to do the same. Feel the Chi from the breath of your partner reach this space, slowly allowing it to open and expand. You will gradually feel the tension go and the muscles relax to allow a deeper and more relaxed breathing.

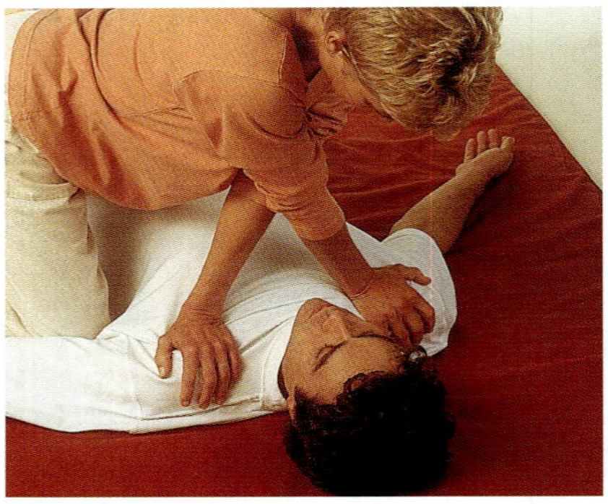

2 Cross your arms over and place the palms of your hands on your partner's shoulders. Ask your partner to breathe in and on the out-breath bring your body weight over your hands, stimulating the first point of the lung meridian and gently opening the chest. Repeat this three times.

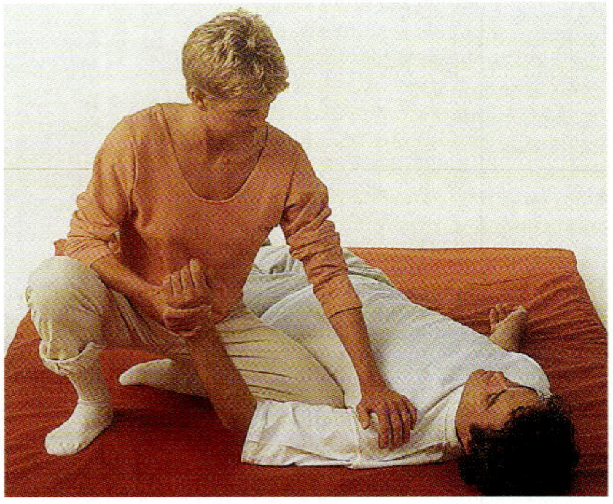

3 Keep your left hand on the shoulder and take a firm hold of your partner's hand with your right hand. Lift the arm from the floor, shake it out, and then finally allow it to relax again.

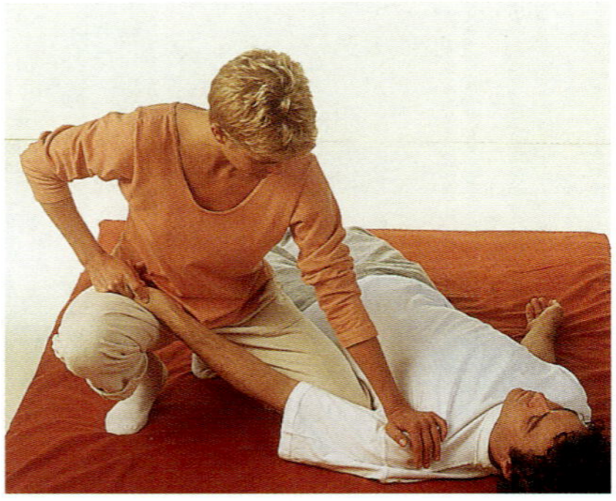

4 Firmly hold on to the thumb and give the arm and the lung meridian a good revitalizing stretch. You can repeat this technique several times.

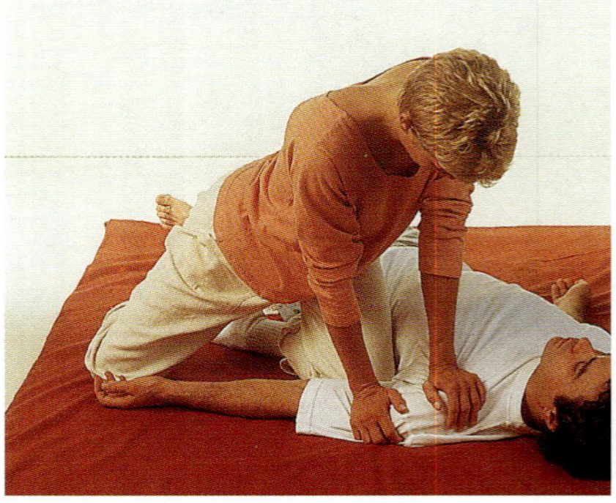

5 Place your partner's arm at a 45-degree angle to the body. Use one of your hands to support the shoulder while the other hand palms along the arm to the hand. Stay on the thumb side of the arm to activate the energy in the lung meridian.

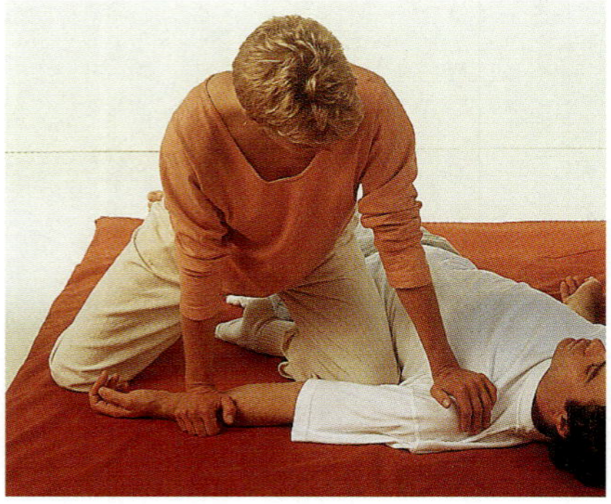

6 Continue all the way down to the thumb (end point of the lung channel). Avoid applying any direct heavy pressure over the elbow joint.

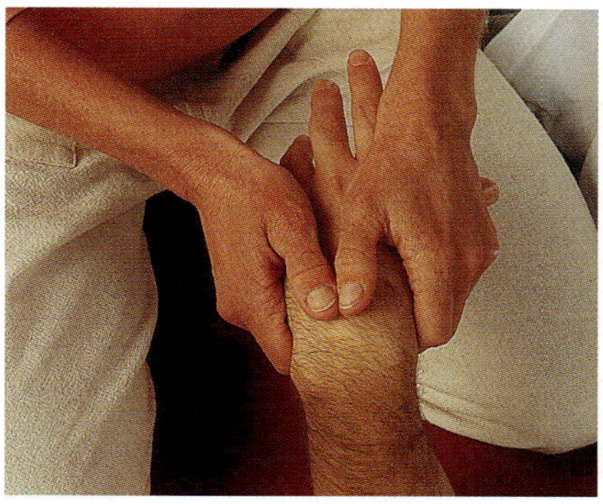

7 Using your thumbs, massage the whole of the dorsal side of your partner's hand.

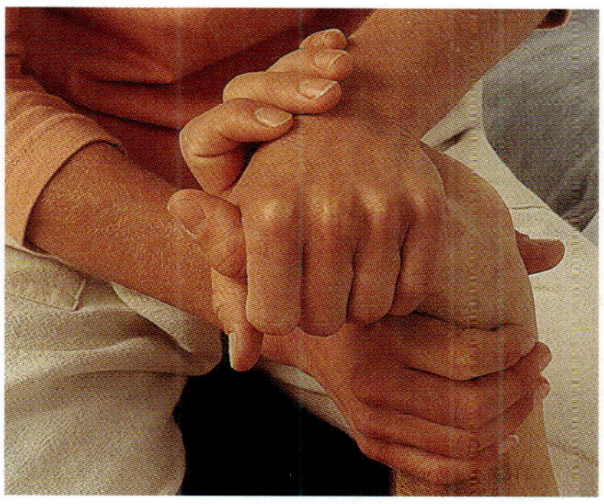

8 Loosen up the wrist joint by slowly rotating the hand.

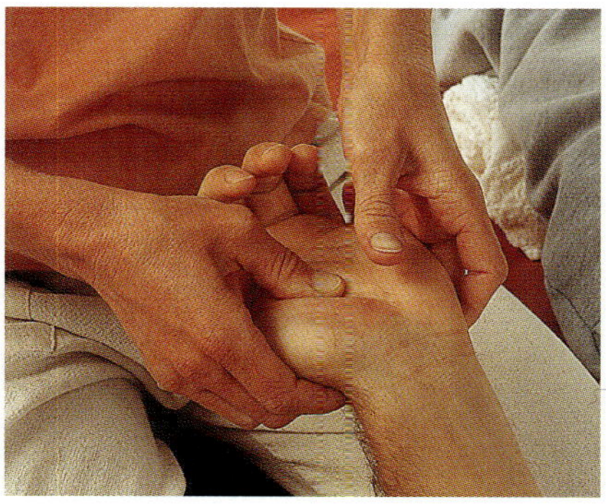

9 Open up the palm of the hand and gently massage. Apply pressure to the point in the centre of the palm, called "Palace of Anxiety". A very good point for calming and releasing tension.

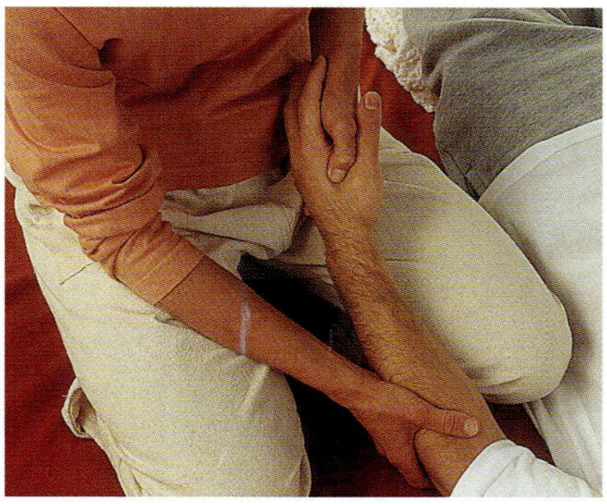

10 Find point LI4 which is located in the web between the index finger and thumb. Stimulating this point with gentle pressure from your thumb will relieve headaches and help clear any mucous congestion taking place in the lungs.

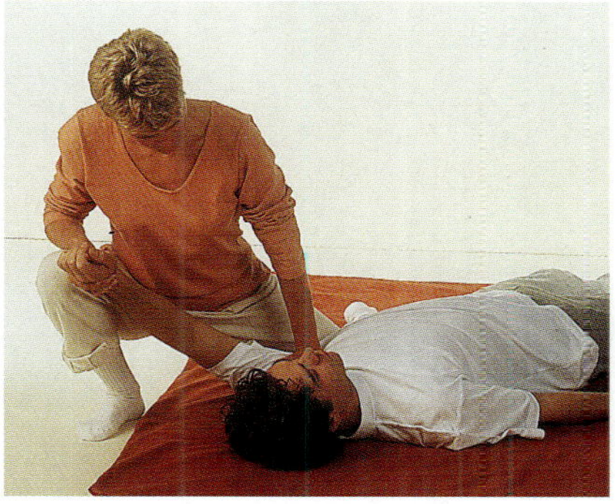

11 Hold your partner's arm by the wrist and support the shoulder with your other hand. Step forward and rotate the arm into an overhead stretch. Before you step forward, you need to apply pressure to the supporting hand at the shoulder. Maintaining this pressure ensures a strong stretch. Step back, allowing the arm to return to the starting position.

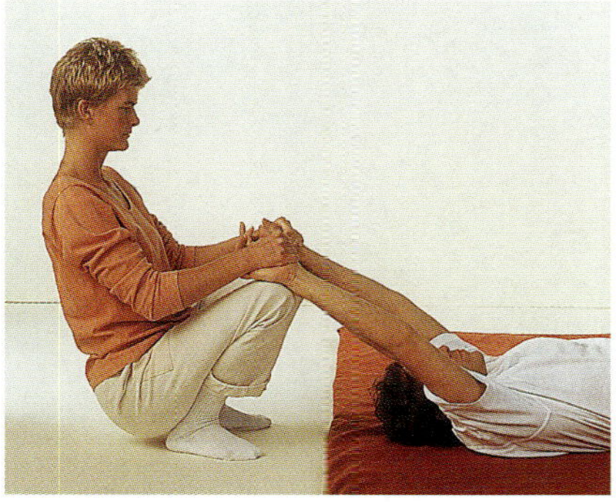

12 Place both hands on top of your knees and stretch the arms by leaning backwards. Let go of the arm you have treated and move over to the other side. Repeat the whole sequence working on the other arm.

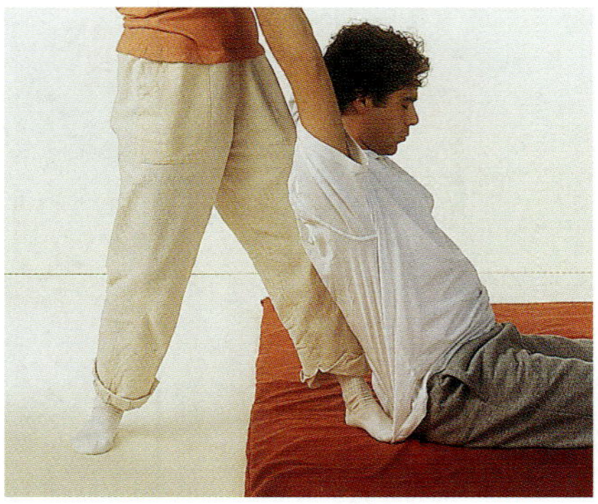

13 Stand behind your partner. Take hold of the hands, gripping around the thumbs, and as you both exhale, lift up from your knees and lean backwards until your partner feels the stretch.

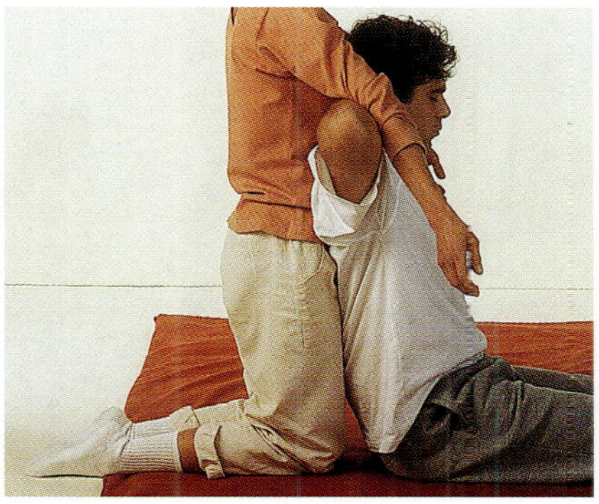

14 Kneel down behind your partner and ask them to clasp the hands behind the neck. Bring your arms in front of your partner's arms, and on the out-breath gently open up the elbows to the sides.

15 Bring one knee up to support your partner's lower back. Take hold of the lower arms, and on the out-breath bring the elbows towards each other behind your partner's back.

self-help breathing enhancers

The lung energy controls our intake of fresh air and Chi from the external environment. However, when your stress levels are high for a period the bronchial tubes expand to let in more air and the end result is that we tend to "over-breathe", or hyperventilate. By working on the lung meridian and practising these breathing exercises, you will facilitate deeper, more satisfying breathing.

1 Link your index finger and thumb on both hands. Step forward with your right foot and reach to the ceiling. Step back, relax the arms and repeat with your left foot. Repeat 3 or 4 times on each side.

2 Stand with your feet apart. Lift your arms to the sides with elbows bent, and make loose fists. Take a deep breath in, opening your chest by bringing your arms back as far as is possible.

3 On the exhalation, cross your arms over in front of you and relax your head down. Keep your knees bent, press back the area in between your shoulder blades. Repeat four or five times.

4 Stand with your feet shoulder-width apart and knees bent, and spread your feet slightly apart so that your toes point out. Hook your thumbs together behind your back, and inhale as you look up.

5 On the exhalation, bend forward and stretch your arms over your head. Breath in and feel the stretch along the back of your legs, back and arms, Slowly exhale. Stay down and repeat twice more.

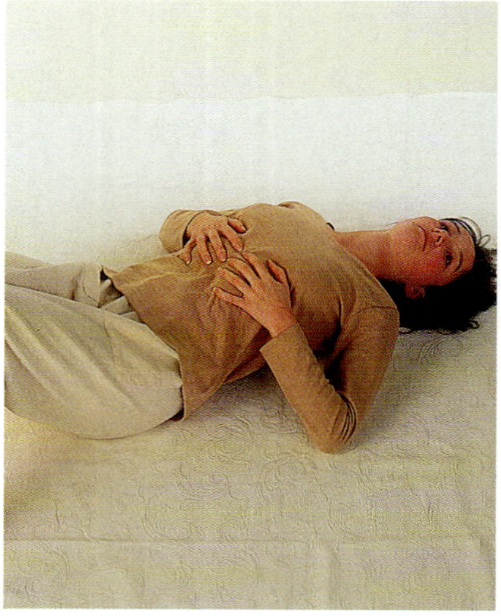

6 Lie down with a rolled-up towel along your spine, allowing the head to drop back on to the floor or a pillow. Place your fingers along your ribs, gently pressing as you breathe out.

immune system revivers

The immune system includes your spleen, thymus gland and lymph nodes. It is responsible for moving proteins and fats around the body, and is also responsible for filtering body fluids, producing white blood cells and immunity. However, periods of stress will weaken your immune system and leave you prone to infections. These simple shiatsu techniques will help awaken your immune and lymphatic systems.

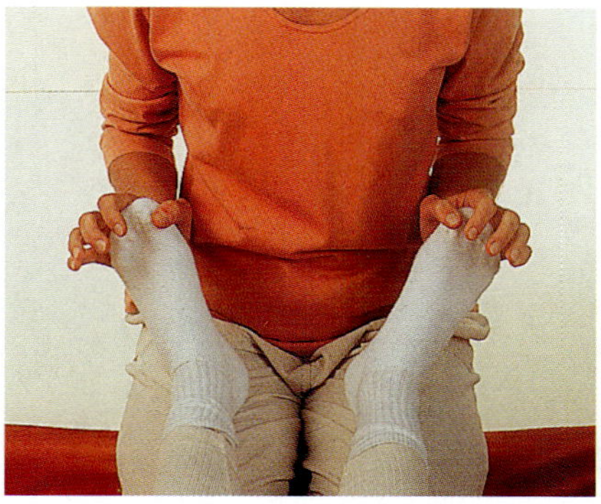

1 Ask your partner to lie down on the back with legs straight. Place your palms over the soles of your partner's feet. Intermittently rock the feet towards the head in a rhythmic motion of about two movements per second for 3-4 minutes.

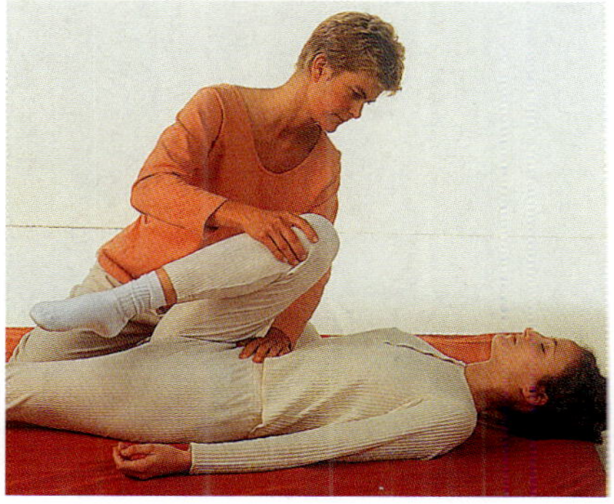

2 Bend your partner's leg and move yourself up to the side. Hold the leg just below the knee. Slowly rotate the hip joint, moving from the centre of yourself. Keep a fixed distance between your chest and your partner's knee.

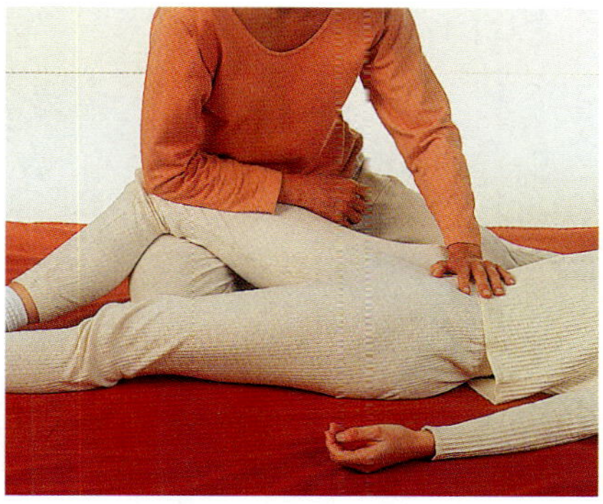

3 Place your partner's foot against the opposite inside ankle so that the leg is bent, exposing the inside leg. Ask your partner to inhale and gently use your forearm to stretch open the spleen meridian on the out-breath.

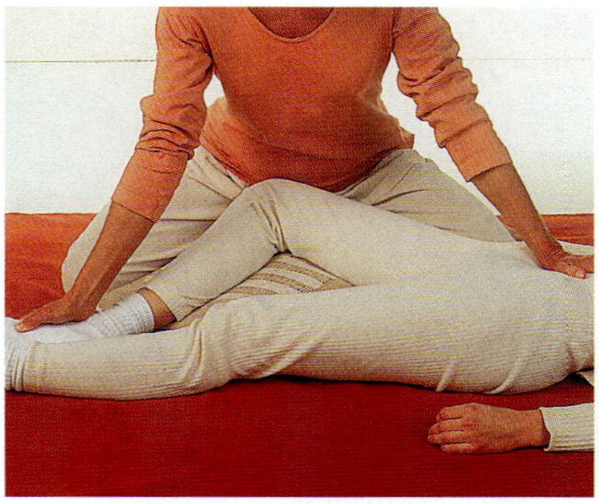

4 Support the lower leg with a cushion and, starting from the inside of your partner's big toe, use your thumb to apply perpendicular pressure along the medial part of the foot.

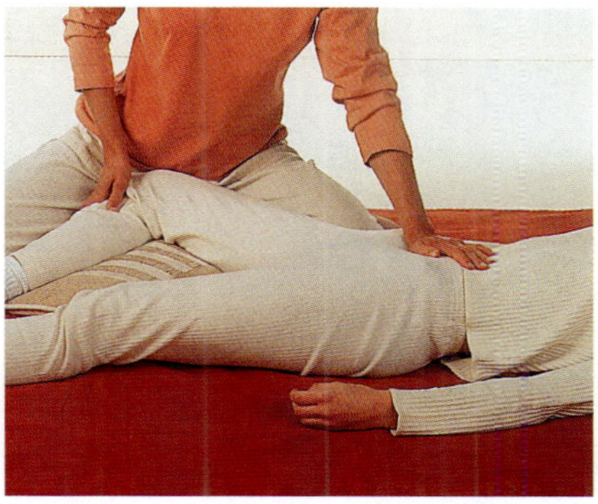

5 At the top of the shin bone on the medial side of the leg is SP9, another powerful point on the spleen meridian. Press this point to treat abdominal and menstrual pain, or local pain in the knee.

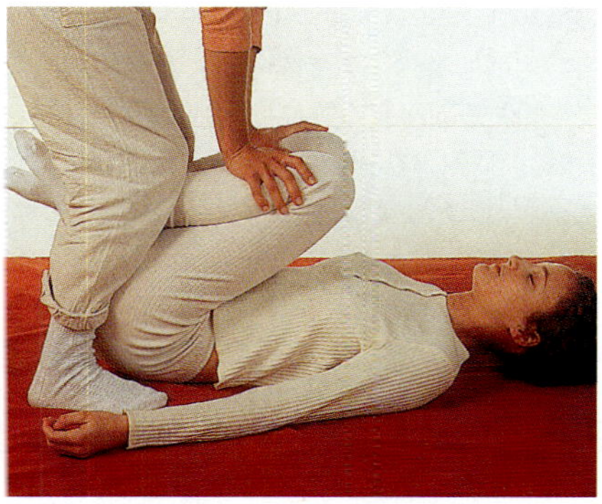

6 Rotate the leg you have worked on and then bend the other leg as well. Come to a standing position, bring your feet close to your partner's hips for support and gently bring the knees to the chest. Ease up on the stretch and rotate both legs. Move over to the other side, stretch out the treated leg and repeat the sequence for the other leg.

working on the digestive system

The stomach and spleen energy channels are associated with the highly important functions of ingestion and digestion of food. In traditional Chinese medicine, the stomach corresponds to the entire digestive tract, from the mouth to the small intestine, and it creates Chi energy. The following exercises are aimed at fine-tuning and improving the health of your digestive system.

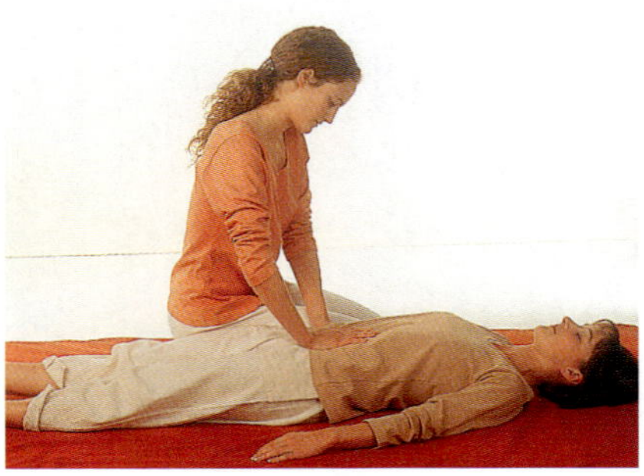

1 Sit in the Seiza position at your partner's side. Take a few moments of stillness to "tune in" and observe. Be aware of any tension and note the breathing rate: fast and shallow indicates tension; slow and deep shows relaxation.

Trace the borderlines of your partner's *Hara* (vital body centre). Start at the ribcage just below the breastbone and move slowly out to the pelvis.

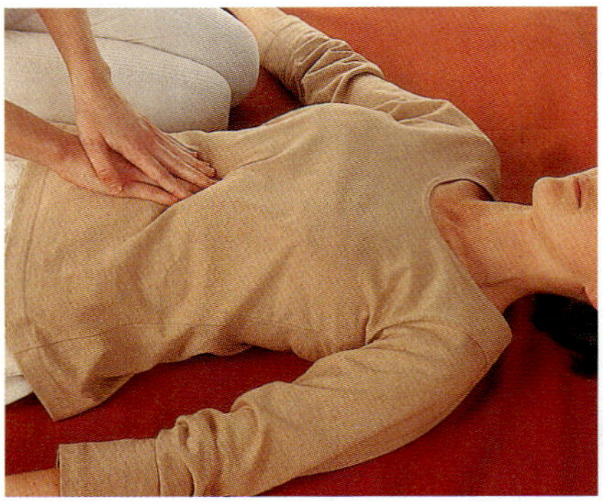

2 Using two hands, one on top of the other, apply finger-pad pressure in a clockwise movement around the Hara, as shown. Where you find tension, apply gradually deeper pressure to dissolve it.

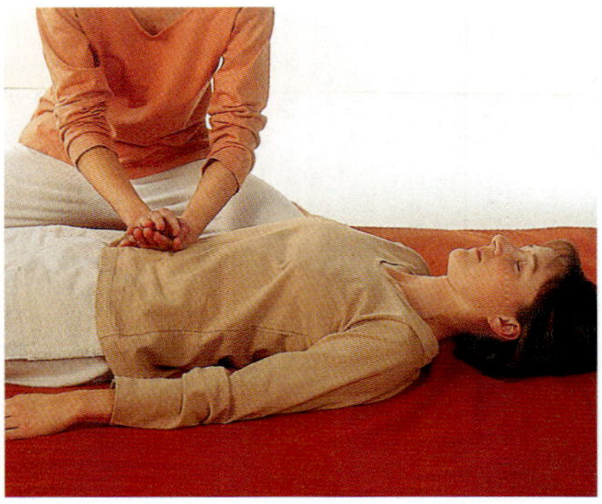

3 With one hand on top of the other, make a rocking and pushing type motion like rolling dough, from one side to the other, and pull back using the heel of the hand. Repeat for relaxation.

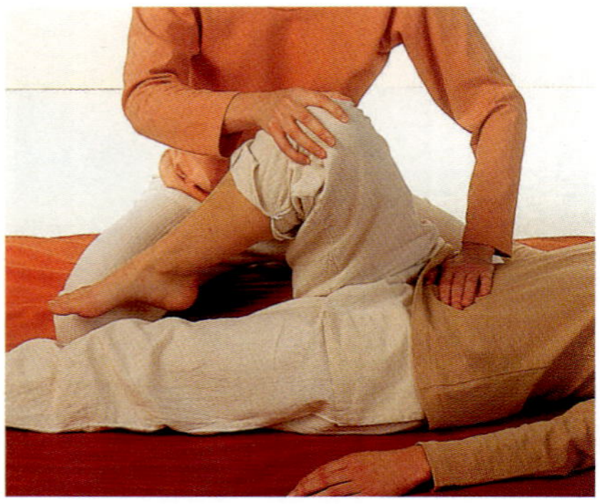

4 One hand holds the right leg just below the knee. Move from your centre, using your whole body, not just your arm muscles, to rotate your partner's leg. Keep a fixed distance between your chest and your partner's knee to ensure a balanced rotation of the hip.

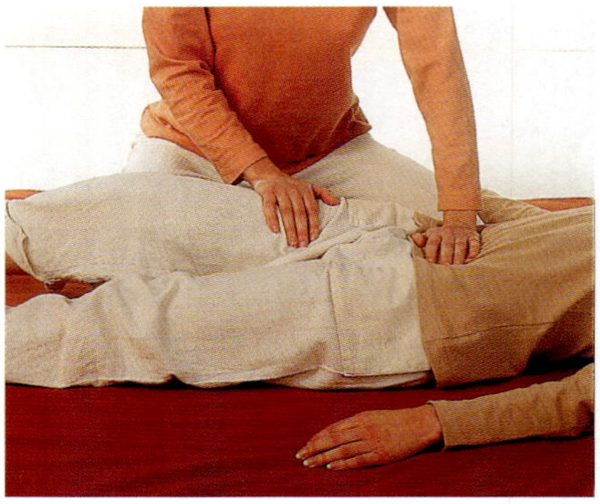

5 Stretch your partner's leg out, and place your knee underneath your partner's knee for support or use a pillow. Apply palm pressure along the outside frontal edge of the leg following the stomach meridian. Start from the top of the thigh and work to the foot. Repeat three or four times.

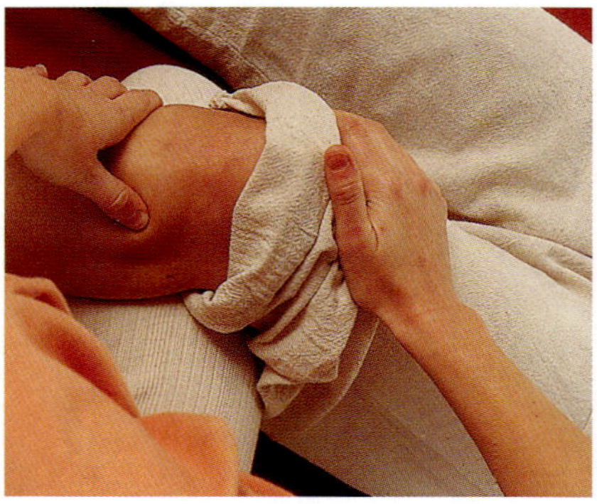

6 Stimulate ST36, "Leg Three Miles", using thumb pressure. The point is located four fingers' width below the knee-cap on the outside of the shin-bone. The name refers to this point's remarkable effect. It has been used since ancient times to build up endurance.

circulatory system enhancers

The heart organ, the heart and heart governor channels are the central focuses for regulating circulation, according to traditional Chinese medicine. However, heart energy can be surprisingly weakened in several circumstances. One excellent way of tackling the problem is by using wonderfully specialized shiatsu techniques. Dual functional, they will help calm the mind and cure such problems.

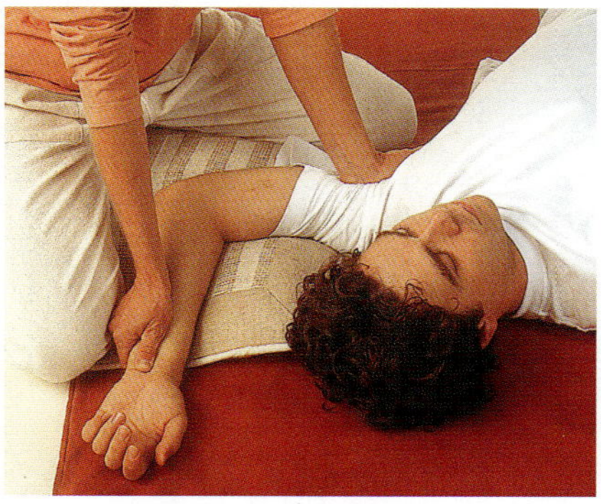

1 To expose the energy channel, place your partner's arm with the hand above the head, palm facing upwards. Support your partner's elbow with a cushion, and kneel in an open Seiza position. To improve the blood circulation to the skin generally and to the peripheries in particular, give yourself a daily body scrub. Use a dry loofah, skin brush, rough face cloth or even a towel.

2 To balance the energy in the heart meridian, sit on the floor, bend your knees and bring the soles of your feet together in front of you. Hold on to your ankles and straighten your spine. Inhale and lean forwards, keeping your back as straight as possible. Breathe out as you bring your head towards your feet and your elbows in front of your legs. Open up the axilla (armpit) and relax.

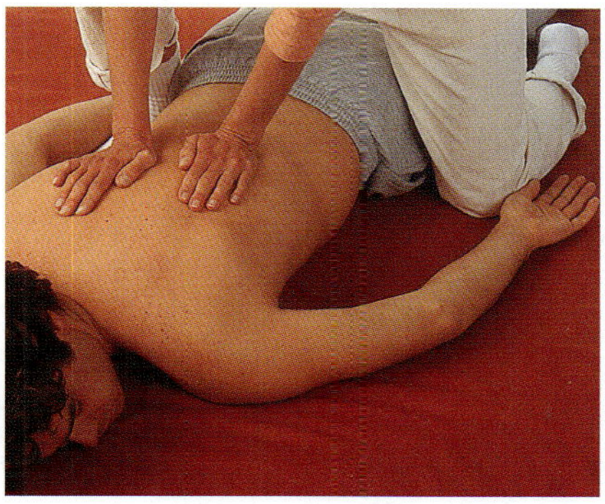

3 Use both palms in a technique known as palm rubbing to apply pressure quite firmly and rub down either side of the spine.

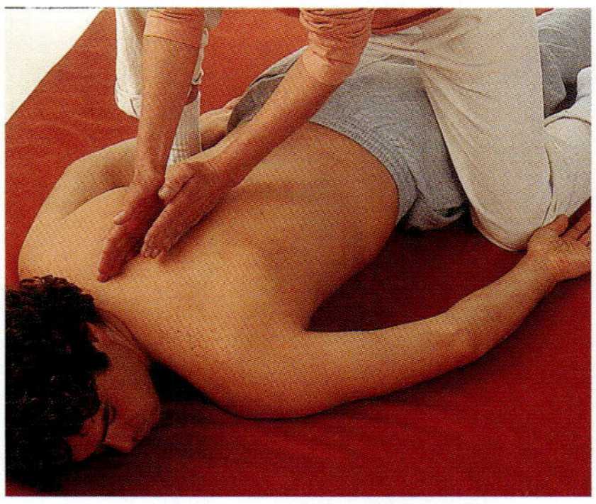

4 To rub, use the little finger side of your hands and vigorously rub down either side of the spine a few times until the area begins to redden.

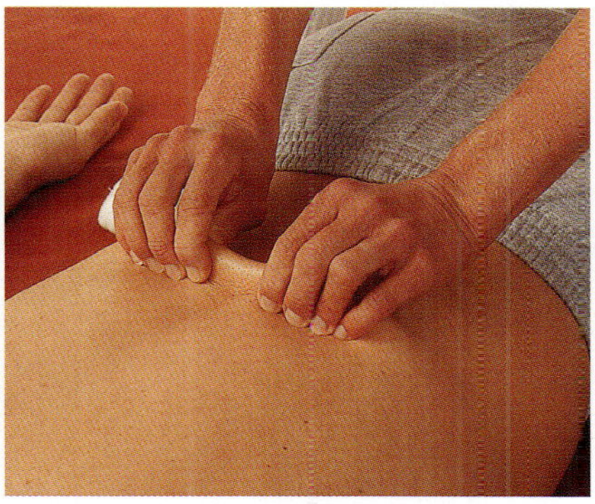

5 Rolling the skin involves pinching and taking hold of the skin on the lower part of the spine (lumbar area). Lift the tissue and gradually "roll" it up the spine. Repeat three or four times. Then roll the skin from the spine, the centre line, out towards the sides to the back.

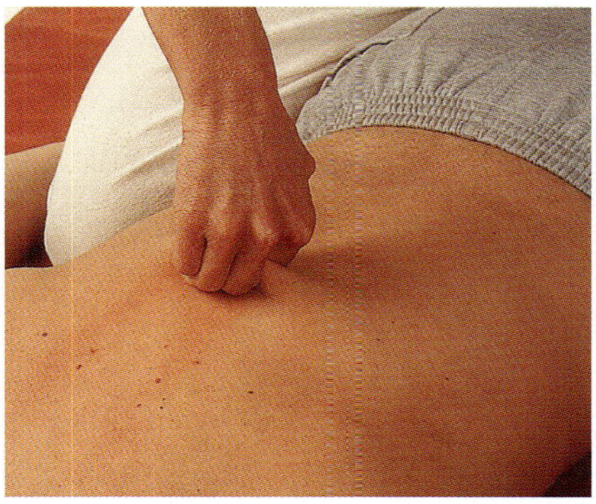

6 When pinching, use your index and middle fingers to pinch and take hold of the tissue. Twist and lift the skin at the same time. Work within your partner's pain threshold. Cover the whole back using this technique. You will see the area redden as the circulation improves.

reflexology

Using our hands to release and alleviate tension in our bodies is something that we do instinctively. When you bang your shin it is an automatic response to hold your hurt leg or rub it better. You are thus releasing the disturbed energy from the traumatized part of your body through contact with the undisturbed energy of your hands. In effect you are re-balancing the traumatized part to restore it to its natural state of well-being, with harmony between the flow of energy circulation and muscle tension.

Our hands have been a means of caring, comfort and giving since we first ceased to need them to walk on, and started to use them for focused, specialized activities. They are the tools of many natural therapies. In reflexology you can use them, specifically your fingers, to apply pressure-point therapy to certain key points, usually on the feet, although often on the hands. There are reflex points elsewhere, notably on the head, but these are used far less frequently.

The word "reflex" means to reflect. Pressure points on your feet and hands reflect all the parts of your body, both external and internal: organs and glands as well as limbs, torso and head. Each point actually reflects the activity of another part of the body. By learning to read the right signs and act accordingly, it is therefore possible to effect a wide range of cures.

how reflexology works

Reflexology acts on parts of the body by stimulating the corresponding reflexes with compression techniques applied with the fingers. Where there is inhibited functioning we find congestion in the form of deposits that have not been cleared away by the venous circulation and the lymph. Both feet together hold the reflexes to the whole body. The part that corresponds to the spine runs along the instep of each foot.

Head and Neck

Your head is represented on the toes; to be more precise, the right side of your head lies on the right big toe and the left side on the left big toe. In addition to the whole head being fully represented on the two big toes, the eight other toes hold the reflexes to specific parts of your head for fine tuning.

Your neck reflex is actually found in the "necks" of all the toes: if you find tension in one area of your neck, you will find tension or discomfort, or be able to feel congestion, in the corresponding areas of your toes. The correspondence between the head and toes may be initially difficult to understand because you have only one head while you have ten toes (or two sides to your head and five toes on either side). However, reflexology is a long-lived, well-known art, and you will quickly come to appreciate these close connections.

Gently working on the spinal reflex which in fact runs right along the instep of each foot.

Pelvis

The whole of your heel all around your foot contains the reflexes to your pelvic area: they lie on the sole and the sides of your heel and also across the top of your ankle.

Limbs

The limbs are clearly represented on the outer edge of your foot but also, and most particularly, on the corresponding upper or lower limb. There is no part of the foot that actually resembles the limbs. The arms and legs, however, follow the same basic structure, and as such each limb holds and contains the reflexes to the other limb on the same side. Shoulders reflect hips and vice versa. Elbows and knees, wrists and ankles and hands and feet are related in the same way. These are known to practising, experienced reflexologists as the cross reflexes.

Torso and Spine

It is much easier to comprehend how the torso is reflected in or fits on to the body of the feet once you have grasped the concept of your two feet together representing your whole body. The key to such understanding lies in the fact that the spinal line runs right down and along the insteps of your feet, where they finally meet if you put them firmly together. In your feet the whole of you comes together.

Chest

The ball of each foot represents one side of your chest. So in the balls of your feet, and on the same area on the top of your feet, lie the reflexes to your lungs, air passages, heart, thymus gland, breast, shoulders and everything contained in your chest. The whole area is bounded by your diaphragm, the important reflex that lies across the base of the ball of each foot.

Abdomen

In your instep, where your feet are not weight-bearing and are therefore not padded like the ball, you will find contained all the reflexes to your abdominal organs – those concerned with digestion and those dealing with the maintenance and well-being of life. This crucial area is clearly bounded by the diaphragm line above, and also by the heel line that lies below.

zones on the feet

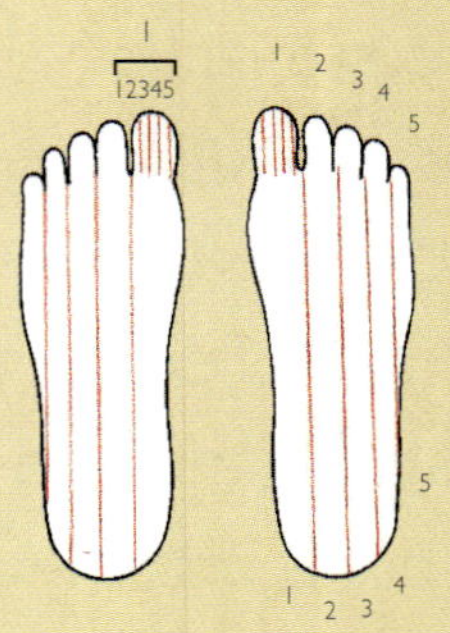

ABOVE: This diagram clearly depicts the zones running along the feet. The big toes represent the whole head, as well as lying in Zone 1. The right side of your body lies on your right foot, and the left side of your body is positioned on the left foot.

zones on the body

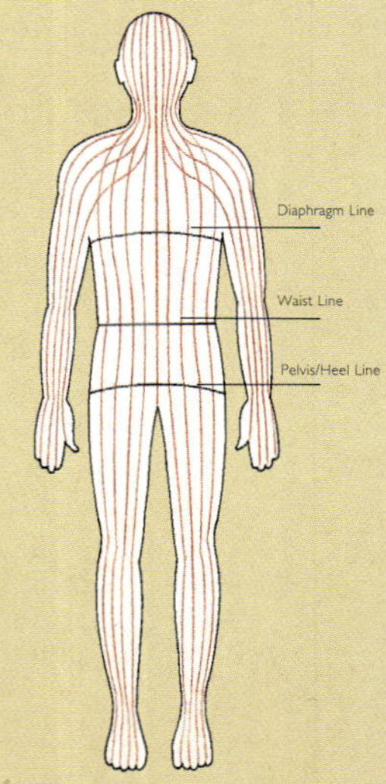

ABOVE: The zones run vertically through the body, from head to feet and hands. Also note the transverse lines on the body.

the benefits of reflexology

Reflexology works quite simply, and in a highly effective, efficient way. It manages to relax and overcome any build up of excess tension in the muscles. Consequently, during a treatment, all parts of the feet will be stimulated and the significant dual effect is to relax your muscles and also to increase the efficiency of the circulation to all parts of the body. You will quickly notice the effects.

REFLEXOLOGY AND YOU

Working along holistic principles, reflexology takes into account body, mind and spirit as they are all interrelated. Whatever happens to you will affect all levels of your being, whether you notice or not. If you feel under pressure or are stressed, the effect on your body will be detrimental, as your muscles remain tense and taut, constricting the circulation and nerves, and compromising their functioning. Similarly, if you have a physical mishap, your feelings will be affected by the degree of pain you experience, the way in which the accident happened, and the effect it has on you afterwards.

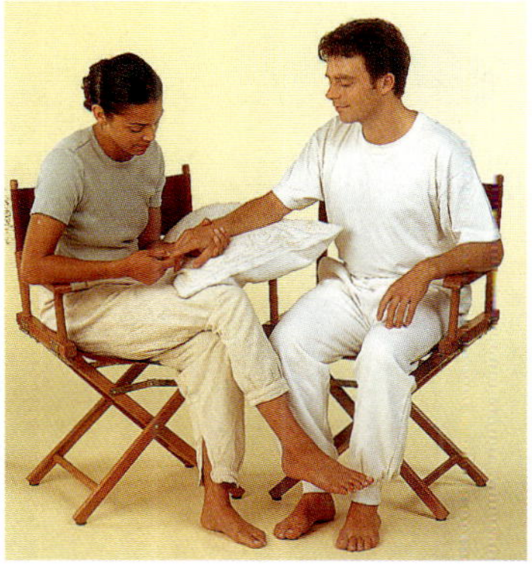

Through working the hands (or feet) you are working the whole body.

Although you are working mostly on the feet in reflexology, you are affecting the whole of the body, both inside and out, through the treatment. This is achieved by working the reflexes to the internal organs and glands as well as to the surface of the body. It appears that you can have a more far-reaching effect by working the reflexes than by working directly on the corresponding body part. Such referral treatment, as it is sometimes called, is highly effective.

Pain in the back, for instance, may be due to the onset of structural problems in which the bones are actually out of place and misaligned, and should be checked by an osteopath, cranial osteopath or chiropractor. If the pain results from muscular problems, or if manipulation has already been done but muscular strain remains, the next step is to identify the muscles involved and then begin work to relieve the situation with massage and reflexology. As a follow-up treatment it is highly effective.

Massage has an immediate and profoundly relieving effect, but the pain and discomfort is likely to recur when the effects of the massage have worn off. Benefits resulting from working the reflexes to the relevant area of the back will be more long term than those produced by working directly on the muscles themselves. This is because through the reflexes you are stimulating the body from within, rather than exercising and soothing the muscles from without. Stimulating the reflex to a troubled area will promote healing. Reflexology uses both massage and specific stimulation of the reflexes to gain lasting relief.

Always wash your feet before any treatment to refresh the skin.

What Treatments Involve

Reflexology is not just a foot massage, but this technique is certainly incorporated. Sweeping whole hand movements on the whole foot will relax the entire person and prepare the feet for reflex work. During the working of the reflexes, massage soothes and relaxes the area where congestion or discomfort is to be found. It actively links the treatment together into a continuous, flowing whole, and manages to relax and stimulate the whole of the body while various individual parts are being treated specifically. Equally beneficial is the use of whole hand massage movements which is used to complete a reflexology treatment, and to give a feeling of well-being to the entire person before ending the session.

A reflexology session can be both relaxing and stimulating for the patient. As muscle tensions are relaxed, and the nerve supply freed from constriction, the body slips into a deep state of relaxation. At the same time, the circulation is being stimulated to bring nutrients to all parts of the body, and to remove waste products that interfere with the healthy functioning of the parts and the whole. Energy is able to flow more freely around the body, and feelings of total well-being result.

giving reflexology

Anyone new to reflexology will immediately notice a marvellous difference in the way treatment is given. Instead of being seen as an assembly of parts with one or two needing a quick overhaul, the whole body is considered, and the whole is carefully fine-tuned to get you back into shape. It is the recognition of the way in which every part of the body interacts with another that makes reflexology such a success.

THE HOLISTIC APPROACH

Reflexology works on the whole of the body, stimulating the reflexes to the internal organs, glands and body parts, as well as massaging the outside of the body. Through working on your feet as a whole, healing is stimulated throughout the body rather than just in one part that may well be influenced, or have influence on, other parts or systems. This is what makes the holistic approach of natural medicine so completely effective.

When you have a problem, natural therapies do not address you as a machine - repairing or replacing the part that does not work, but treat you in your entirety to deal with the cause of the problem, rather than merely alleviating the symptoms locally. If you have a raging toothache you may be able to relieve it by taking painkillers, but you will not make the abscess to go away unless you deal with the poison that gave rise to it in the first place.

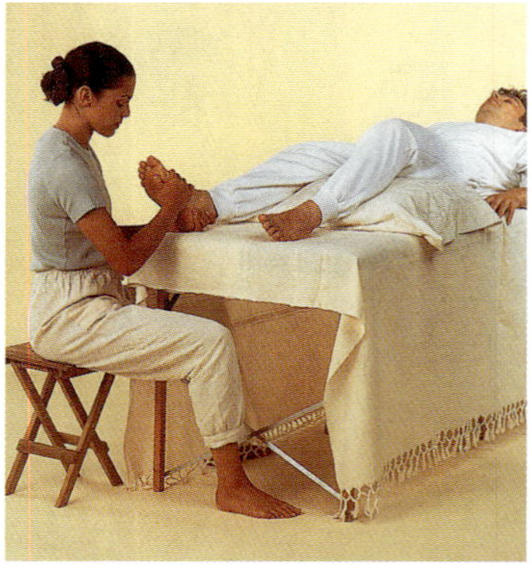

Make sure that your partner is comfortable, with pillows under their head, neck and knees for support.

Locating the Problem

If you develop a headache you may or may not know its cause. Where in your body is the trouble seated? Does it come from tension in your neck or lower down your spine, from digestive disturbance, or even from held-in tension in your legs? Many headaches have such roots even though we do not notice the beginning of the trouble until the pounding in our head attracts our attention. Recurrent headaches happen because their causes have not been recognized and dealt with.

If you massage the reflexes to the head you might give temporary relief, but you will probably not cure the headache. Stimulating a related reflex, however, is effective. You will only find it if you work the whole foot, and do not spot-work for one symptom.

The feet must be where you can comfortably reach them.

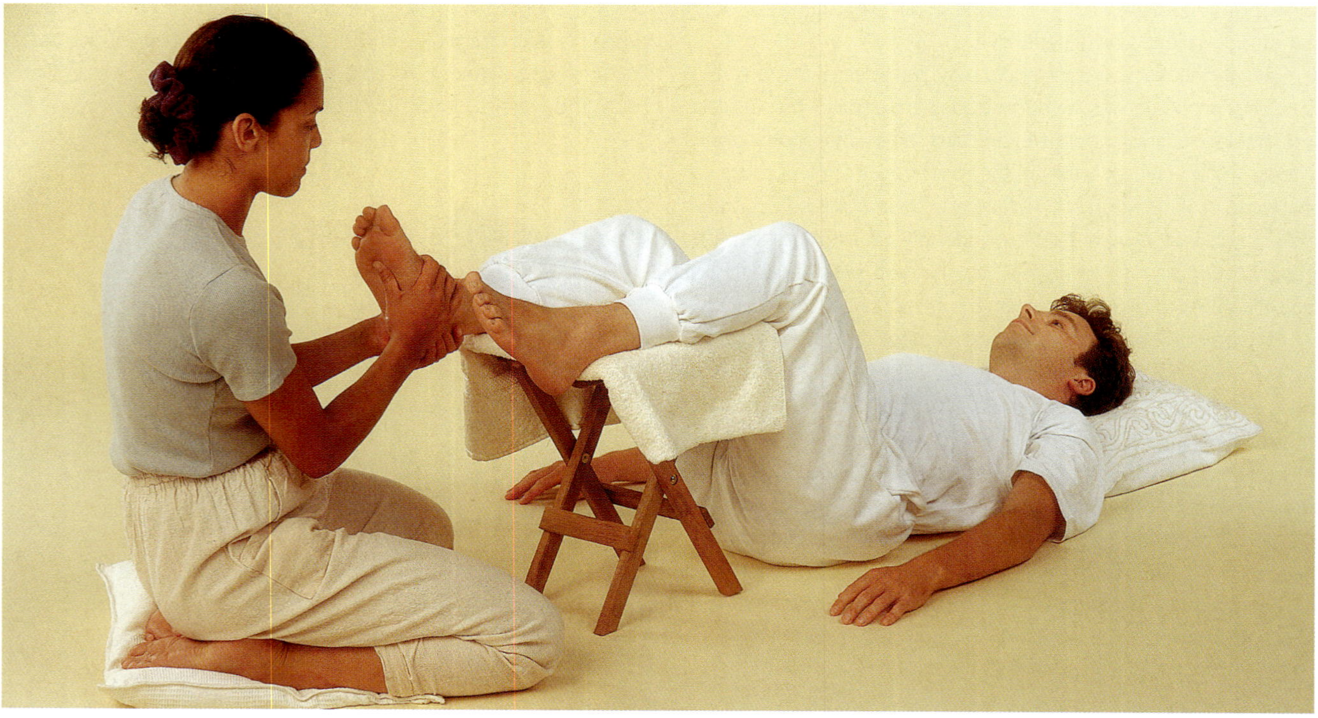

basic techniques

Make sure that the room you are going to use is warm and quiet without any interruptions from telephones, faxes, pagers, you name it, with people coming and going. Once you have created the right conditions you can proceed with the basic techniques for the hands and feet. They make an excellent introduction. Once mastered you will quickly pick up reflexology's movements. They are straightforward and highly effective.

HAND AND FOOT TREATMENTS

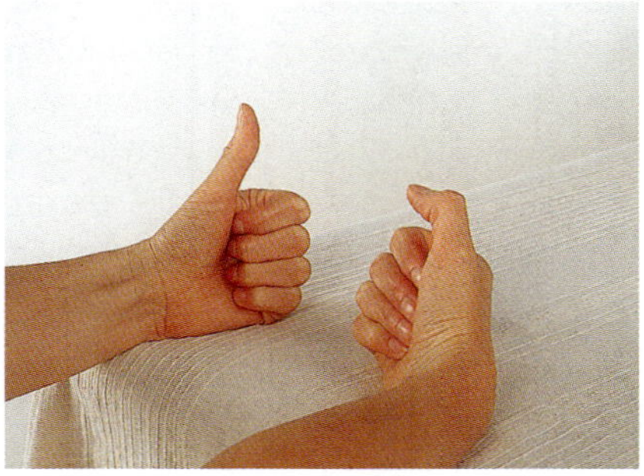

1 To thumbwalk, hold your two thumbs straight up and bend one at a time at the first joint. Repeat several times.

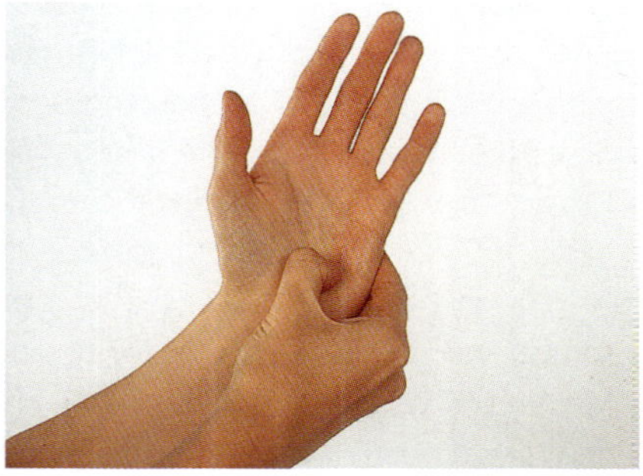

2 The therapeutic movement is on the firm downward press with your thumb bent. Use one hand only.

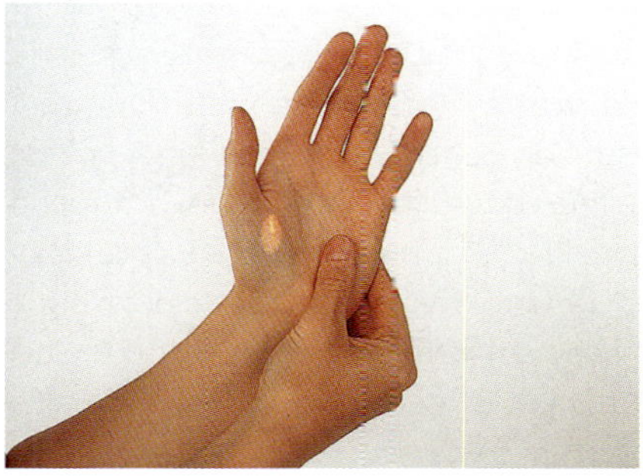

3 Slide forward as you straighten your thumb. The technique is sometimes called caterpillar walking.

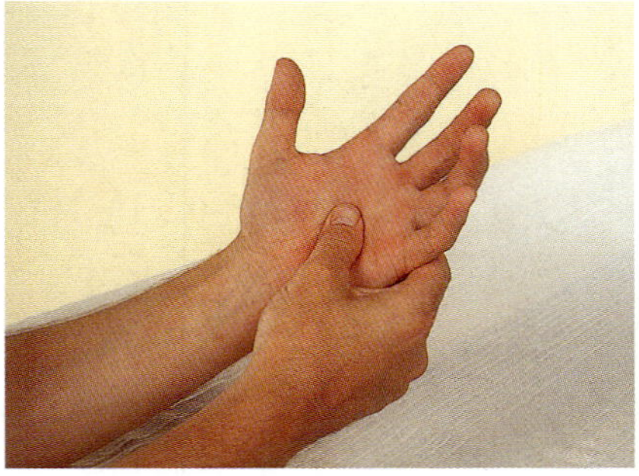

4 To rotate, place your thumb on part of your hand and gently rotate it on the spot. Try exerting a little more pressure.

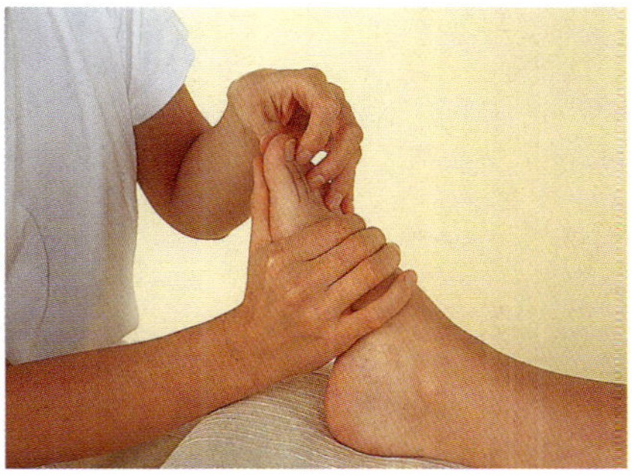

5 To fingerwalk, use the index finger. The technique is as for thumbwalking but using one or more fingers.

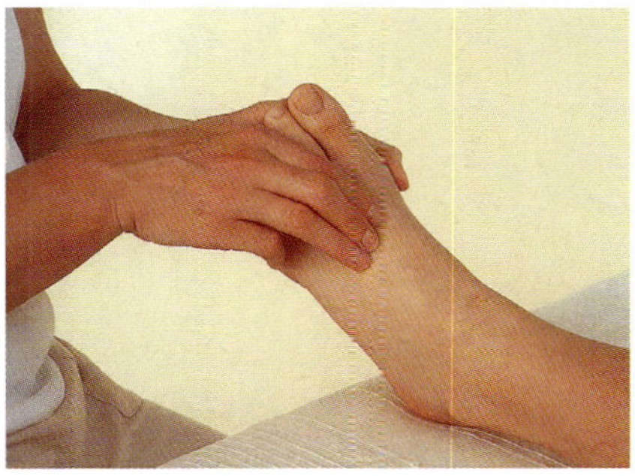

6 Continue the fingerwalking exercise, but this time keep the three middle fingers together.

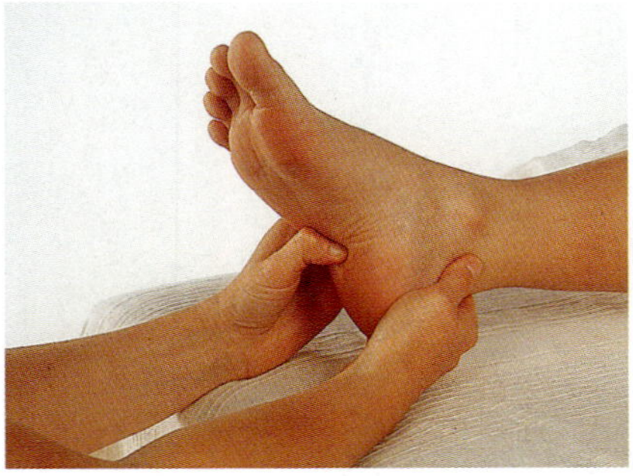

7 To pinpoint, use your thumb and fingers. Move them together and apart, like a pincer, then press in the thumb.

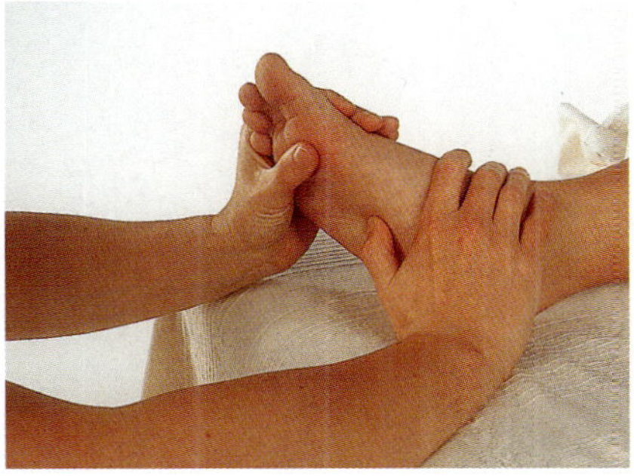

8 To hold and support, use one hand to hold the foot securely. This will help you give more sensitive treatment.

Getting Relaxed

Make sure that you find a comfortable position for the person whose feet you are going to treat. They may be lying on a sofa, with cushions to support their back, head and neck in one corner, and their feet at the opposite end so that you can reach them easily. If they are sitting in an armchair, find an upright chair or stool of a suitable height and support their legs with a cushion. Be sure you sit comfortably too.

warm-up foot massage

It is always of great benefit to the patient if their feet are massaged right at the beginning of a reflexology treatment. This gives them time to get used to your touch, and to leave behind the cares of the day. Their overall mood is extremely important, and you should do your best to make sure that they are feeling relaxed. Give another massage at the end of the reflex work, and then at the end of the session.

THE FIRST STEPS

Massage prepares the feet for reflex work: it warms and relaxes the tissues, accustoms the receiver to your touch and soothes and relaxes the whole body. Massage will also loosen tensions in the muscles and stimulate the blood supply to and around the feet. Consequently, when the reflex points are worked the tissues will not be strained, and they will respond fully. Do not miss out this stage, as it is extremely important.

During treatment use plenty of massage to link the movement from one reflex area to the next, to soothe and relax the foot in between working the reflex points, which may produce sensations of tenderness, and use it where any tenderness or discomfort is found.

Oil and Massage Treatments

When you have covered all the reflex points, end with a massage on both feet to instil a sense of deep relaxation. Use 2–3 drops of essential oils mixed in with some almond oil. Do not use the oil beforehand because once on your hands it will counter any accurate hand reflexology movements.

When it comes to massage movements, note that there is no one set sequence. The prime object is to fit movements together in a way that is customized to your individual needs. They should feel good to you and to the person you are working on. The first few movements are good as an introduction, and you should always rotate the ankles as this frees up the blood and nerve supply through the ankle to the foot.

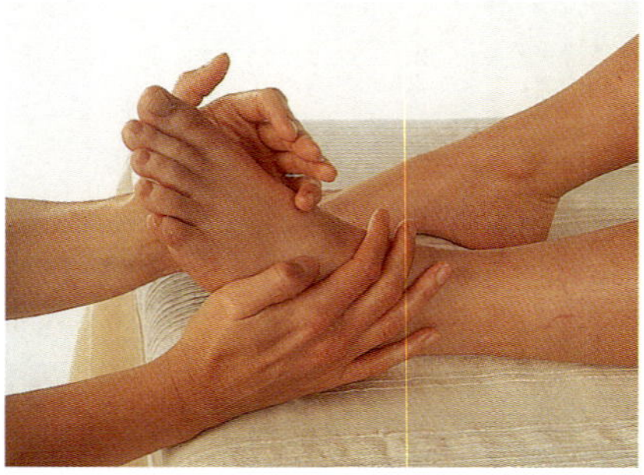

1 Stroking movements, or effleurage, are just as they sound, sweeping and soothing, and are good all over the foot. Add wherever appropriate.

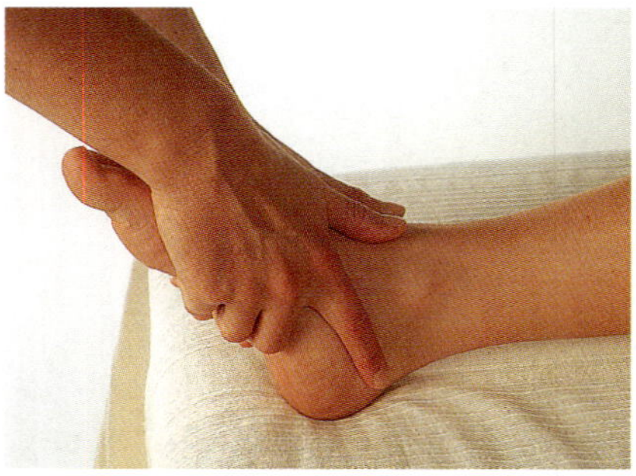

2 To make spreading movements on the top of the foot, draw your thumbs off sideways, keeping your fingers still.

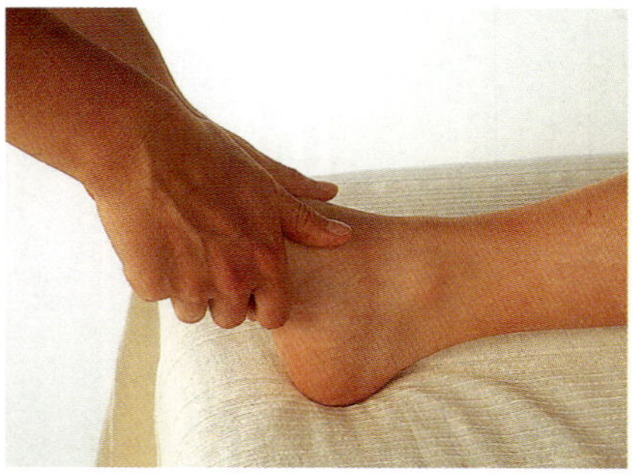

3 Repeat the first movement, gradually working your way down the foot with each subsequent repetition.

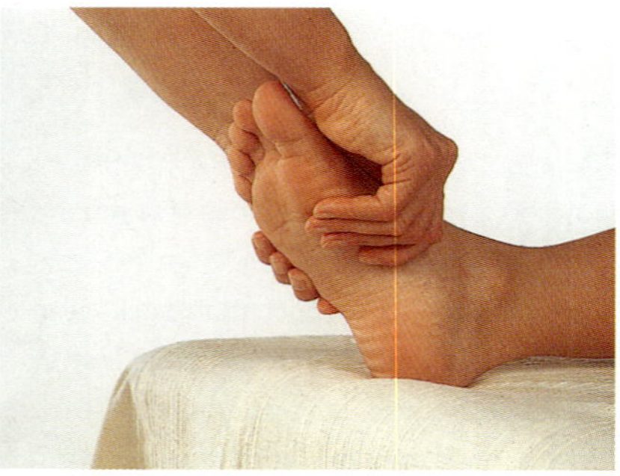

4 To cover the sole of the foot, start in the same position as before, but this time draw your fingers off sideways, keeping your thumbs still.

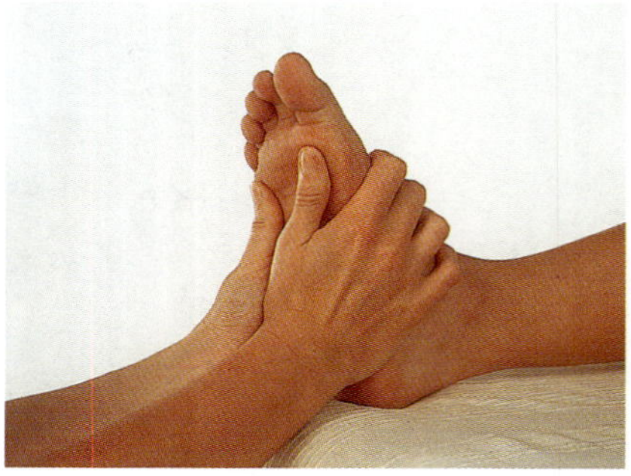

5 Finally, massage into the ball of the foot with your thumbs.

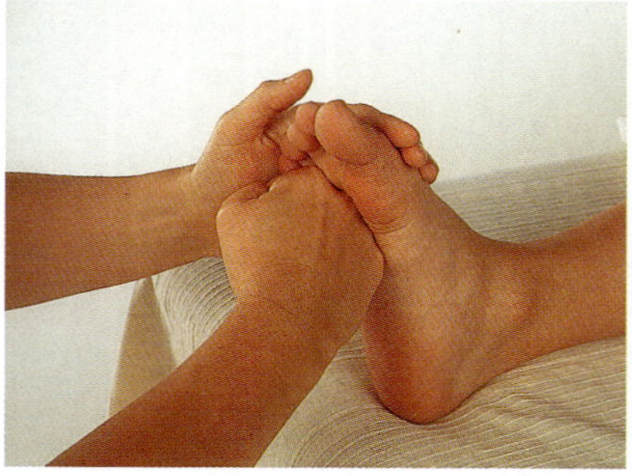

6 To knead, use a movement like kneading dough and work into the sole of the foot using the lower section of your fingers.

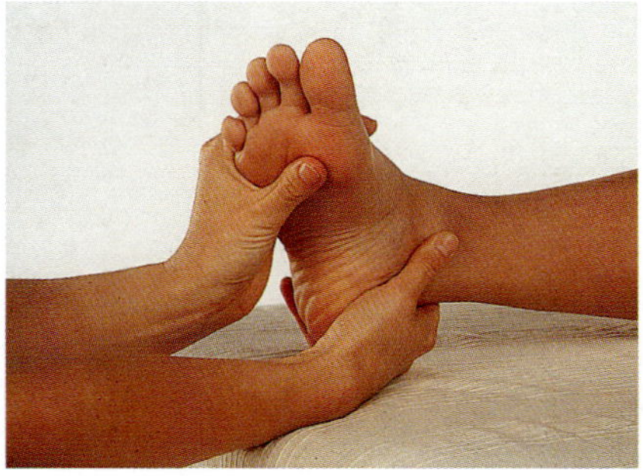

7 To rotate the ankle, rotate the foot clockwise several times, feeling gently as you proceed so that you do not force stiff ankles, but you do manage to exercise the joint.

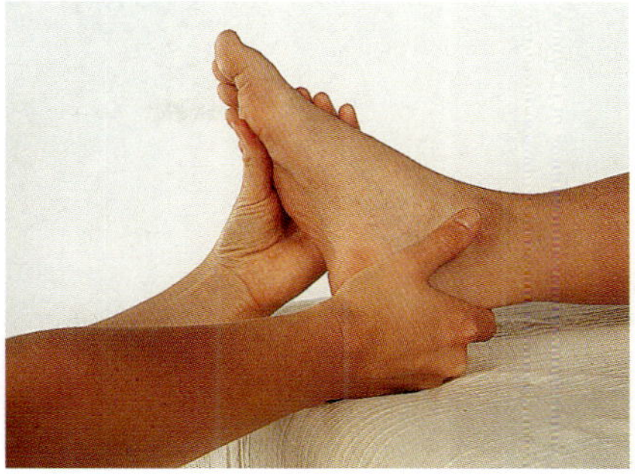

8 Repeat the ankle rotation, but this time in an anti-clockwise direction.

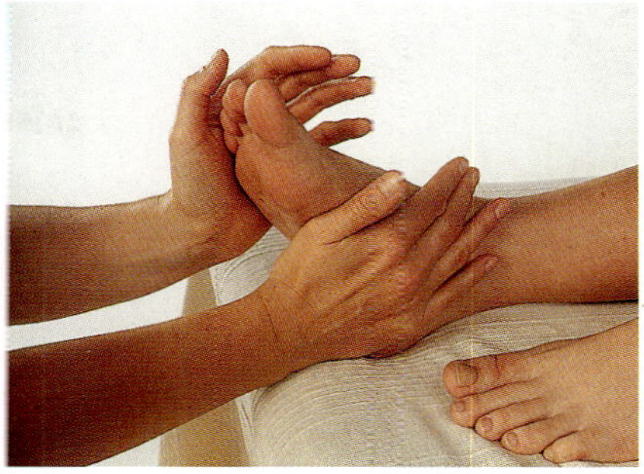

9 To make vigorous, fast movements, massage both sides of the foot, running your hands freely up and down the whole length of the foot. Repeat this technique several times.

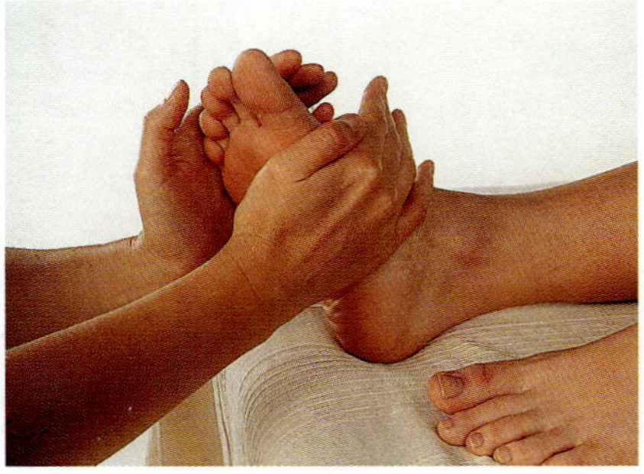

10 With your hands in the same starting position, this time move them alternately up and down from the top to the sole of the foot so that the foot tips from side to side. Do take great care not to twist the ankle.

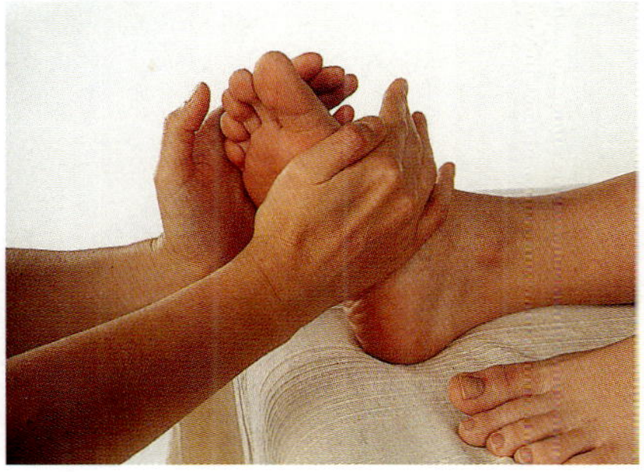

11 With your hands palms up on either side of the foot, move them quickly to and fro, to exercise and loosen the ankle. When this movement is done correctly, the foot will waggle around.

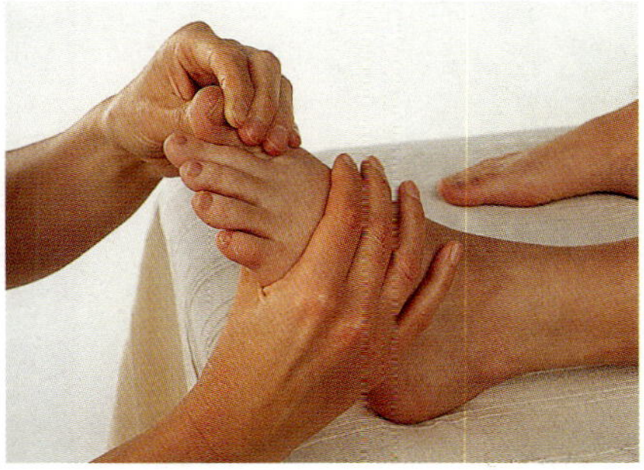

12 To rotate the toes, begin with the big toe, holding it securely but not too tightly and gently rotate. Repeat this movement carefully with each toe.

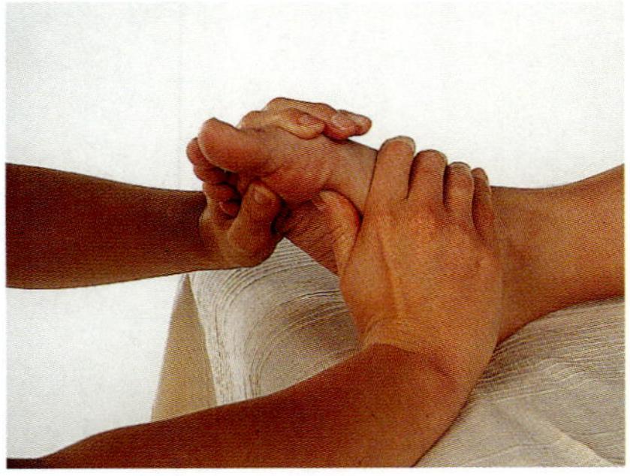

13 To relax the diaphragm, hold the foot and bring it down on to the thumb of your other hand, and lift it off again. Next, move your thumb one step to the side and repeat the movement.

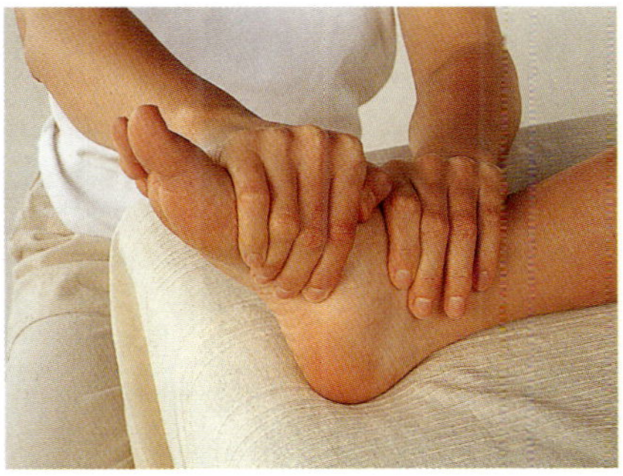

14 To make a spinal twist, the hand on the ankle remains still while the other, lower hand moves to and fro across the top of the foot, round the instep and finally back again. Repeat several times.

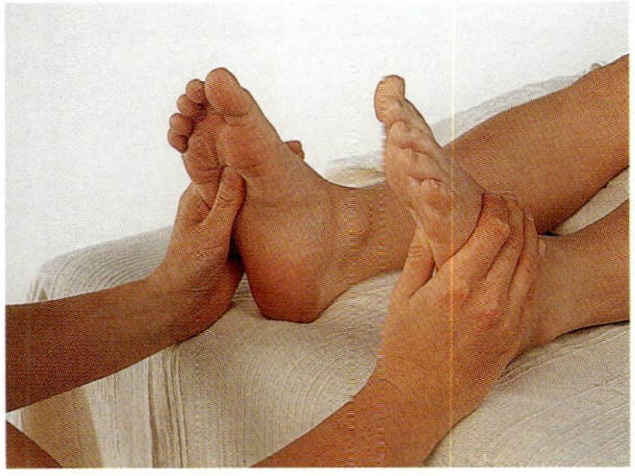

15 For good breathing and to relax the solar plexus reflex, place your thumbs in the natural dent. As your partner breathes in, press in with your thumbs and as they breathe out, release them.

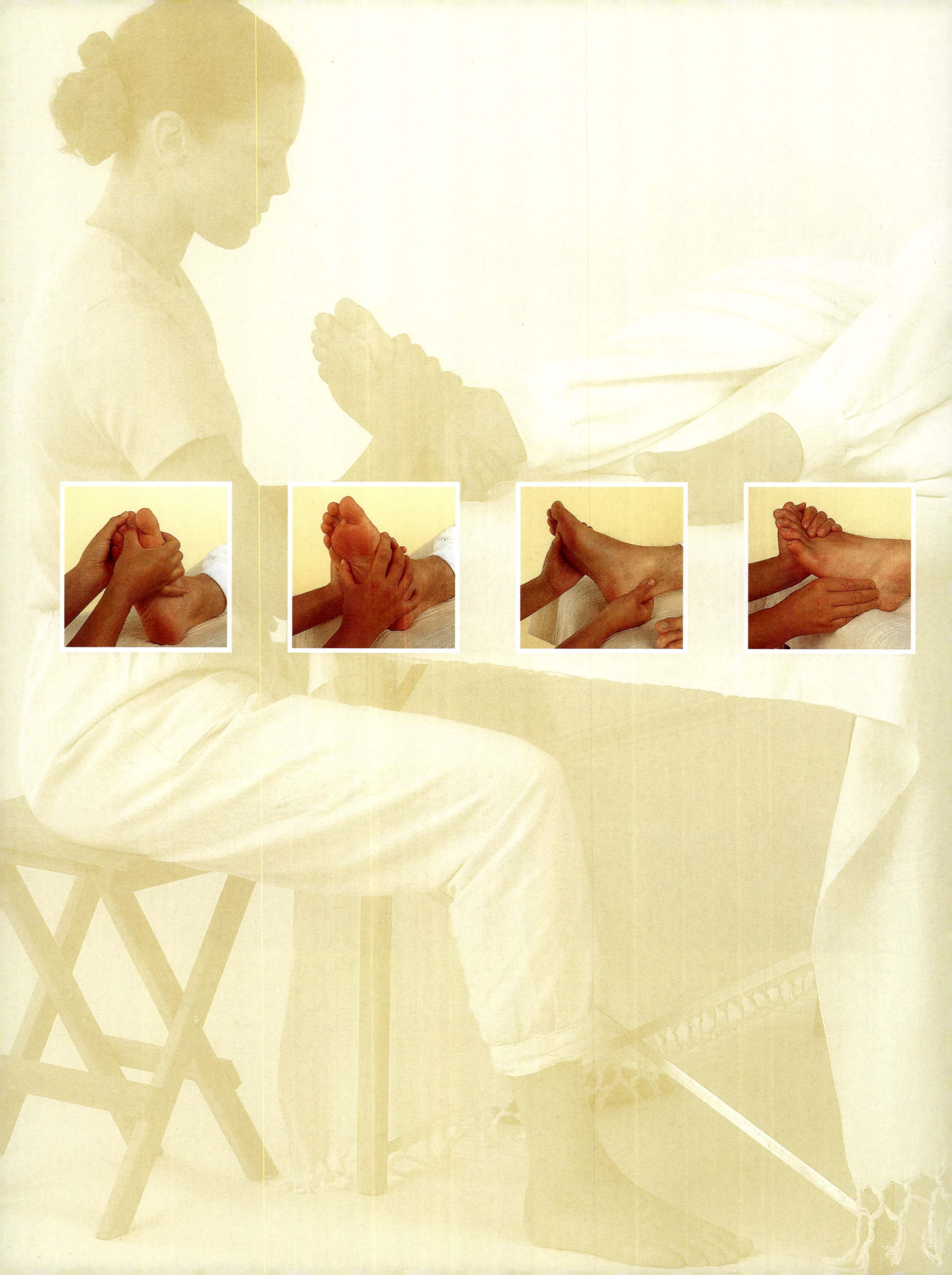

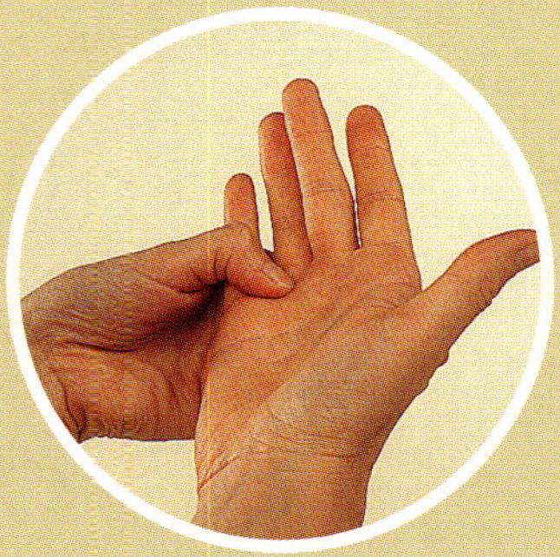

reflexology routines

reflexology routines
reflexology routines

The following pages are a clear step-by-step illustration of the full reflexology routine, which should be performed on your partner before you begin treating specific problems. In fact, the full routine covers most key parts of the body, and includes the spine, toes, chest, abdomen, pelvis and limbs. Depending on how it is given, it can be an invigorating or relaxing beginning to a treatment.

To see how all these parts of the body are reflected and simultaneously contained in your hands and feet, look at the detailed charts shown at the end of this chapter. It is immediately clear that both hands and feet are much more than themselves; they have become highly detailed referral points, in essence being like blueprints to all parts of the body. It obviously takes time to remember the exact whereabouts of all these areas, and to feel confident that you are treating the lungs alone and not, say, the adjacent stomach or even the spleen. Part of the art of reflexology is sensitivity and pinpoint accuracy.

In order to guarantee such accuracy it is important that your hands are not covered with any essential oils or they will glide and slide everywhere, which is not what you want. Also note that though this routine runs before more detailed work, it is not something that can or should be rushed. Besides fully toning up your partner, and making sure that their body is fully tuned in and responsive to what is happening, the routine is an excellent way of helping them relax. It gears up the body for what is to come. Interestingly, many patients claim that this is the high point of the treatment; and it can certainly be highly effective.

When you start giving such treatment there is invariably a stop-start feel to it as you have to remember precisely what to do next. The joy of working with an experienced practitioner is that one routine seamlessly and effortlessly flows into the next, and your body quickly learns to yield itself up to the continuous waves of well-being that the routine soon imparts.

the full reflexology routine

The following step-by-step illustration of the full reflexology routine should be performed on your partner before moving to treat specific problem areas. Always try to treat the areas of the body in exactly the same order as outlined here, from the spine to the limbs. Just occasionally, as a help, fine lines have been drawn on the photographs to highlight the important reflex points.

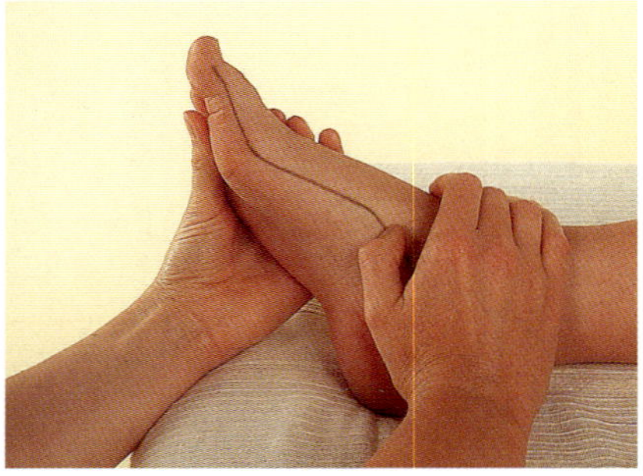

1 To treat the spine, thumbwalk up and down the spinal line as shown here. Repeat several times.

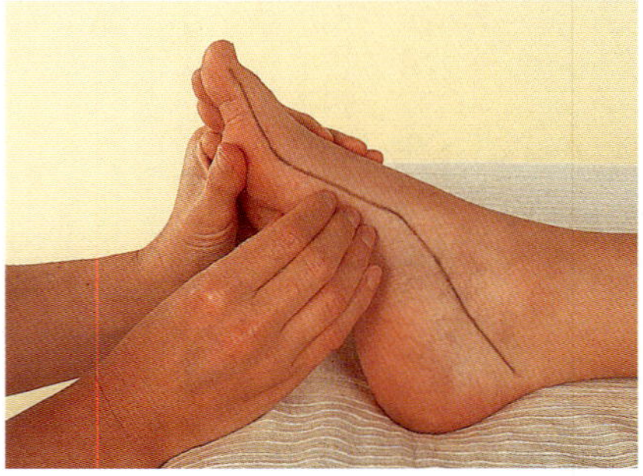

2 Use the three middle fingers to fingerwalk across the spine/instep in stages, from big toe to heel.

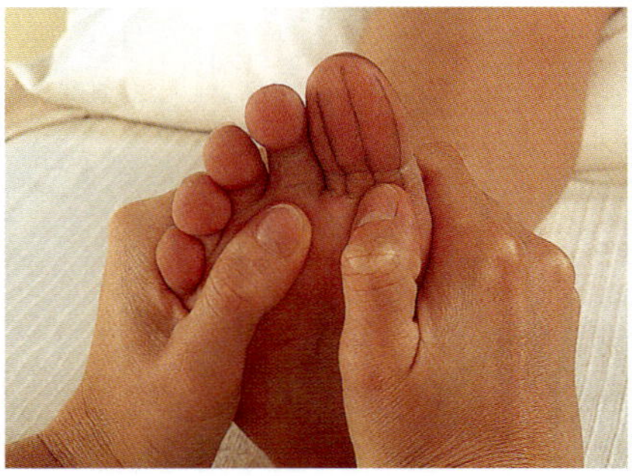

3 To treat the head and neck, work up the back of the big toe, thumbwalking in three lines to cover the whole area.

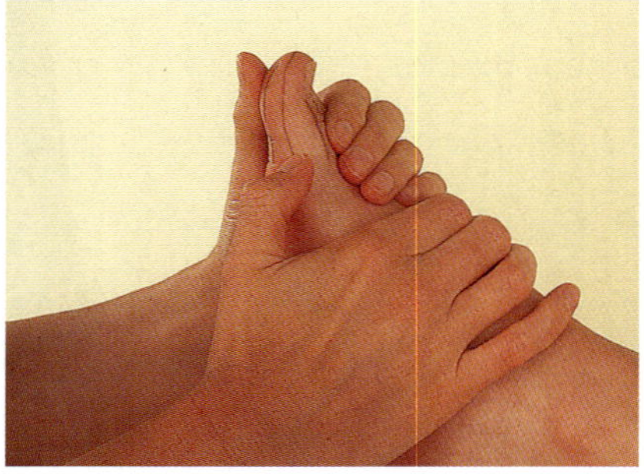

4 Use your index finger to fingerwalk down the front of the big toe again in three lines. Next, work up the side of the big toe with your thumb.

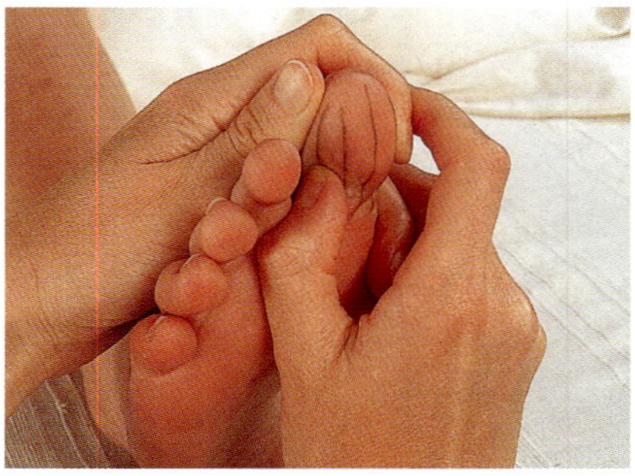

5 For the other side of the toe, approach from the back and tuck your thumb between this toe and the second one. Now thumbwalk the side of neck.

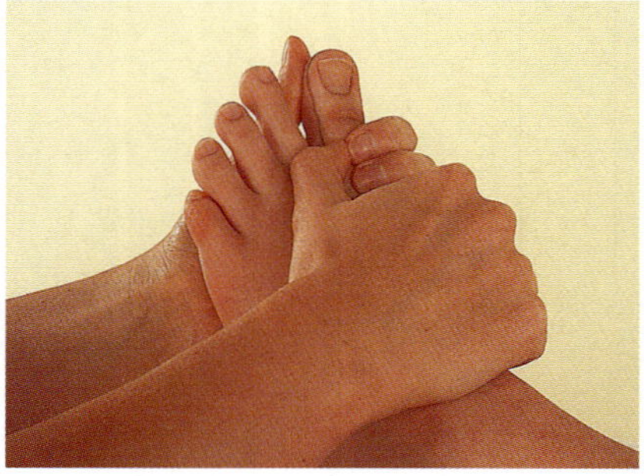

6 Change hands and, using your other thumb, approach from the front and tuck it in between the big toe and second toe again. Work up this side to the top.

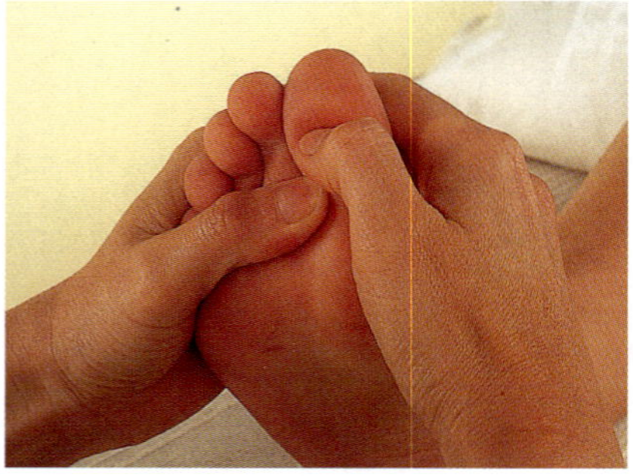

7 Find the centre of the whorls of the big toe print and position your hand for pinpointing the pituitary reflex. Press gently at first, as it can be tender.

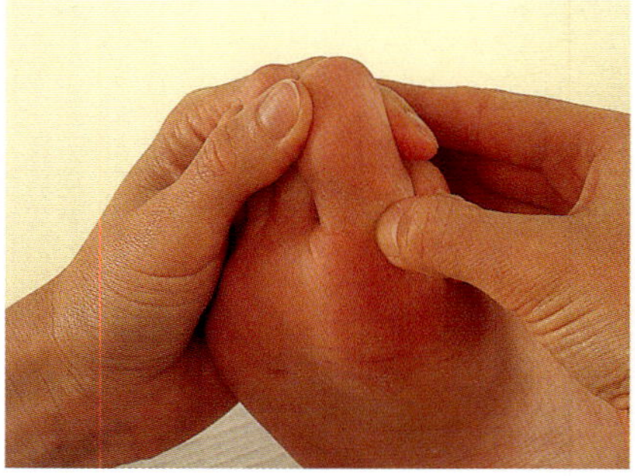

8 Work around the neck of the big toe in two semi-circles: thumbwalk the back part first of all.

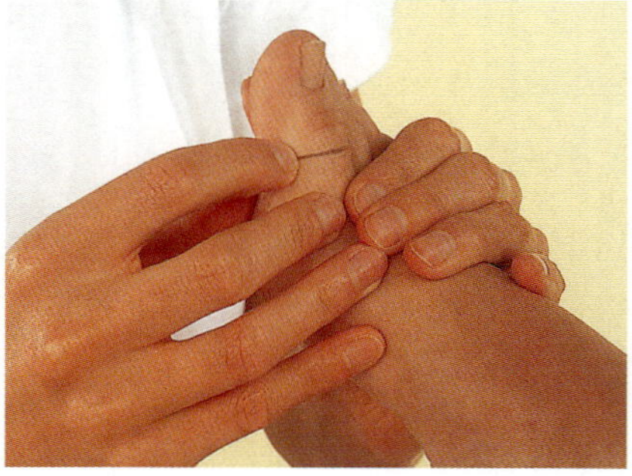

9 Fingerwalk right around the front of the big toe, but this time using your index finger.

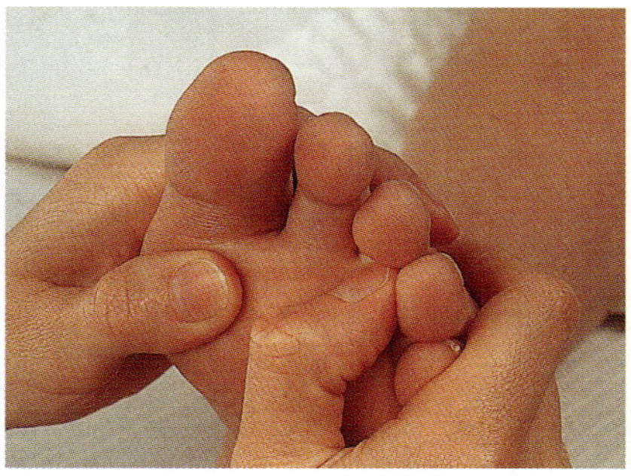

10 For the smaller toes, follow exactly the same routine as for the big toe. These toes can be covered in one line to each surface. Thumbwalk up the back. Fingerwalk down the front.

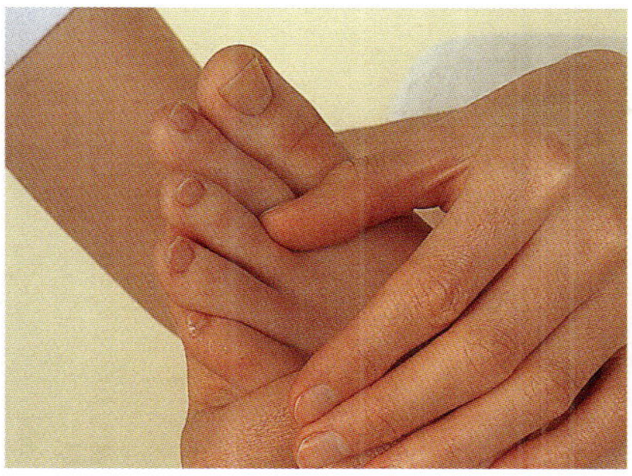

11 Thumbwalk up one side of the toe. Always approach the side from the front. Next, change hands and then gradually work up the other side of the same toe.

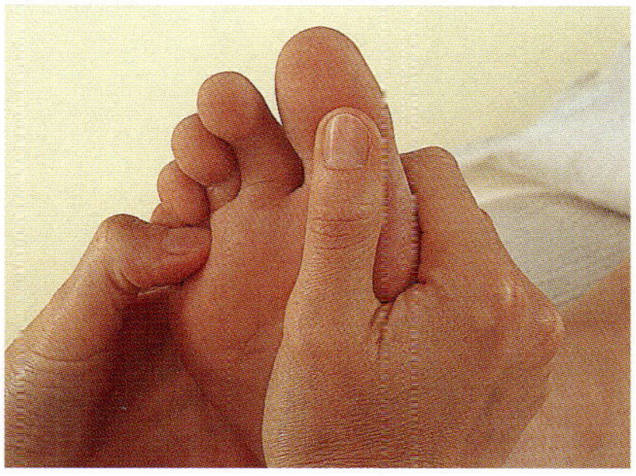

12 Finally, commence thumbwalking the ridge under the little toes. Repeat several times, then culminate this routine.

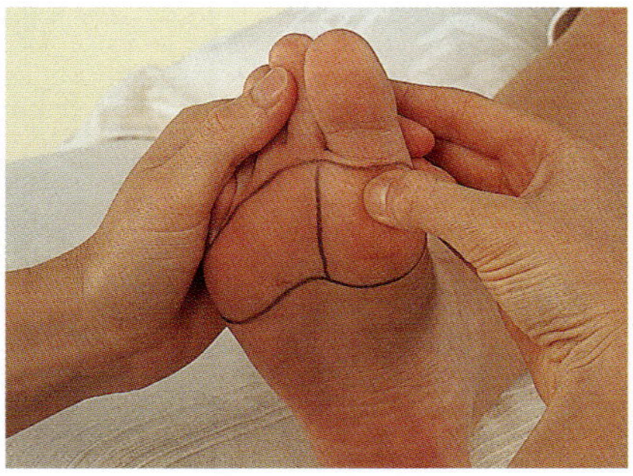

13 To treat the chest, thumbwalk horizontally in from the instep under the big toe, starting just next to the neck. Repeat just below the first line, bordering on it. Continue thumbwalking lines like this until you have covered the ball under the big toe down to the diaphragm line.

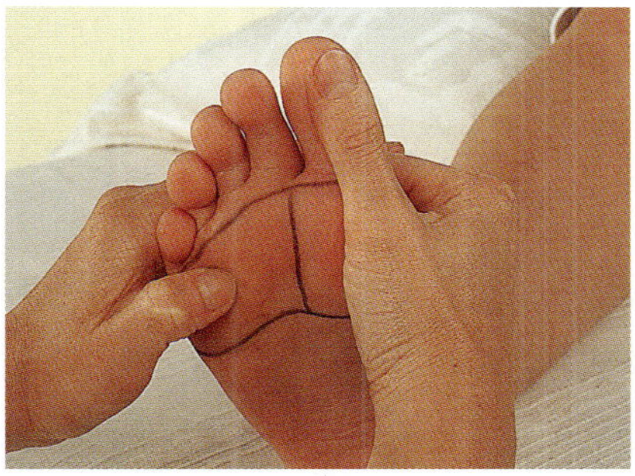

14 Thumbwalk horizontally in from the outside of the foot under the little toes, starting just below the ridge. Cover the whole of this area in the same way as described in step 13.

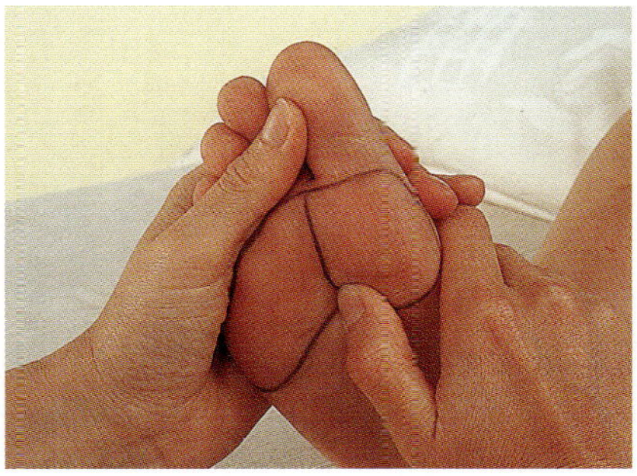

15 Next, work carefully along the diaphragm line under the big toe, and follow the natural line up between the big and second toes to the actual base of the toes.

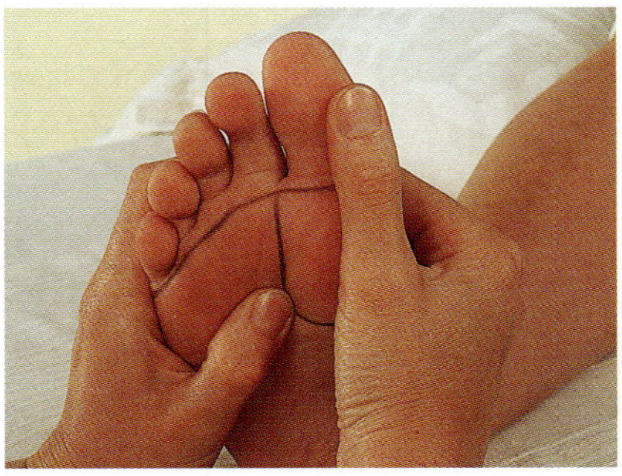

16 Work along the diaphragm line from the outside of the foot, and when you finally meet the line between the big and the second toes you can continue up this line to the base of the toes.

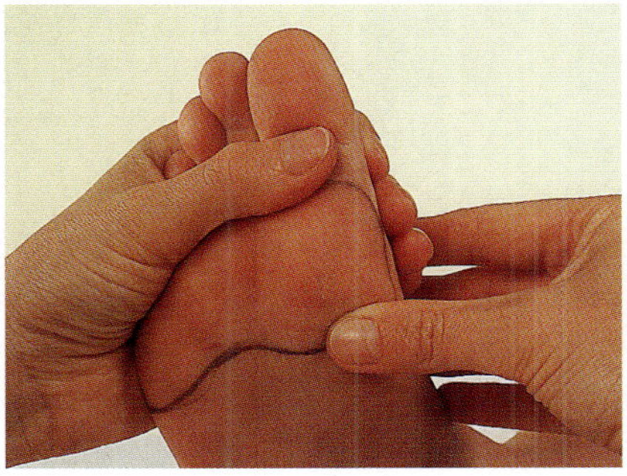

17 Starting from just under the big toe, thumbwalk the whole diaphragm line.

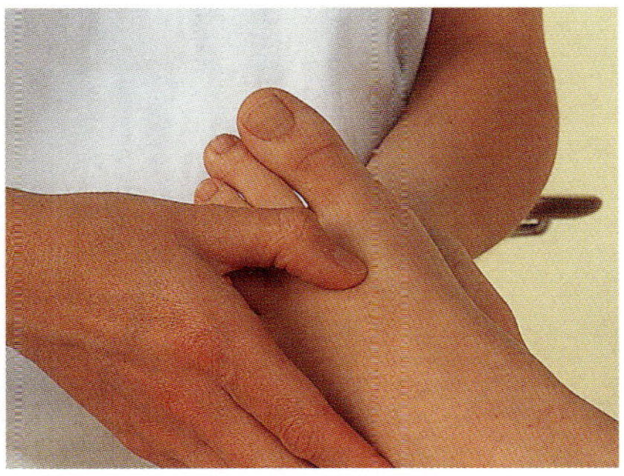

18 When on the top of the foot, you may now commence thumbwalking right along each individual channel that exists between the bones which lead up to the toes.

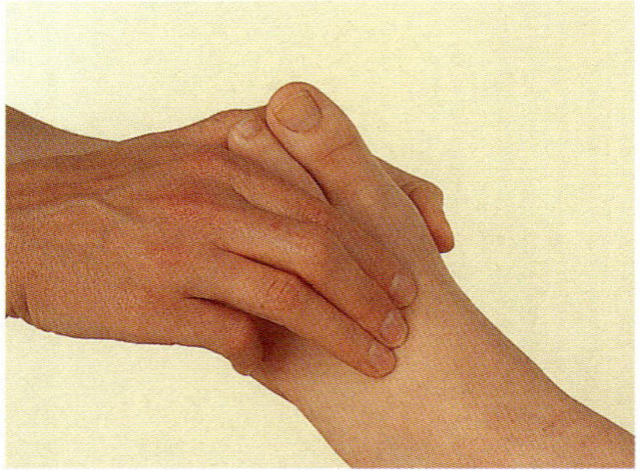

19 The last step involves using the three middle fingers together to fingerwalk the whole of the top of the foot. You should work from the base of the toes right up the foot.

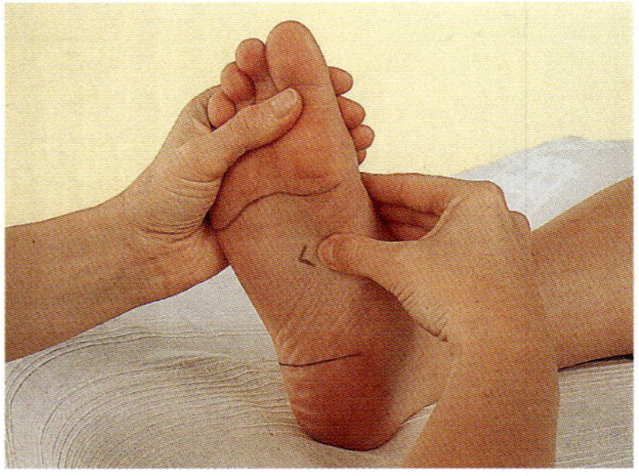

20 To treat the abdomen, thumbwalk from the medial edge, under the big toe, to the outer edge in horizontal lines as you did for the chest, each line bordering the previous one.

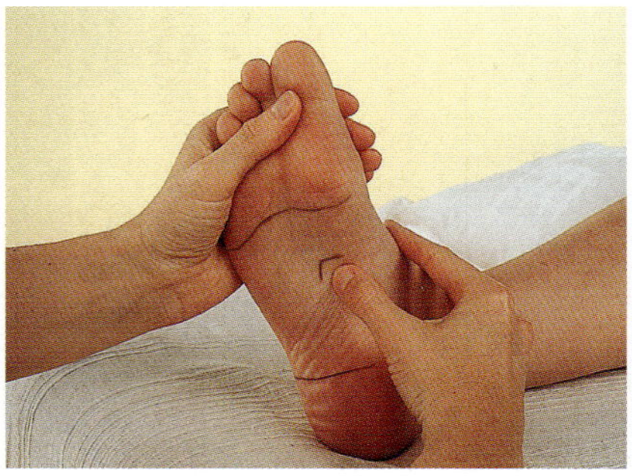

21 Next thumbwalk in diagonal lines covering the same area, as described in the previous step.

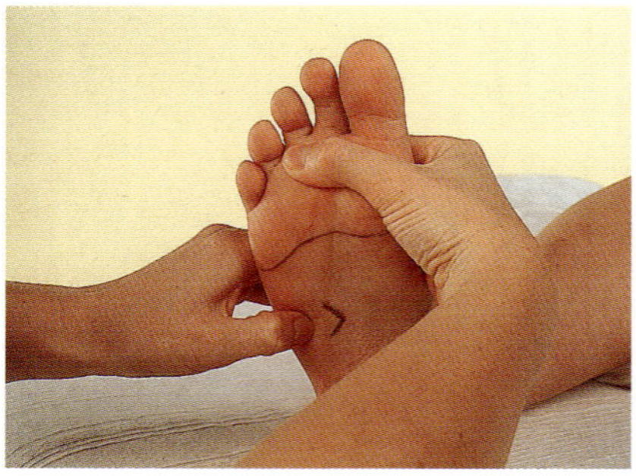

22 Now swiftly change hands and thumbwalk in horizontal lines. You should now be working from the outside of the foot towards the inner (medial) edge, as previously shown.

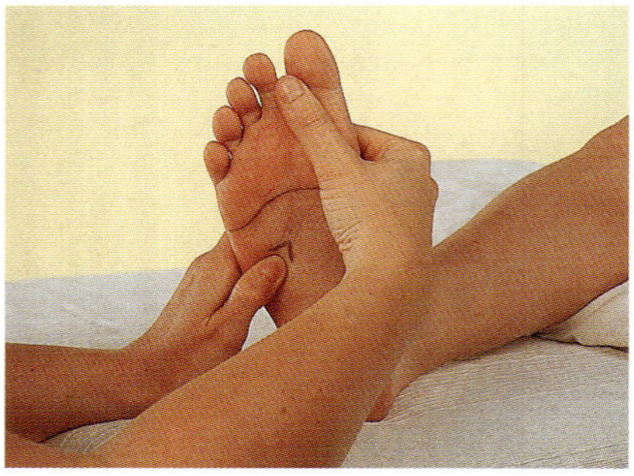

23 Employing the same thumb, begin thumbwalking in diagonal lines and gradually work from the outside towards the inner edge, covering the whole area, as before.

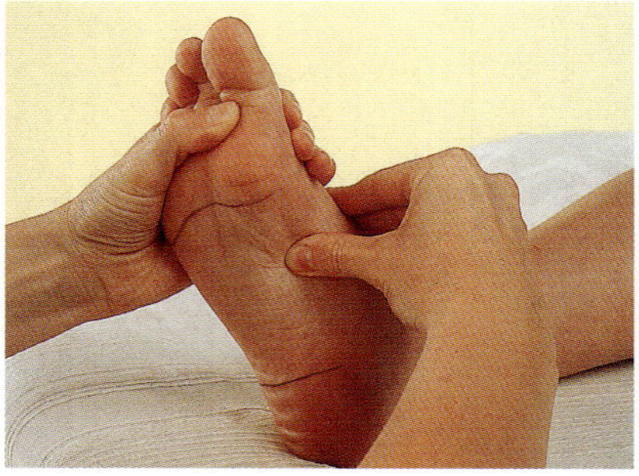

24 While referring to the foot chart, gently begin rotating the reflex to the adrenal glands, pushing in under the tendon running down from the big toe.

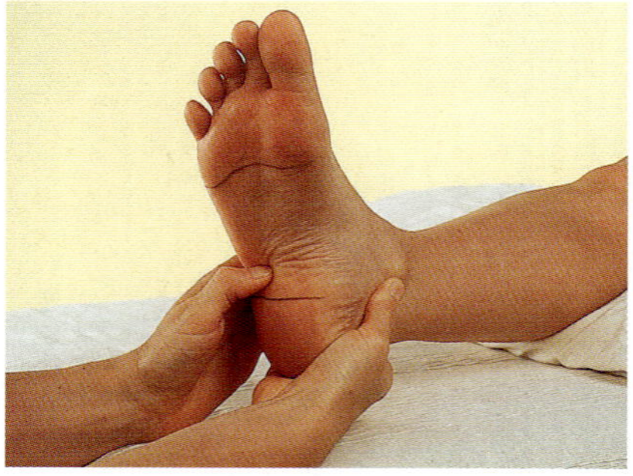

25 Work along what is called the ileo-caecal valve reflex, using the inner corner of your thumb to pinpoint it.

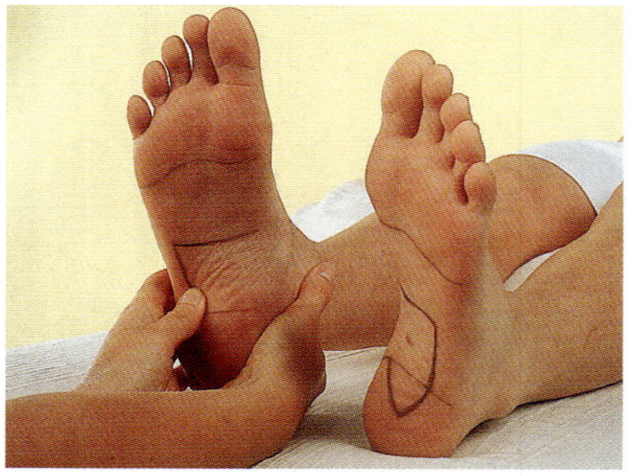

26 Thumbwalk the path of the colon, starting on the right foot at the bottom of the colon line.

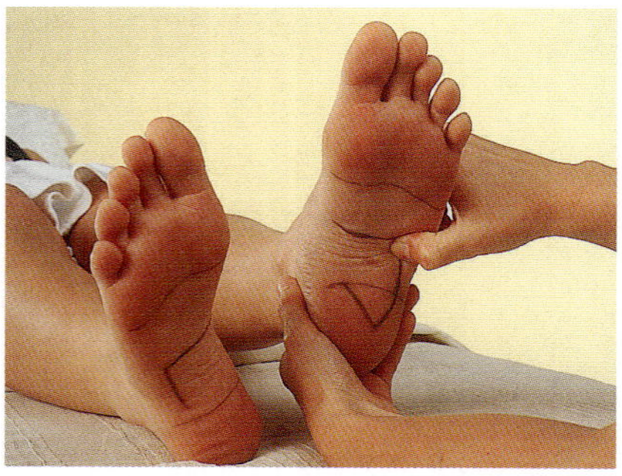

27 Continue on to the left foot, but change from the left hand to right hand at the point above.

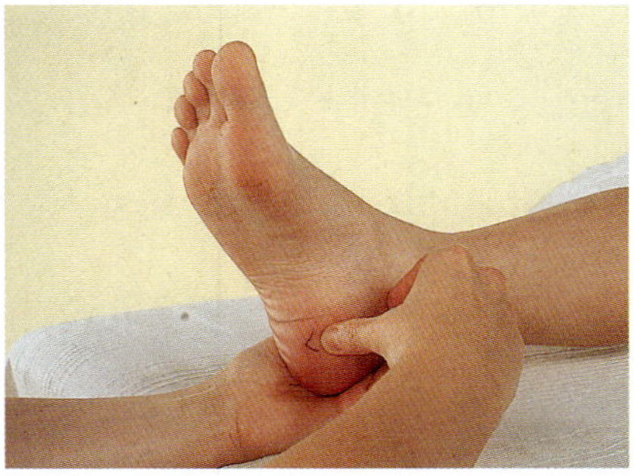

28 To treat the pelvis, begin by thumbwalking the heel across the sole in horizontal, overlapping lines. Note that this can actually be quite hard work.

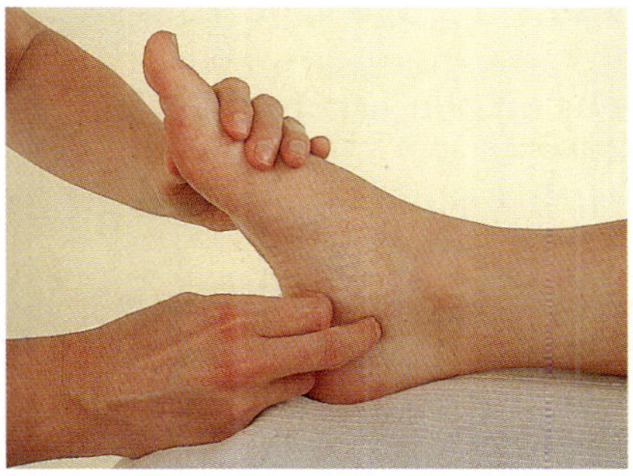

29 Find the little hollow halfway along a diagonal line between the centre of the ankle bone and the right angle of the heel on the inside of the foot, and rotate this point with your middle fingertip. Do not apply too much pressure.

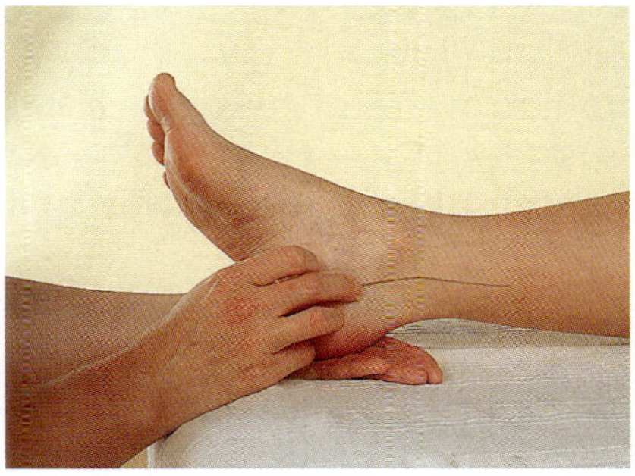

30 From this point, begin the fingerwalking movement using the same finger, going up the line running behind the ankle and up the leg.

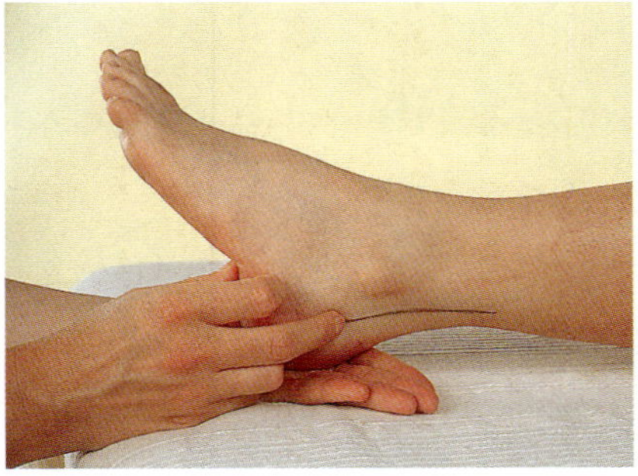

31 Now find the point described in step 2, but on the outside of the foot. Rotate it with the middle finger of your other hand and then fingerwalk up the outside of the ankle and leg, just as you did on the inside.

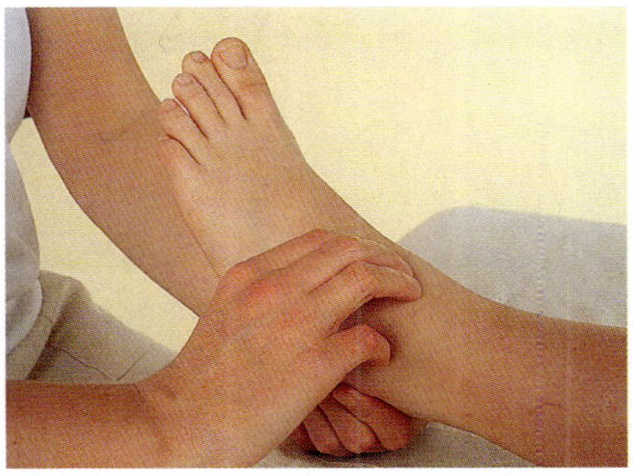

32 Now begin using the three middle fingers, and start fingerwalking right across the top of the ankle.

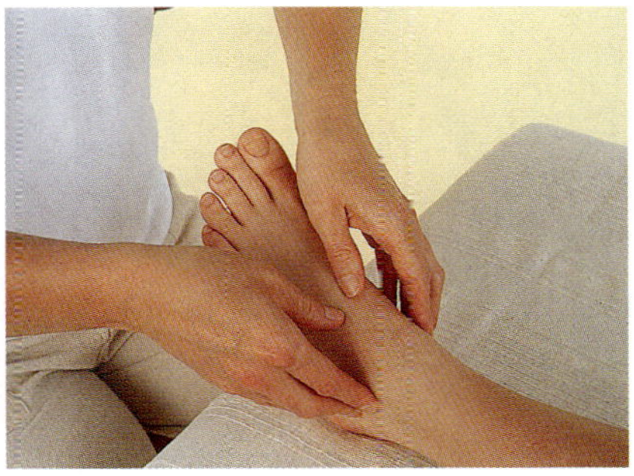

33 Continue the fingerwalking movement, going right round the ankle bone, using the same fingertips.

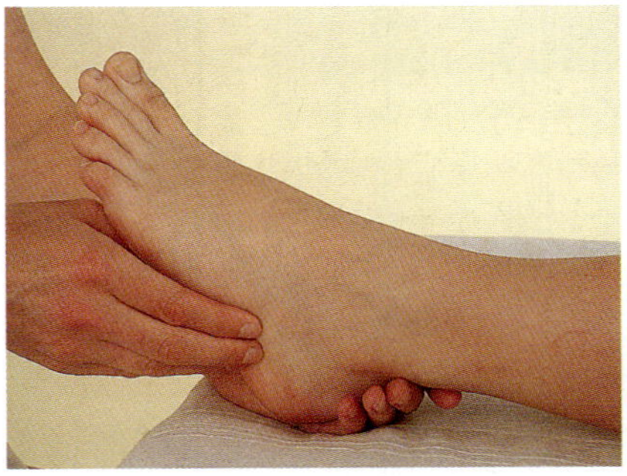

34 Finally, refer to the foot charts to find the hip/knee reflex, and work it by fingerwalking two fingers together.

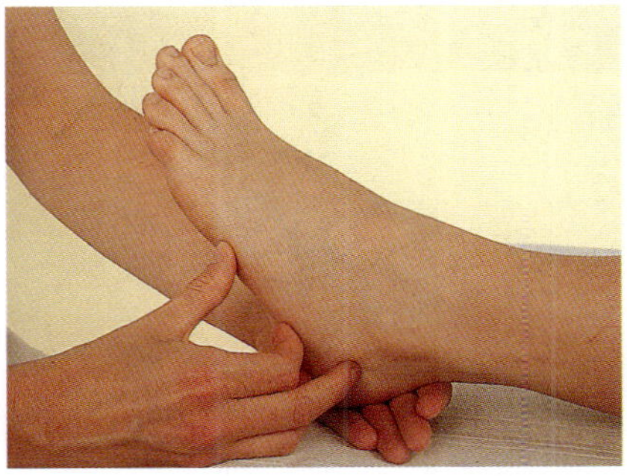

35 To treat the limbs, work the outside of the foot, then begin massaging the relevant cross reflex.

Key Tips

Although the routine is described for one foot only, remember to treat the other foot too. Start with the right foot, as here, then when you have completed the routine, move to the left foot and duplicate what you have done (reversing hands and movements as appropriate to the shape of the left foot). It is always a good idea to start with general foot massage and to incorporate some soothing massage movements into the routine.

tension releasers

We collect far too much tension in our necks. If you are not aware of how much neck tension can accumulate, put your hands to either side of your neck and begin to massage gently. If it feels in any way tight or uncomfortable you may benefit from this sequence as your partner carefully works your feet. When the neck muscles are tense and tight they may lead to pain, noises in the ears, and tired eyes. These releasers will cure that.

NECK AND SHOULDER TENSION

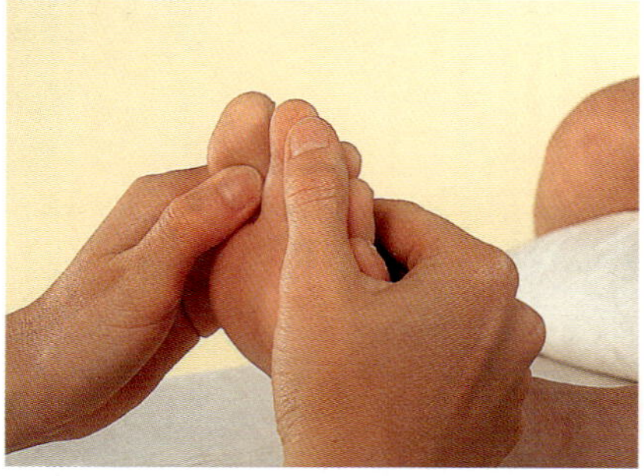

1 Treat neck tension by thumbwalking up and round the side of the big toe, then up the necks of all toes.

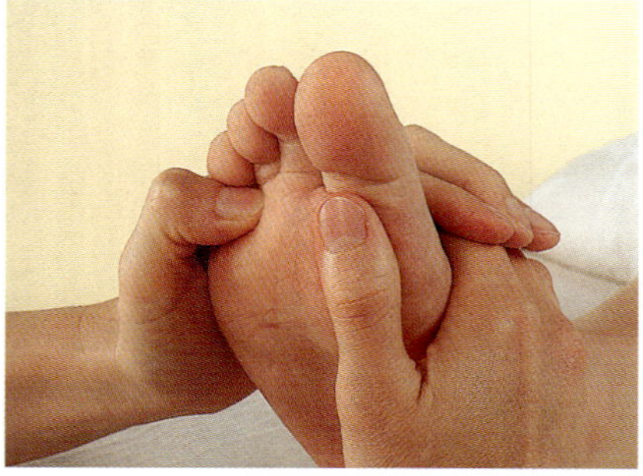

2 Thumbwalk right along the ridge immediately under the toes. Make sure that you are right on top of this ridge.

Self-help

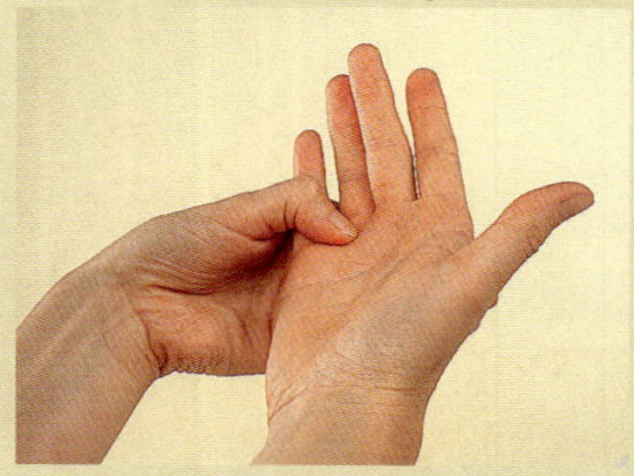

Thumbwalk along the base of your fingers, and repeat several times.

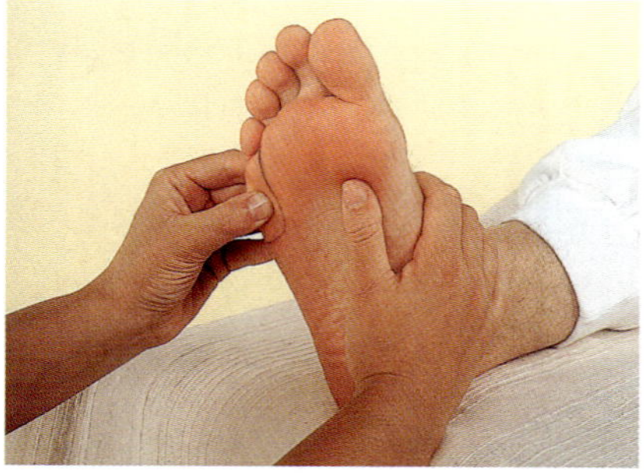

3 Ease shoulder tension by thumbwalking along the line of the shoulders in horizontal, overlapping lines.

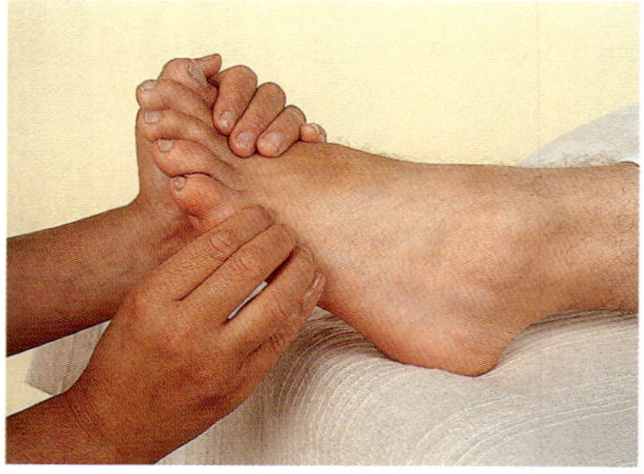

4 Fingerwalk across the same area on the top of the foot with three fingers. Fingerwalk around the mid-back (from the little toe to halfway down the foot).

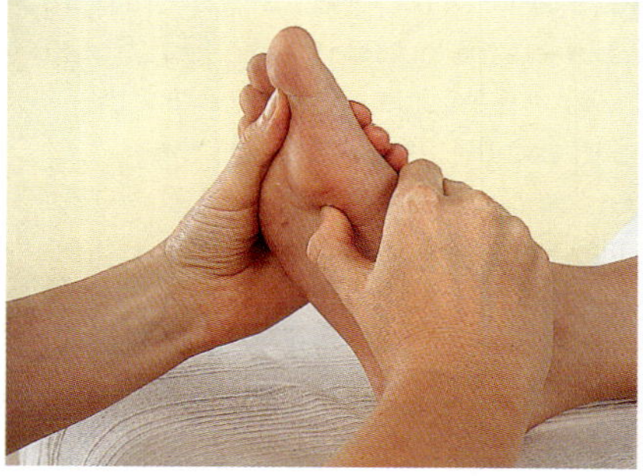

5 To relax the diaphragm, position your thumb on the diaphragm line. Hold the foot, bring it down on to the thumb and lift it off again. Repeat across the foot.

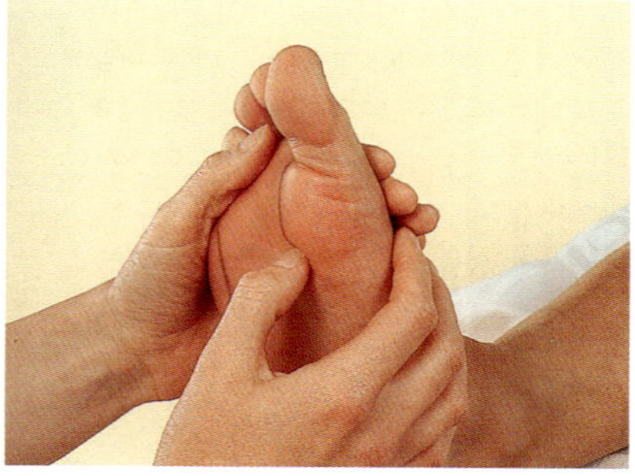

6 Ease whiplash injuries by thumbwalking between the big and second toes.

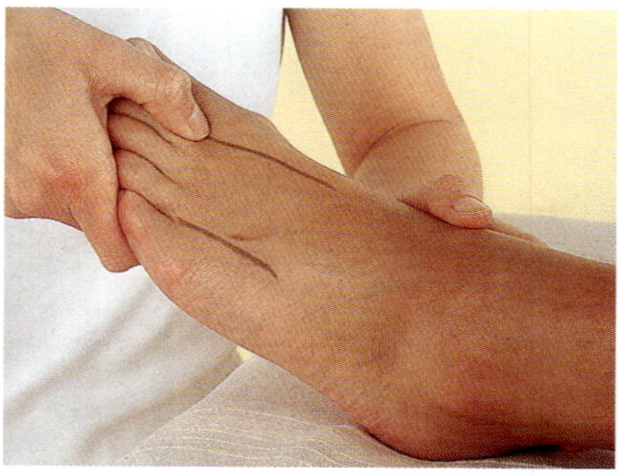

7 Work the same area on the top of the feet with your thumb.

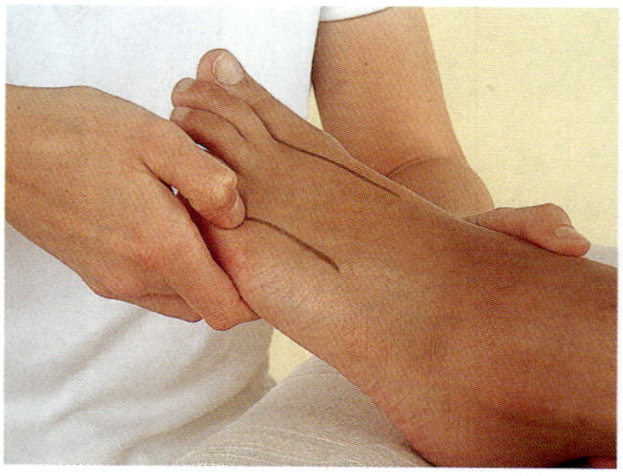

8 Work the shoulder reflex on the top and the bottom of the feet.

BACKACHE RELIEVERS

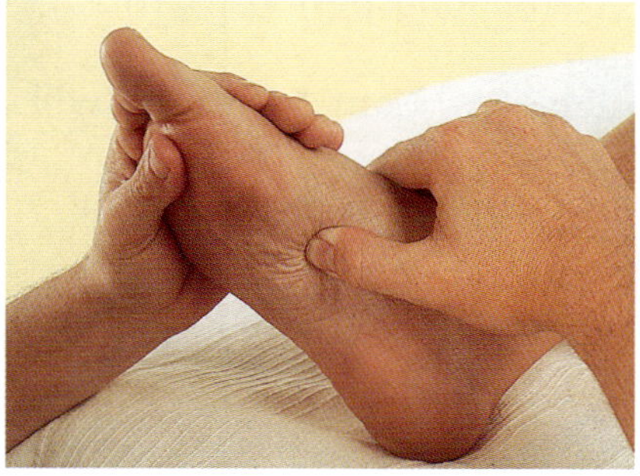

1 Thumbwalk up and down the spine, gently supporting the outer edge of the foot as you work.

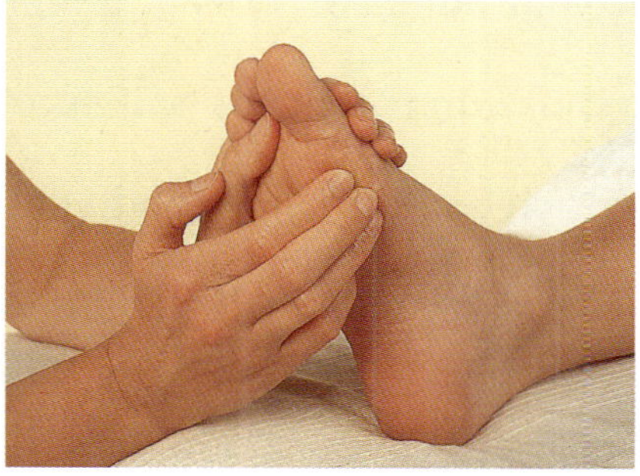

2 Fingerwalk across the spinal reflex with three fingers together, right down the instep in stripes.

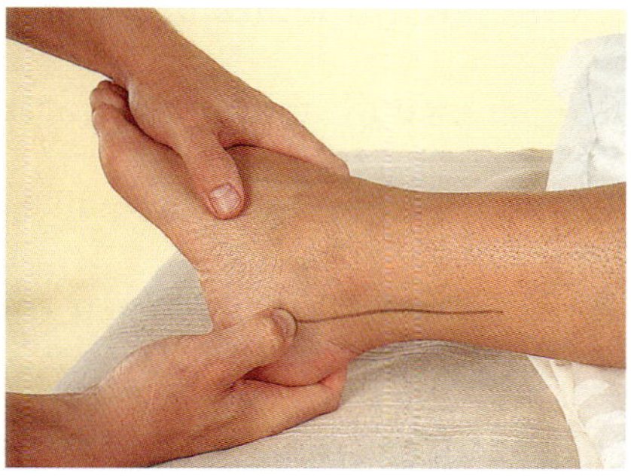

3 Thumbwalk up the helper reflexes for the lower back, behind the ankle bones on either side.

RELIEVING REPETITIVE STRAIN

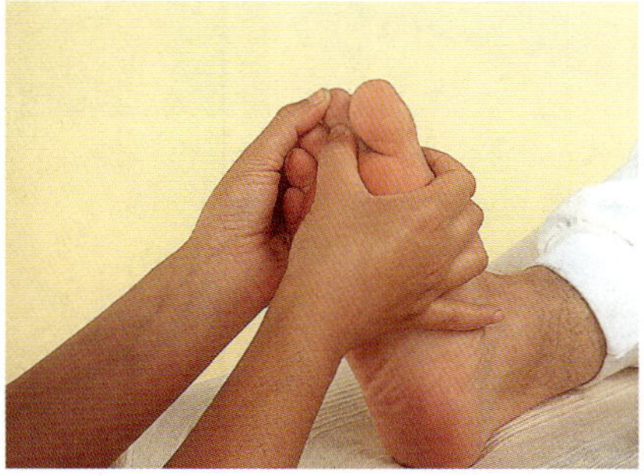

1 Thumbwalk up the back and sides of the second and third toes for the eye reflex. This will also relieve neck tension.

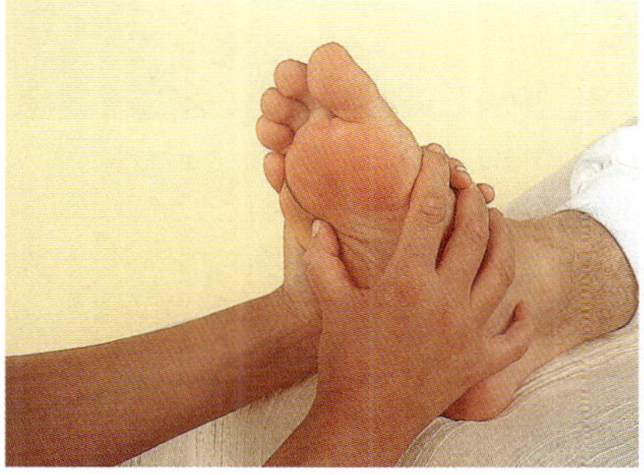

2 Work the shoulder reflexes thoroughly by using the thumbwalking technique. Then fingerwalk across the same area on the top of the foot, with the three middle fingers together.

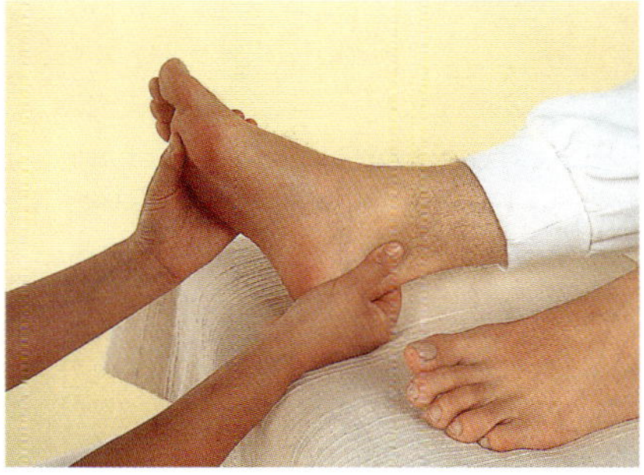

3 Rotate the ankles to ease any aching wrists and to stimulate the healing process within the joints.

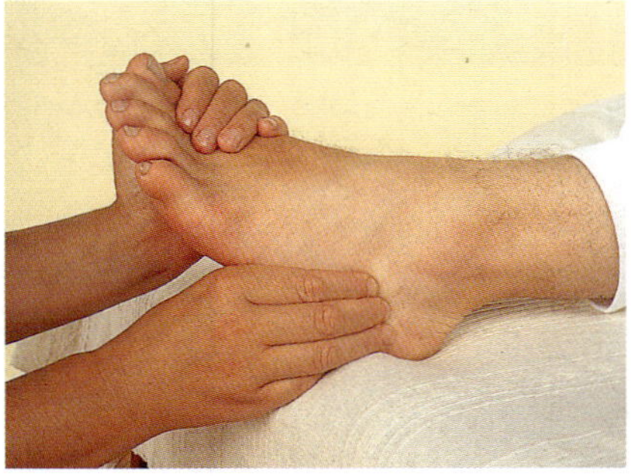

4 For the penultimate step, work across and down the outer foot on both feet to relax shoulders, arms, legs and knees.

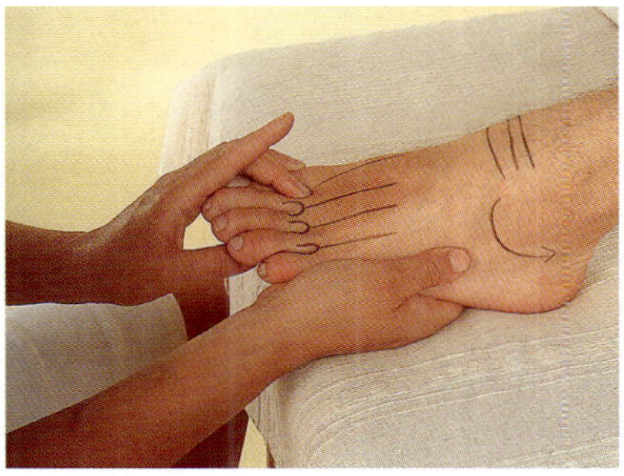

5 Work the lymph system on both feet. Fingerwalk down the lines from the toes to the ankle. Then work round the ankle.

Self-help

Use the detailed hand chart on page 95 when trying to locate the relevant reflex on your hands to give temporary, quick relief for your particular problem. The key point to remember at all times when dealing with repetitive strain is that there is no one particular sequence of movements that guarantees special help. It is completely up to you to work out exactly which part of your body is suffering from the strain. You must then set about locating the relevant reflex on the charts. Then proceed with the treatment.

stress and pain relievers

Excessive stress lies somewhere behind most troubles and illness. If your adrenalin runs at a high level for long periods, with little chance of appropriate action, your adrenal glands will become depleted. Your breathing will also become too rapid or will be restricted and shallow, and your digestion will be upset or strained in some way. When this happens, you know it is time to act and start curing yourself.

RELIEVING GENERAL STRESS

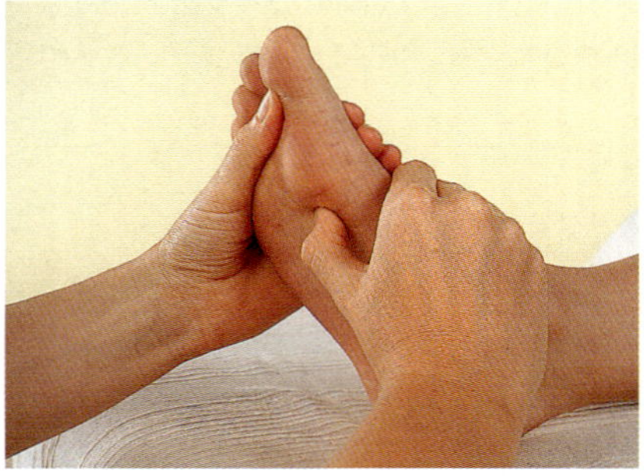

1 Relax the diaphragm by bringing the foot down on to the thumb of your other hand, and then lifting off again. Repeat, moving your thumb to the outside.

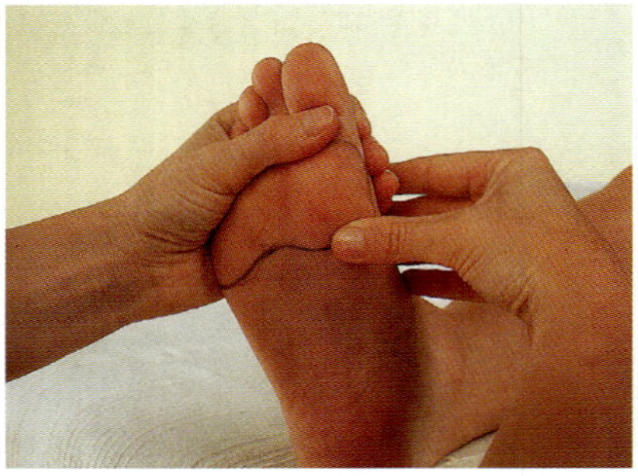

2 Thumbwalk along the diaphragm line. Tension collects in the diaphragm, causing tightness. When the diaphragm is relaxed the abdominal organs are stimulated.

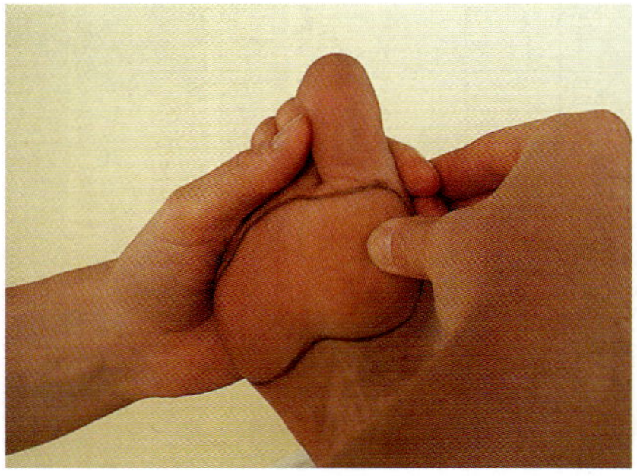

3 Work the lung reflexes on the chest area so that once the diaphragm is relaxed, breathing can be increased. This will help with relaxation.

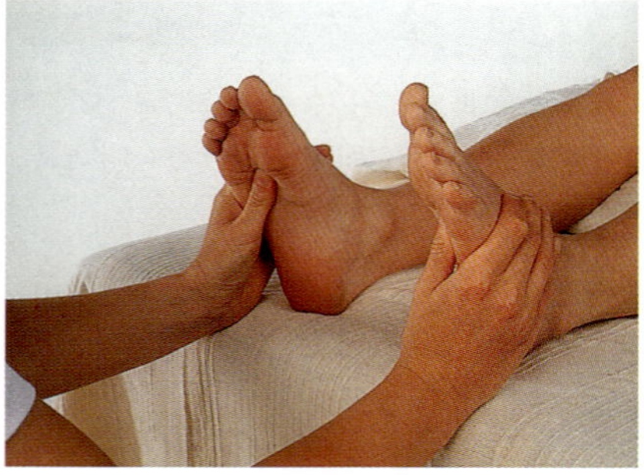

4 With both feet together put your thumbs in the diaphragm line. Press in on the in-breath, and release on the out.

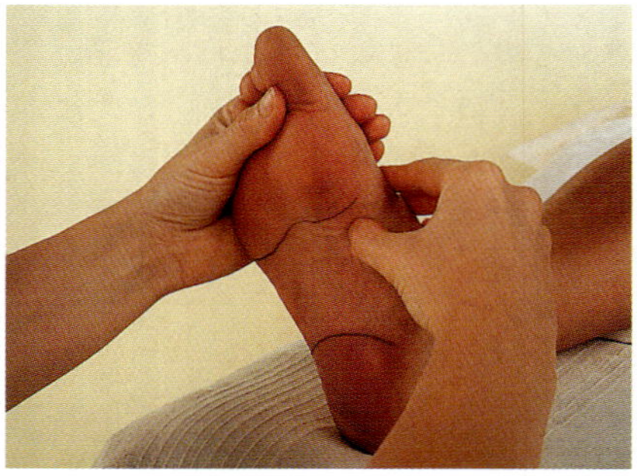

5 Thumbwalk the stomach area and the whole of the instep, which is the abdominal area. This will help digestion.

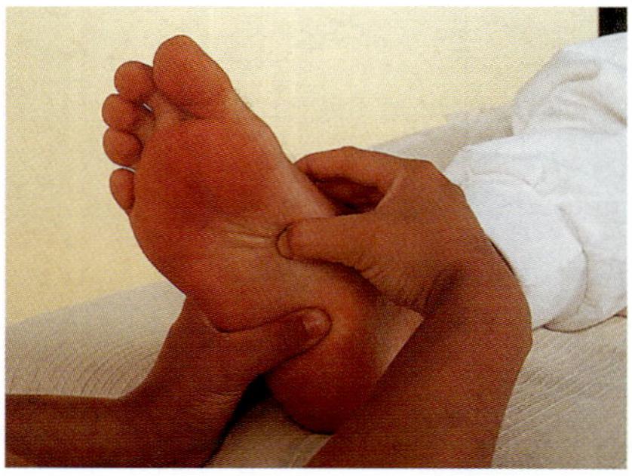

6 Rotate gently on the adrenal reflex.

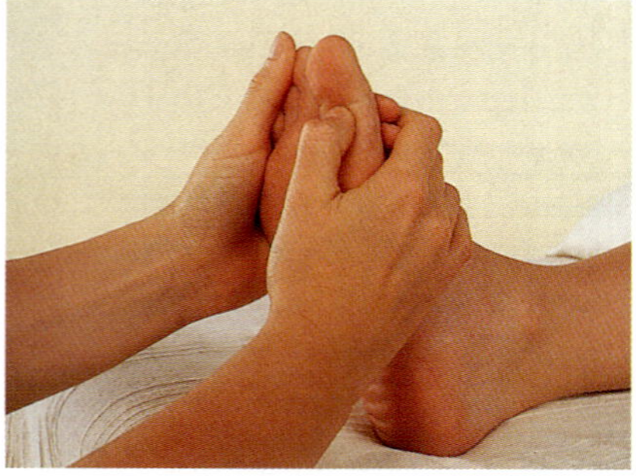

7 Work the neck reflex on the neck of the toes where tension collects.

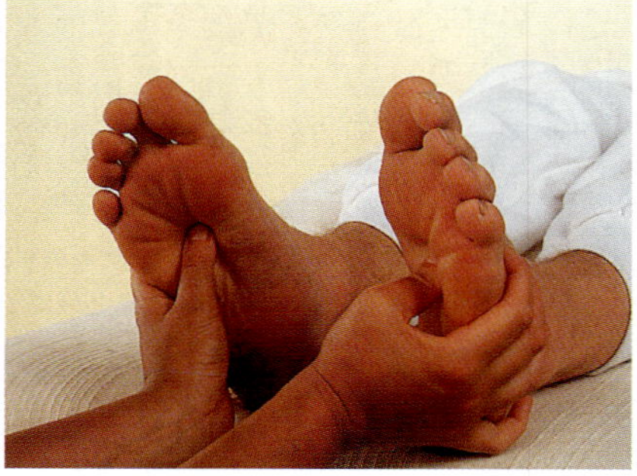

8 Ease stress from anger by working the solar plexus reflexes on both feet.

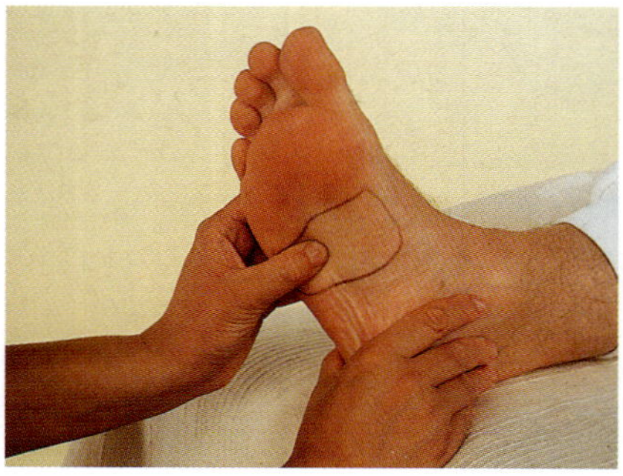

9 Work the liver area.

BACK PAIN

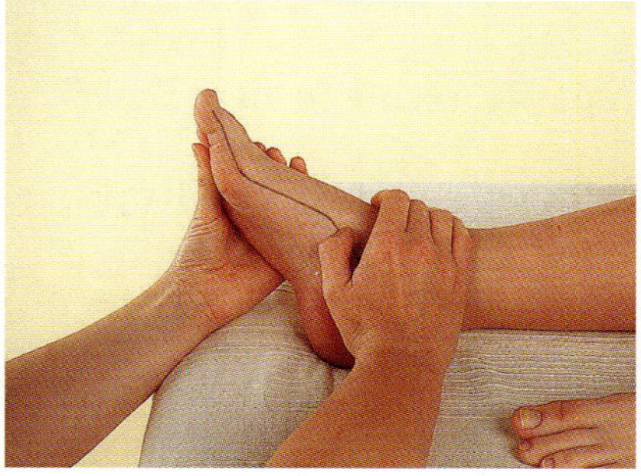

1 Work along the spine and find the tender parts. Work these to try to disperse some of the congestion.

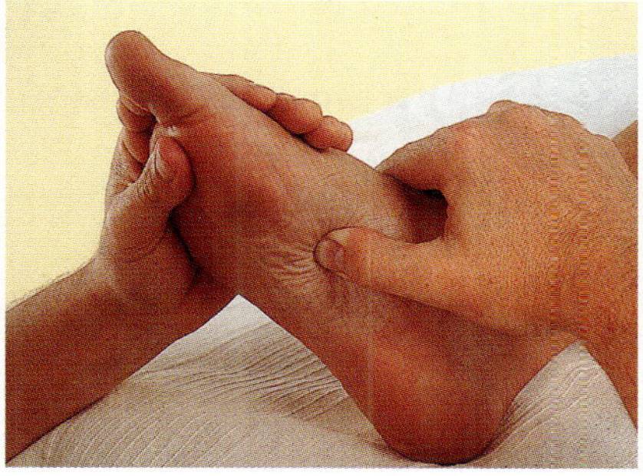

2 Work the adrenal gland reflexes on both feet. These glands deal with inflammation and aid good muscle tone when working effectively.

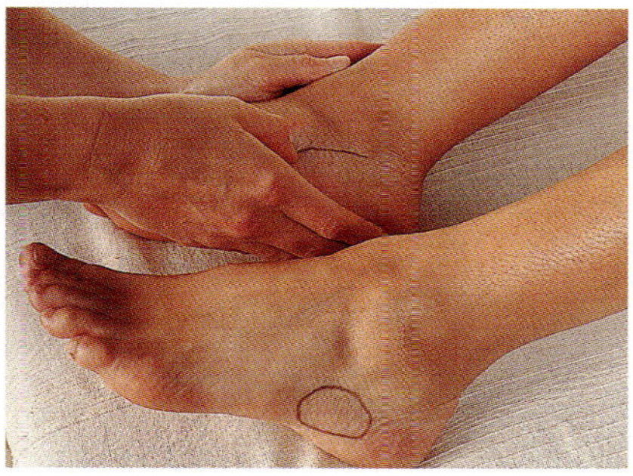

3 For lower back trouble, work the helper area by carefully rotating with your thumb.

NERVE PAIN

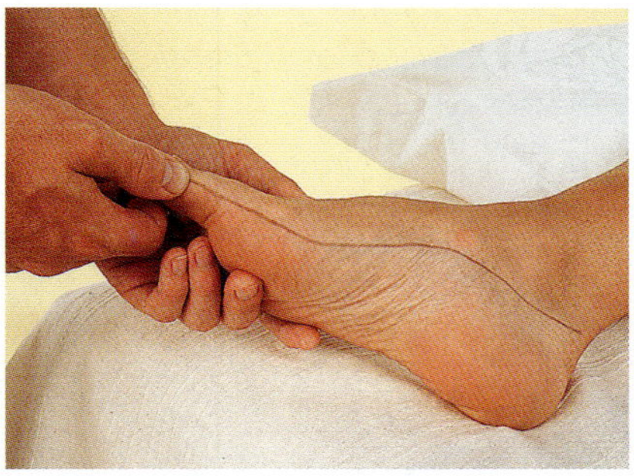

1 Thumbwalk along the spine for the central nervous system in the spinal cord.

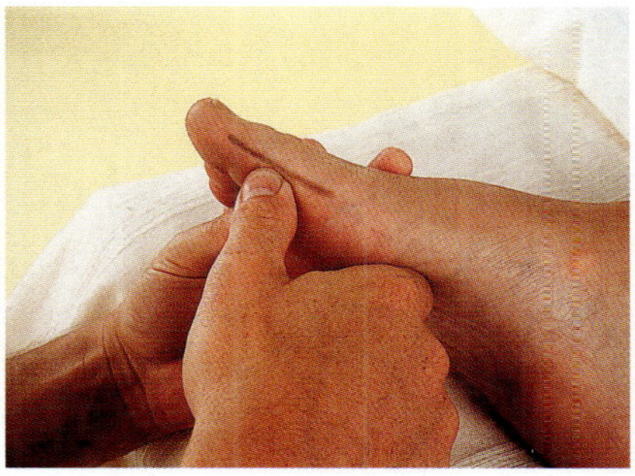

2 Find the local area, for example, for the neck, work the cervical vertebrae and find the part of the neck of the toes that is tender.

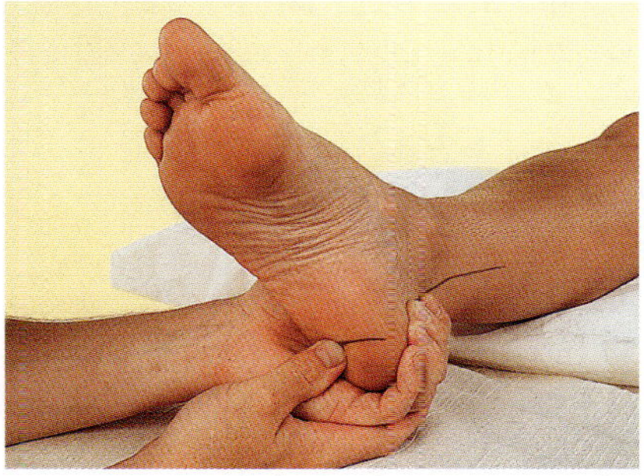

3 To treat sciatic pain, begin working the sciatic reflex as clearly shown in the foot chart.

CRAMP

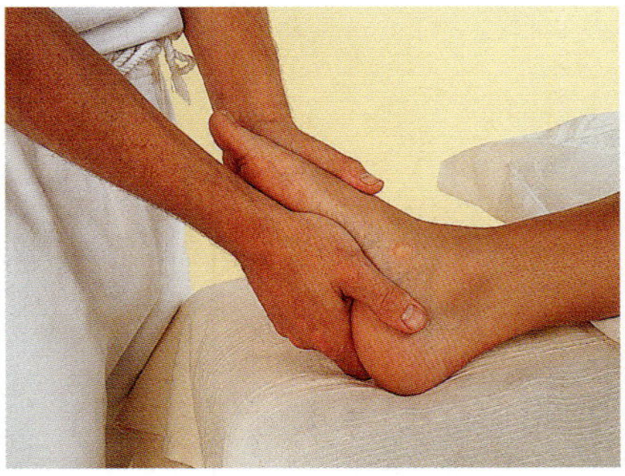

1 Hold the area and massage the appropriate cross reflex. For example, for cramp in the calf, massage the cross reflex on the lower arm.

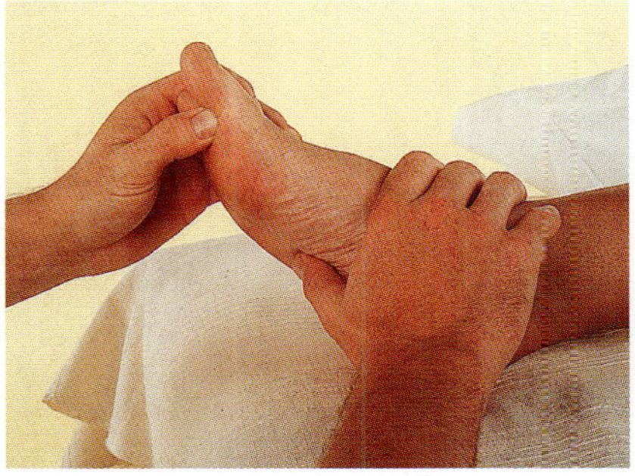

2 Work the parathyroid reflexes round the neck of the big toe.

TOOTHACHE

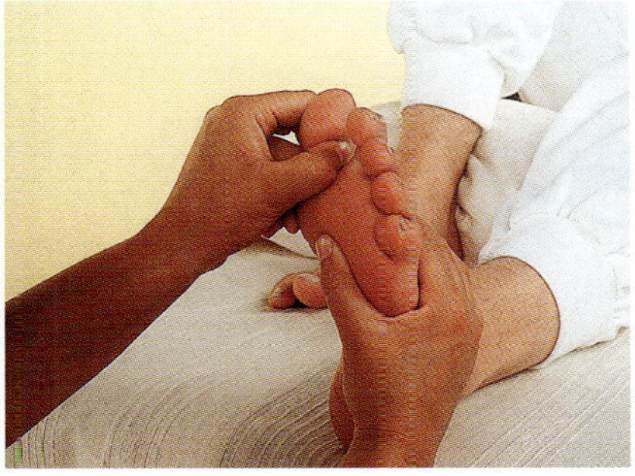

1 Find the toe or finger that has much tenderness, and work that area carefully but thoroughly.

headaches, breathing and sleeping

The three key elements to our continued health and well-being are breathing and sleeping, and a clear head. Poor breathing, possibly caused by too much tension, can easily result in headaches though. A bad night's sleep can also have unpleasant side effects, leading to a heavy head the next day. The following techniques are all excellent ways of helping overcome such problems.

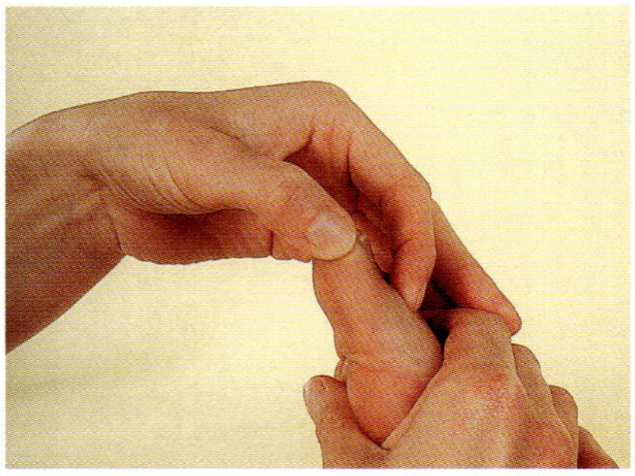

1 Ease headaches by working the hypothalamus reflex, which controls the release of endorphins for pain relief.

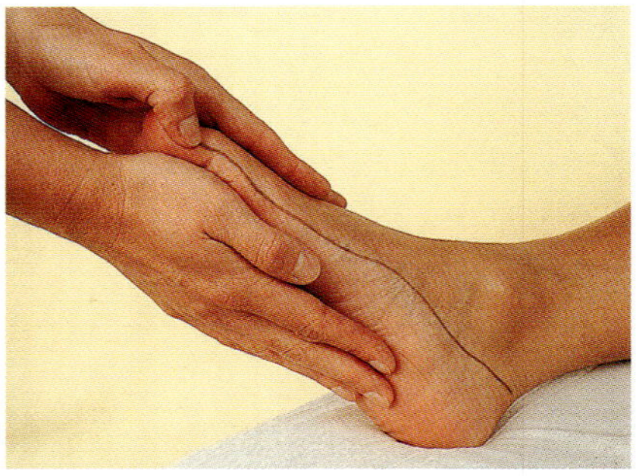

2 Work down the spine to take pressure away from the head. This will draw energy down the body.

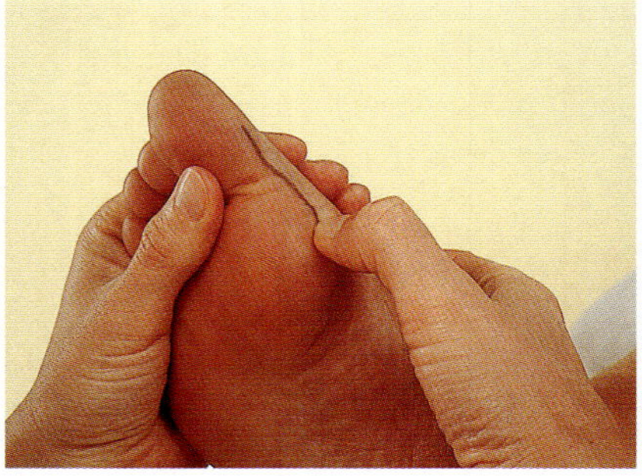

3 Work the cervical spine on the big toe. Work the neck of all the toes to relieve any tension.

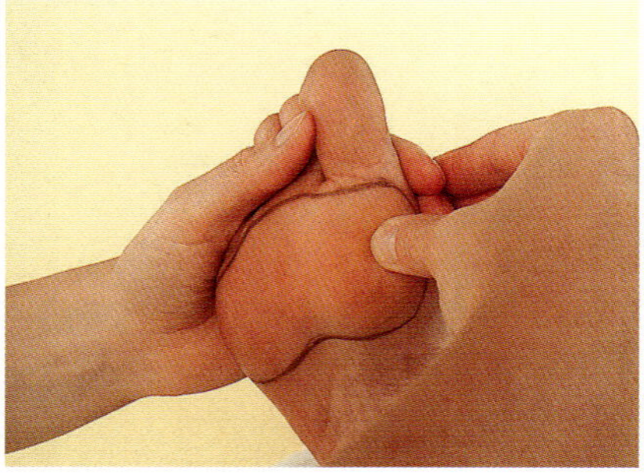

4 Aid efficient breathing by working the whole chest area on the bottom of the feet to relieve the chest and lungs.

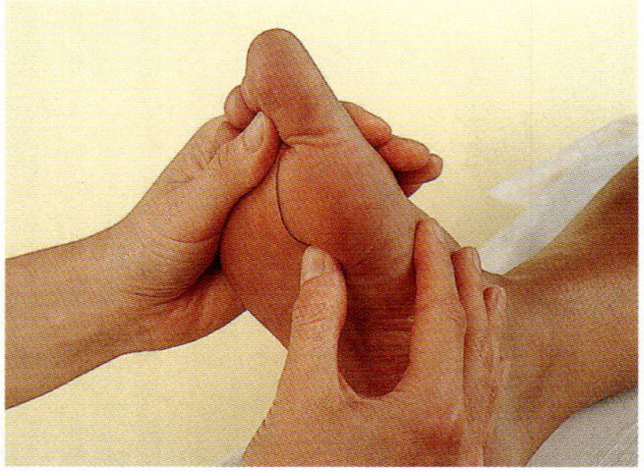

5 Work the air passages. This prompts them to clear themselves.

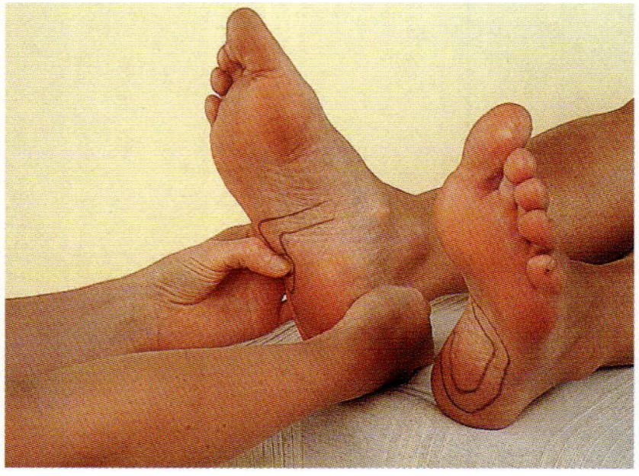

6 Work the ileo-caecal valve and the whole of the colon because this will help balance mucus levels.

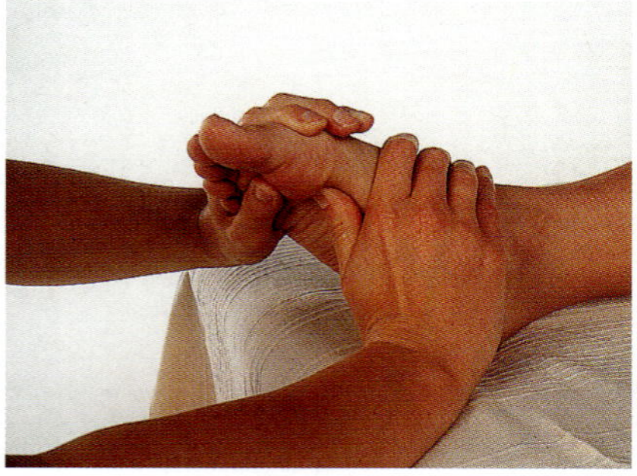

7 For a good night's sleep hold the foot with your outside hand and bring it down on to the thumb of your other hand and lift off. Move your thumb one step to the side and repeat.

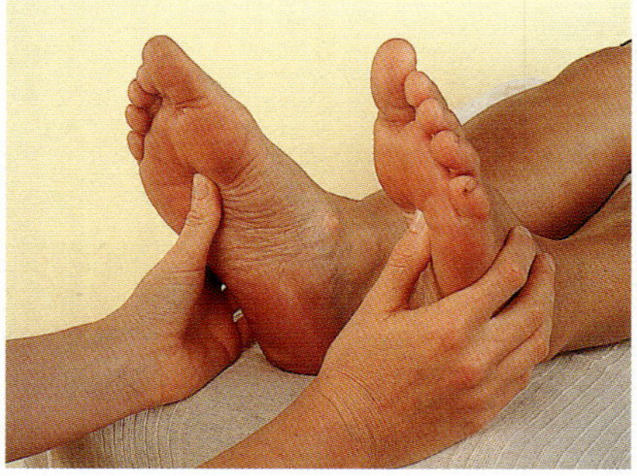

8 Do the solar plexus breathing exercise: take both feet together and position your thumbs in the centre of the diaphragm line. Press in on the in-breath, and release on the out.

Self-help

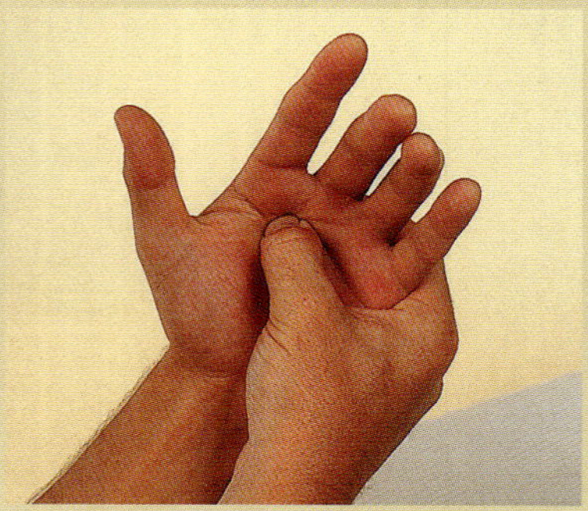

For self-help gently massage the solar plexus reflex in the palms of your hands.

reproductive problems

Reflexology is an excellent way of keeping your reproductive side in good working order. Surprisingly, it is far too often ignored, yet there are simple but highly effective techniques that will cover a wide range of problems including menstrual cramps, painful breasts, and even attacks of nausea. Note that all these reflexology movements concentrate on the feet, particularly on the area around the ankle.

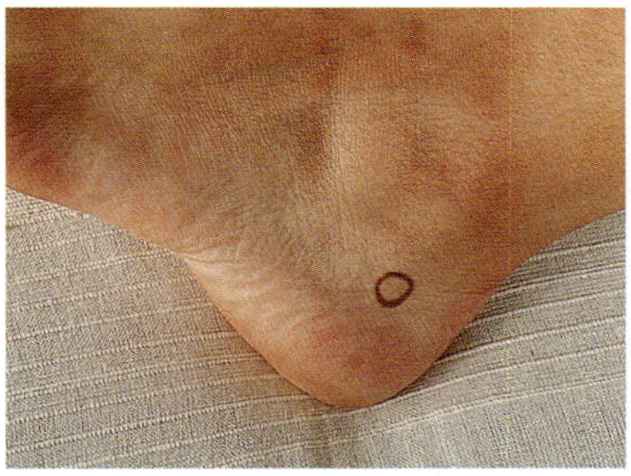

1 Work the ovaries or testes on the outside of the feet.

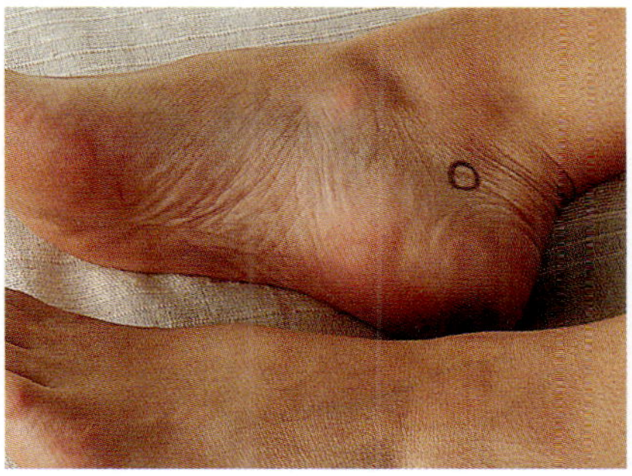

2 Work the uterus or prostate gland on the inside of the feet.

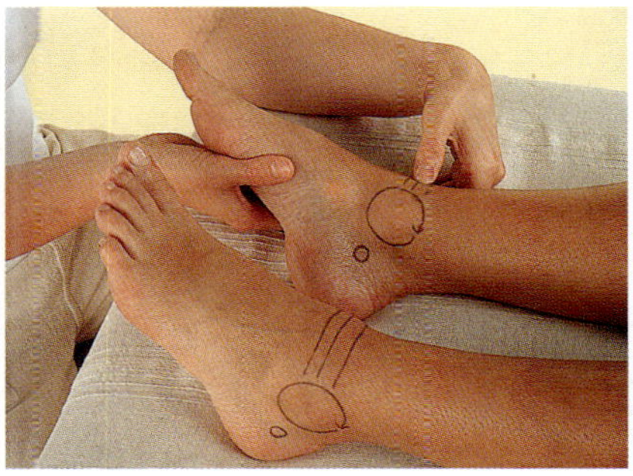

3 Work the fallopian tubes or vas deferens across the top of the ankle.

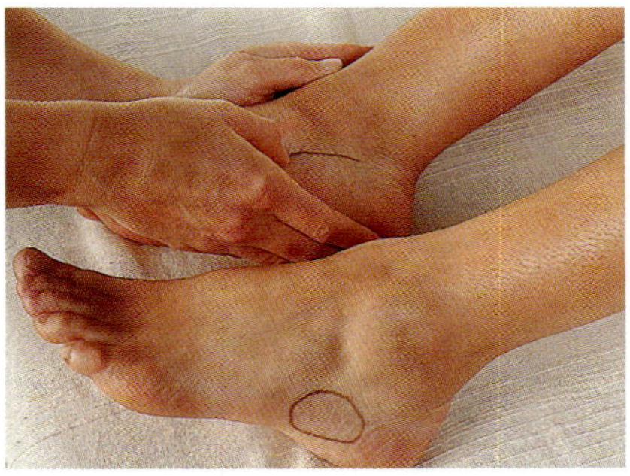

4 Ease menstrual cramps by working the lower spine for nerves to the uterus.

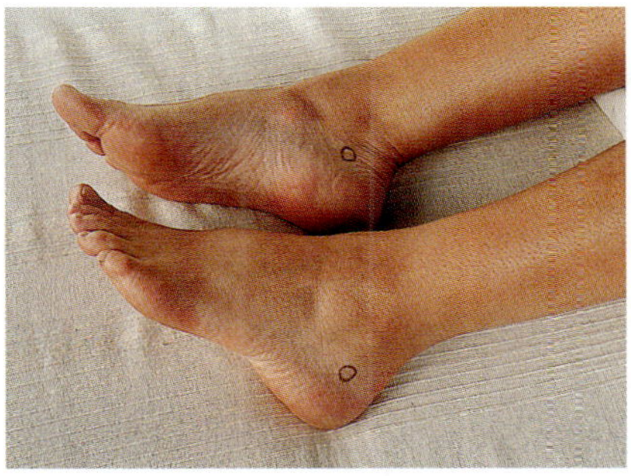

5 Work the uterus reflex area on the inside of the feet.

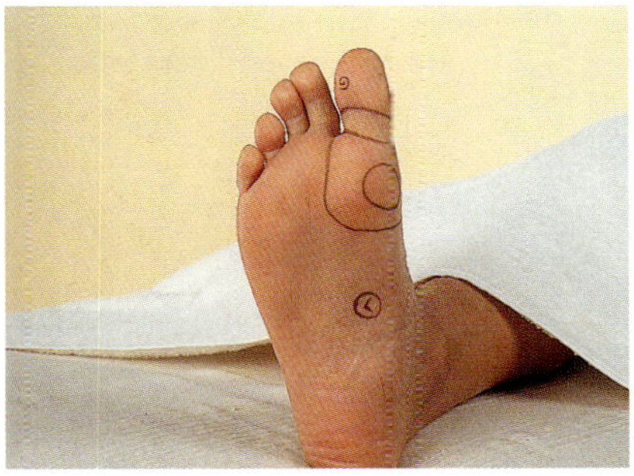

6 Work the glands on both feet, on the areas marked above.

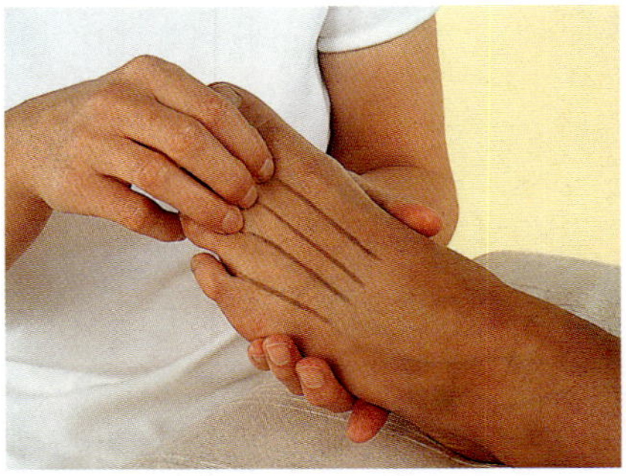

7 Ease painful breasts by fingerwalking up the chest area on top of the foot with three fingers together.

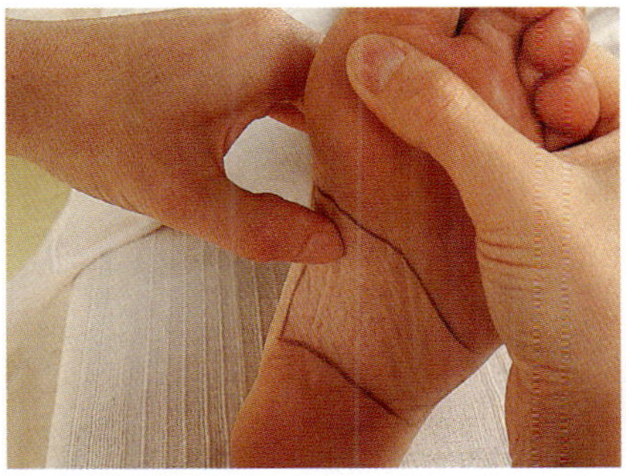

8 Relieve nausea by working the whole abdomen, especially where it seems tender. Do this gently and with care.

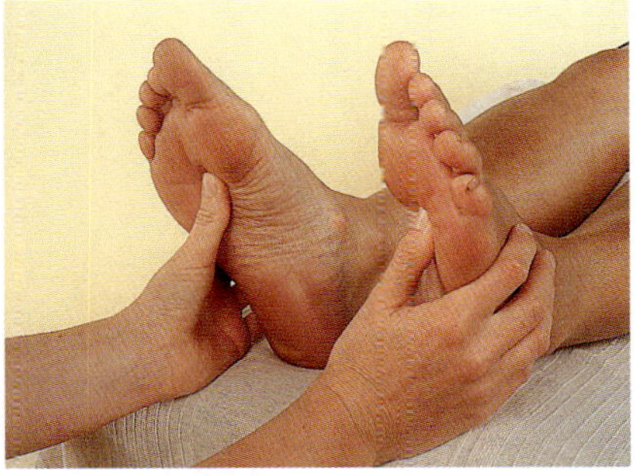

9 Do the solar plexus breathing exercise: press in with your thumbs, and release on the out.

colds, throats and sinuses

It is virtually impossible to avoid minor colds and the whole battery of side effects that go with them. Suddenly you are laid low by relentless outbreaks of sneezing and then sore throats and sinus problems. Fortunately, you do not have to grin and bear it. There are some excellent reflexology techniques that will help you overcome all these nasty extras. They will soon have you on the road to recovery.

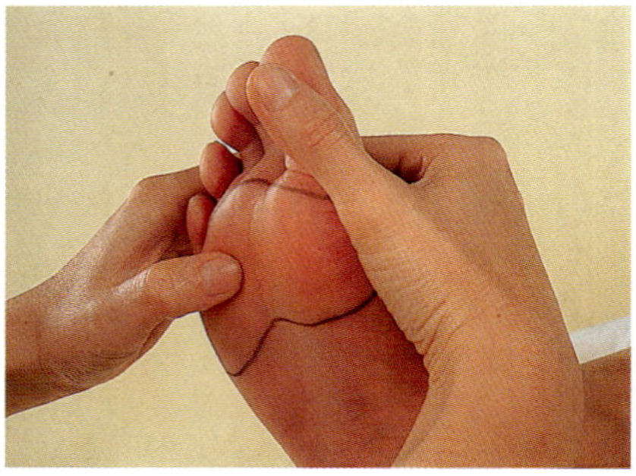

1 Ease colds by working the chest area fully to encourage clear breathing.

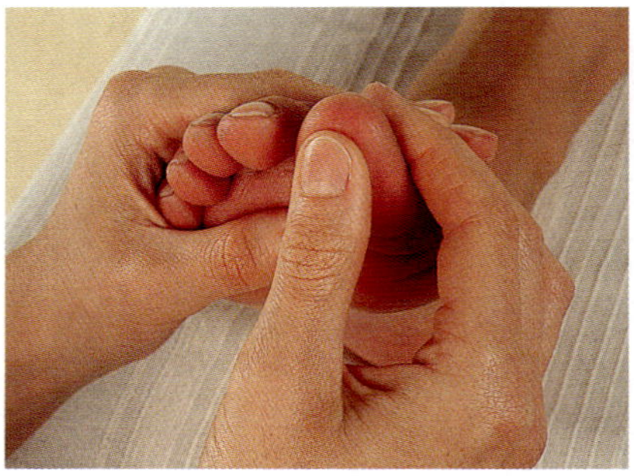

2 Begin with the big toe and work the toe tops to clear the sinuses. Pinpoint the pituitary gland in the centre of the big toes for the endocrine system.

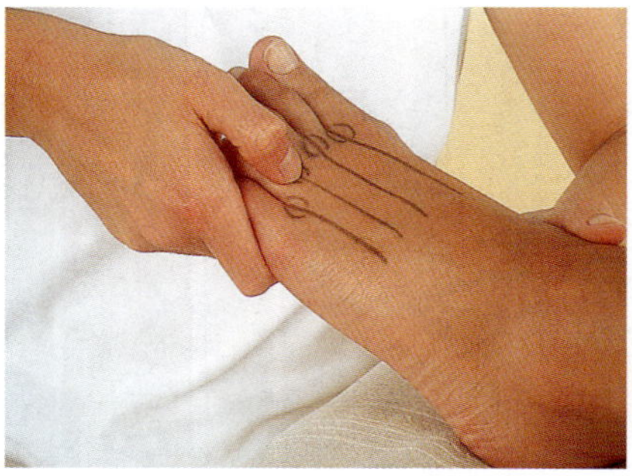

3 Work the upper lymph system to stimulate the immune system.

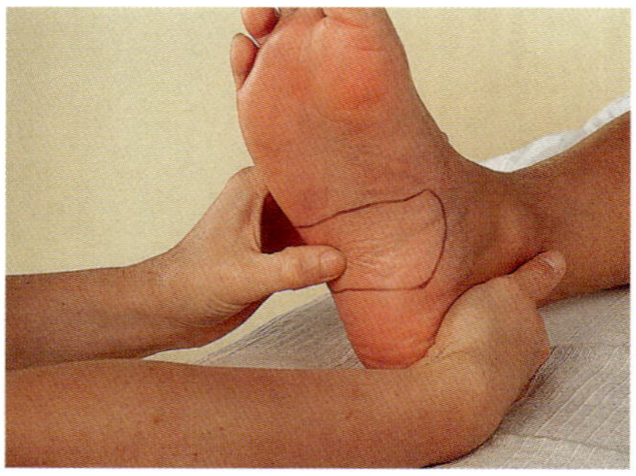

4 Work the small intestines to aid elimination of toxins and uptake of nutrients. Then work on the colon to aid elimination.

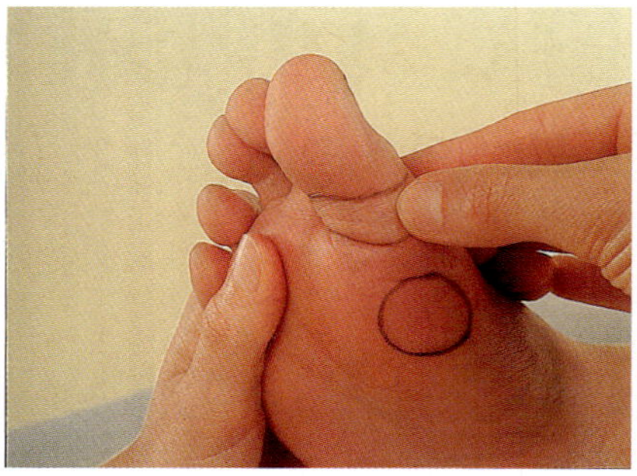

5 Help sore throats by working the upper lymph system, the throat by working the neck, and the thymus gland for the immune system.

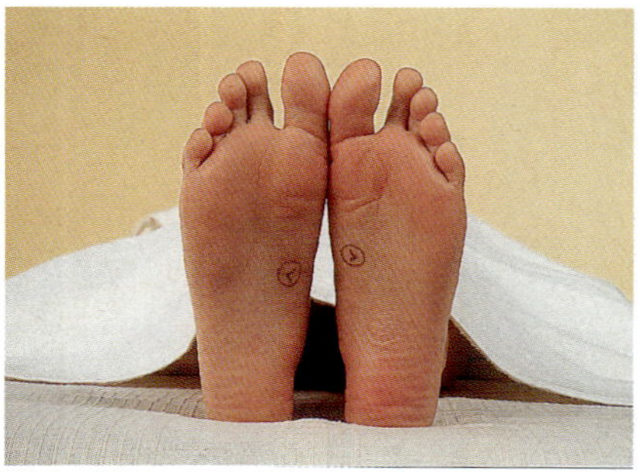

6 Rotate the adrenal reflex in the direction of the arrow.

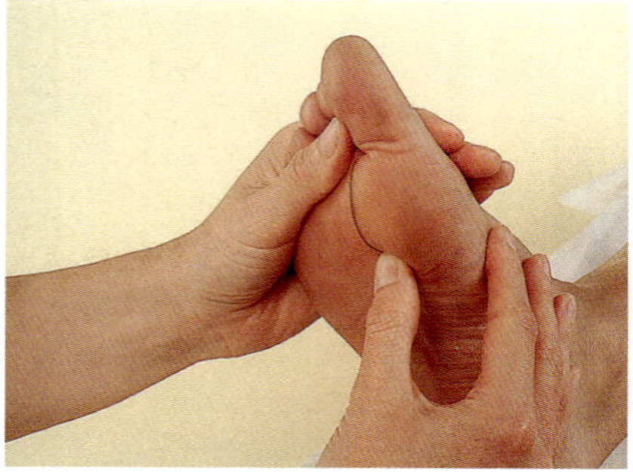

7 Work the trachea and the larynx to stimulate them. Work the thyroid area in the area of the chest under the big toe.

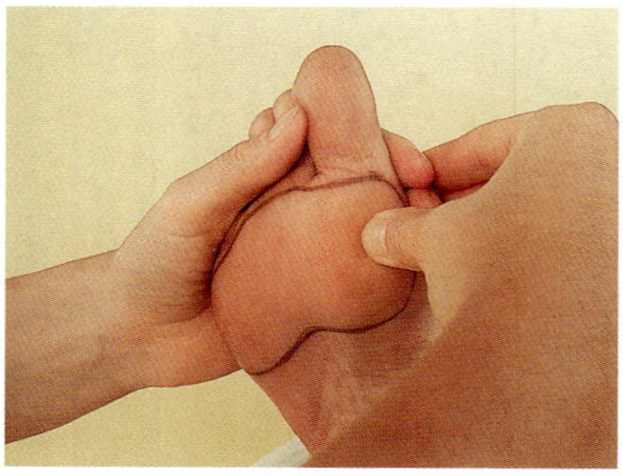

8 Ease sinus problems by working the whole chest area in order to aid good respiration.

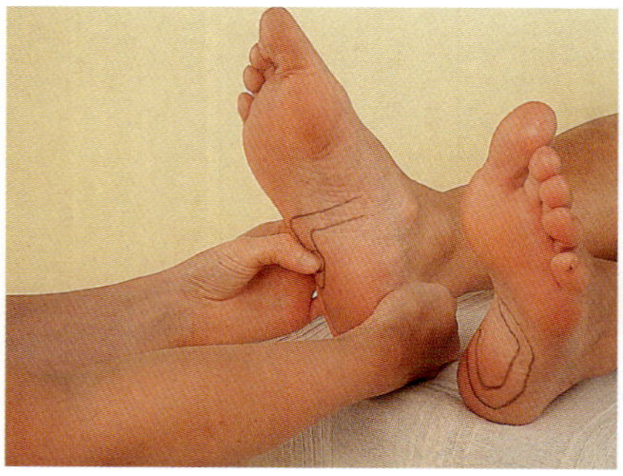

9 Pinpoint the ileo-caecal valve to balance mucus levels. Work the whole chest and rotate the adrenal reflex.

improving the digestion

The digestive system is all too frequently overlooked, yet it is vital that it is operating in a smooth and efficient way. To avoid any irritating problems, try carrying out the following quick and easy routines, and make them part of your daily or weekly reflexology session. One of the extra benefits is that they will help fine-tune the rest of you, leaving you feeling wonderfully calm, refreshed and invigorated.

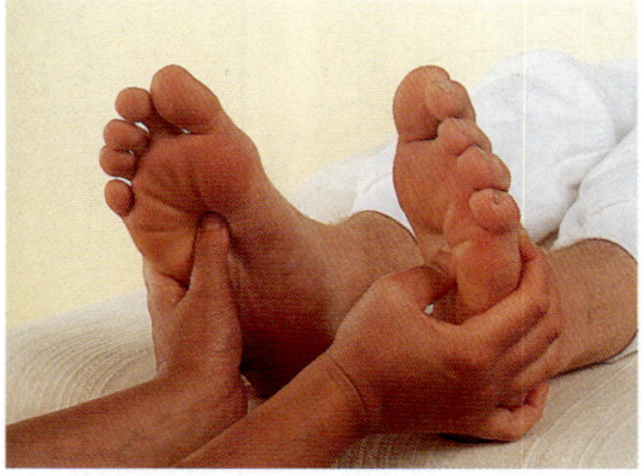

1 Aid any indigestion by working the solar plexus to relax the nerves to the stomach area.

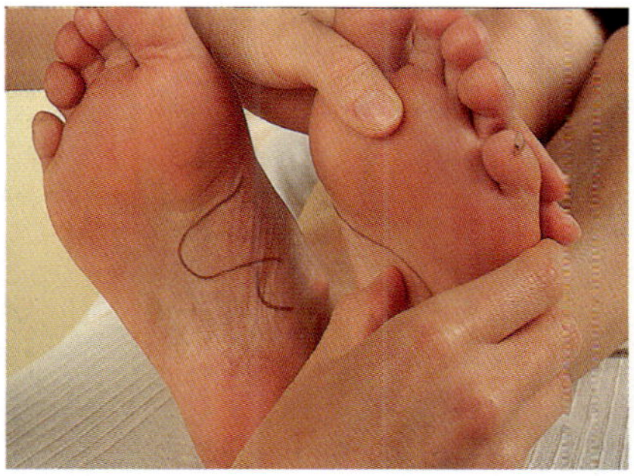

2 Work the stomach, where digestion really begins. Then work the duodenum, the first section of the small intestines.

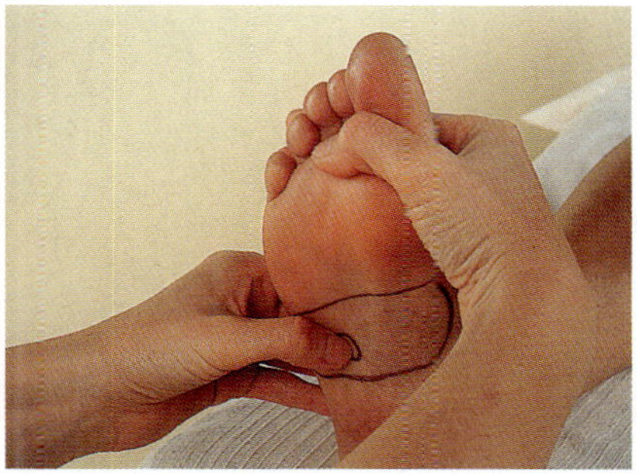

3 Work the liver and the gall bladder: the liver area is shown above, with the thumb rotating on the gall bladder reflex. These deal with digestion of fats.

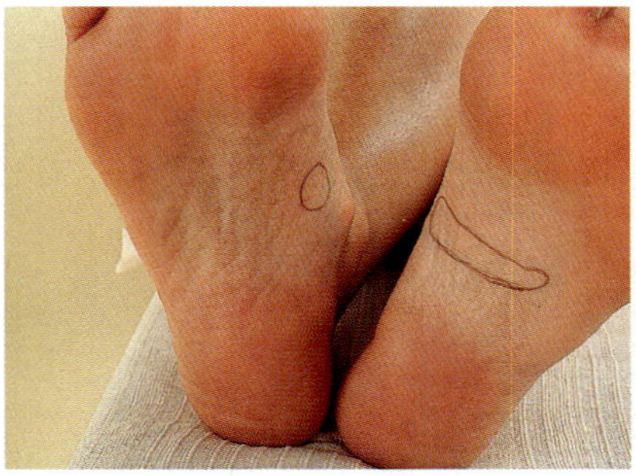

4 Work the pancreas which regulates the blood sugar levels and also helps aid digestion.

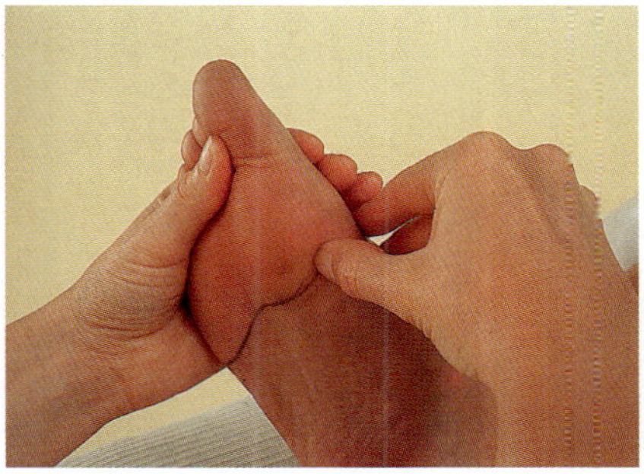

5 Ease constipation by working the diaphragm area in order to relax the abdomen.

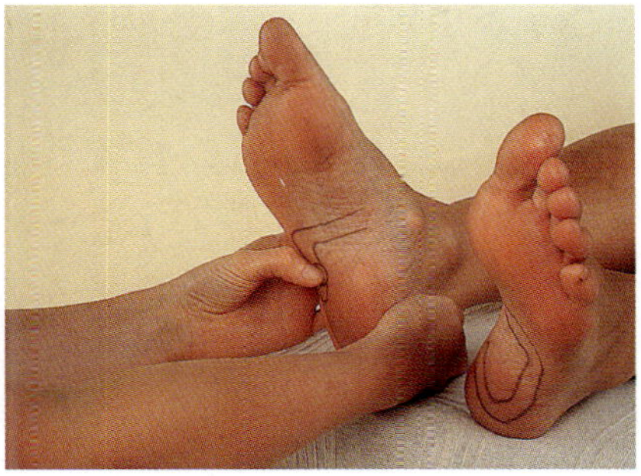

6 Pinpoint the ileo-caecal valve, which links small and large intestines. Work the colon or large intestine.

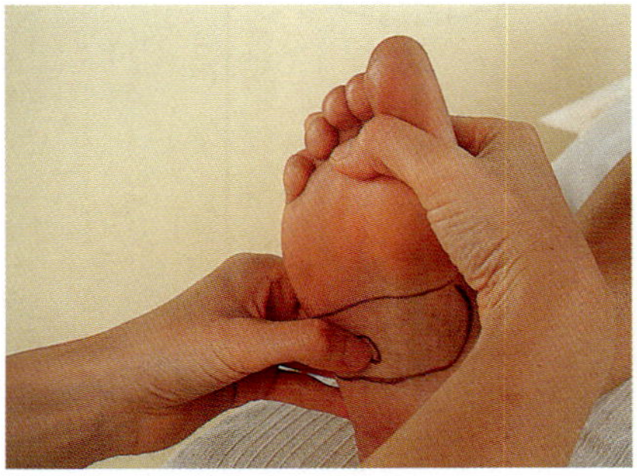

7 Work the liver and gall bladder: the liver area is shown above, with the thumb rotating on the gall bladder.

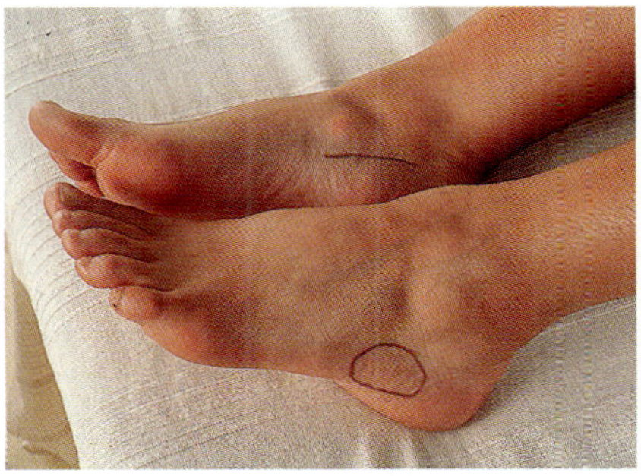

8 Work the lower spine and its helper areas for the crucial nerve supply to the colon.

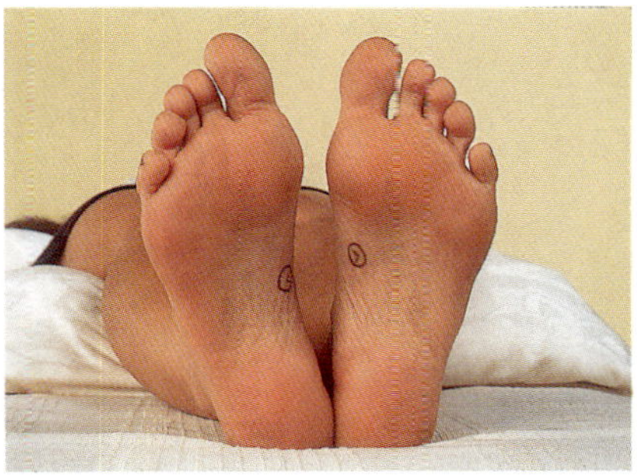

9 Work the adrenals for muscle tone. Rotate the reflex with your thumb in the direction of the arrows

charts

The foot charts are marvellous guidelines for interpretation. When you find a tender part of the foot you can look for that part on the charts and see approximately which reflex the tenderness lies on. Do bear in mind though, that every pair of feet is different and will not be the same shape as your chart. Also, the charts are two-dimensional and your body is three-dimensional. Nonetheless, the charts are every reflexologer's means to success.

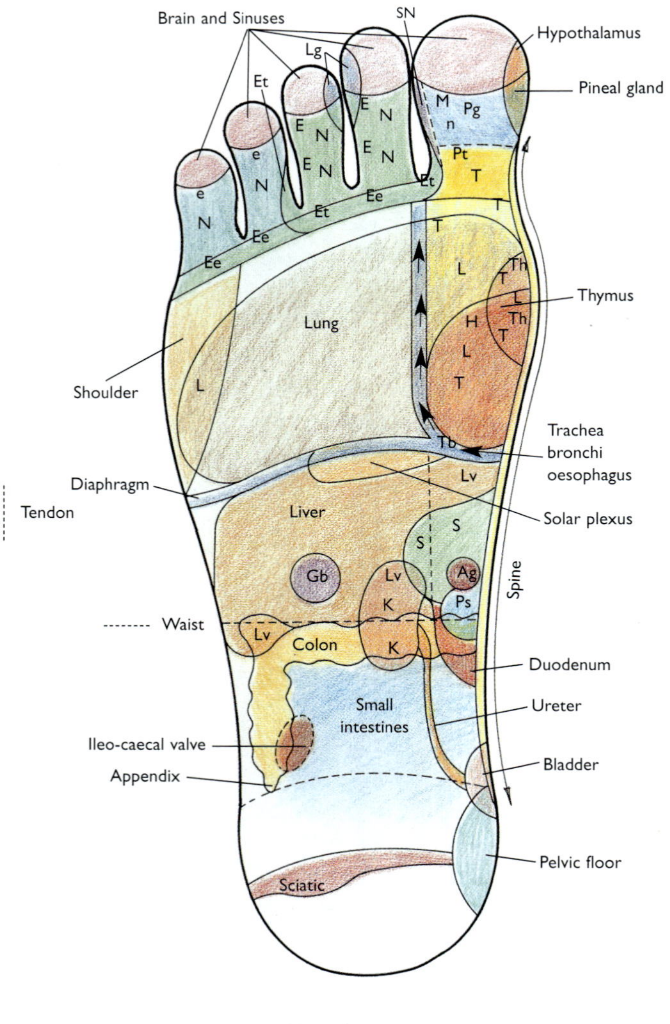

Right Foot

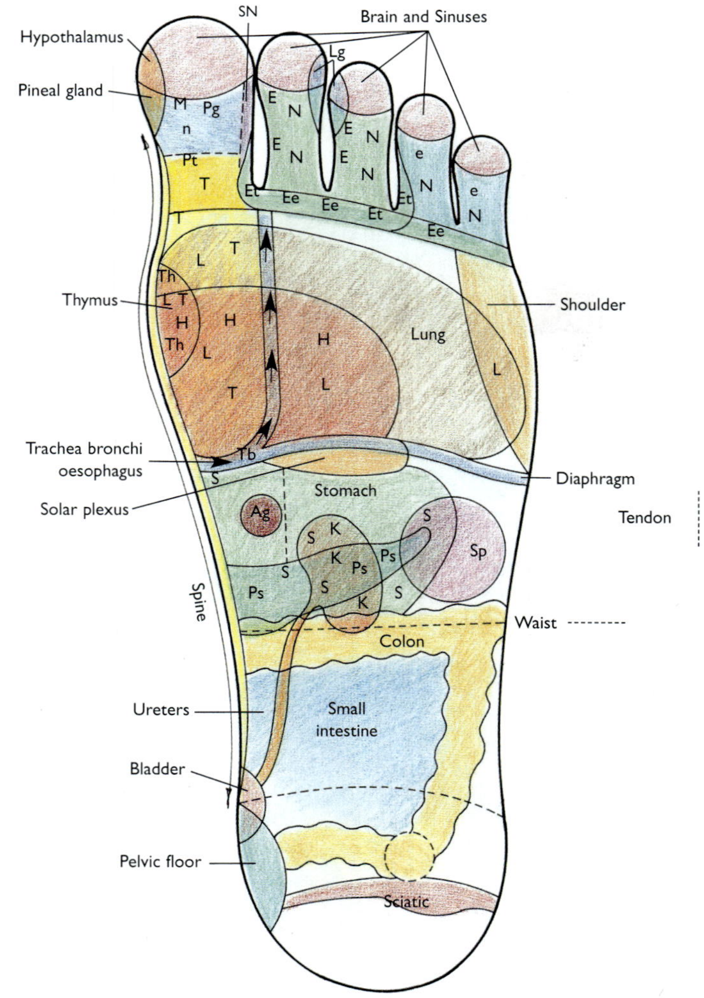

Left Foot

Key

Ag Adrenal glands	**H** Heart	**N** Neck	**Sp** Spleen
e Ears	**K** Kidneys	**n** Nose	**S** Stomach
Et Eustachian tubes	**Lg** Lachrymal glands	**Ps** Pancreas	**Tb** Trachea bronchi oesophagus
Ee Eye/Ear helper	**Lv** Liver	**Pt** Para-thyroid	**Th** Thymus
E Eyes	**L** Lungs	**Pg** Pituitary gland	**T** Thyroid
Gb Gall bladder	**M** Mouth	**SN** Side of neck	

TOP AND SIDES OF FOOT

The spinal reflex (bottom) is especially important and should always be massaged, and the reflex worked thoroughly. Not only is our spinal column our main boney support but it also contains the spinal cord, and through the central nervous system the whole body may be treated on the spinal reflex.

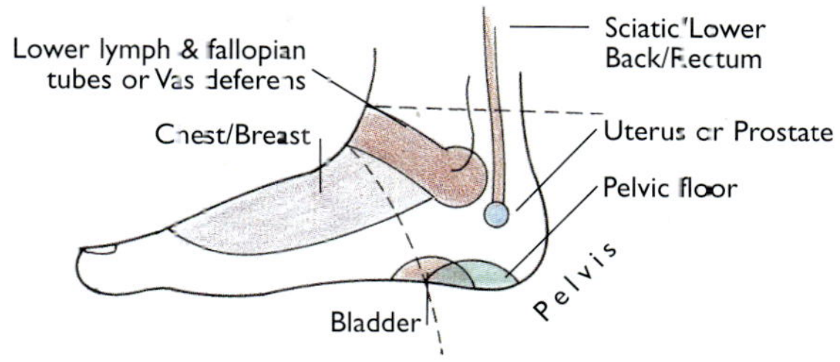

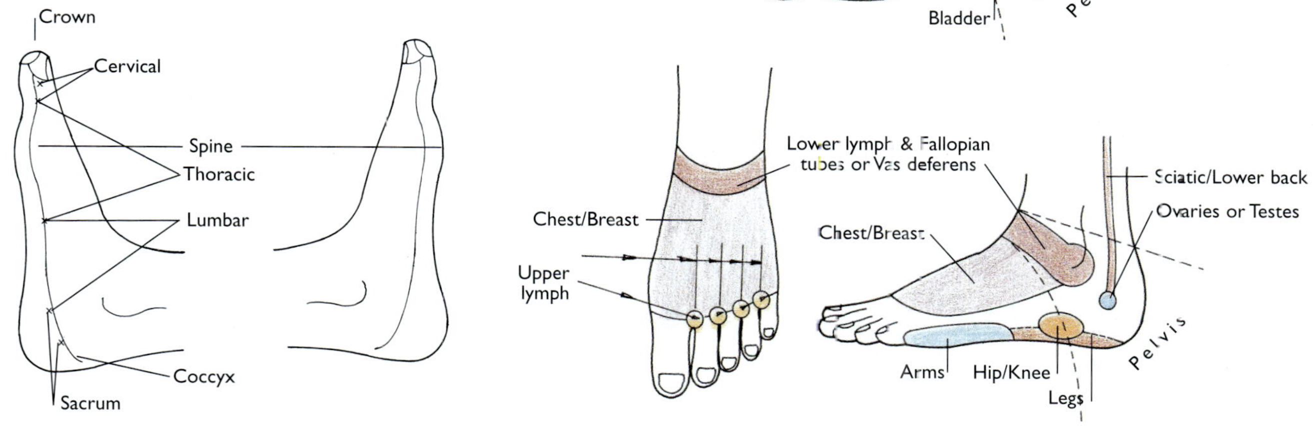

HAND CHART

The hands reflect all the body, as do the feet. They are a very different shape to feet, but once you have adjusted to that and learnt the basic layout, the location of reflexes is quite straightforward. Use the reflexes on the hand when it is impossible to work the feet, such as when only the hands are accessible or when the feet are damaged or diseased.

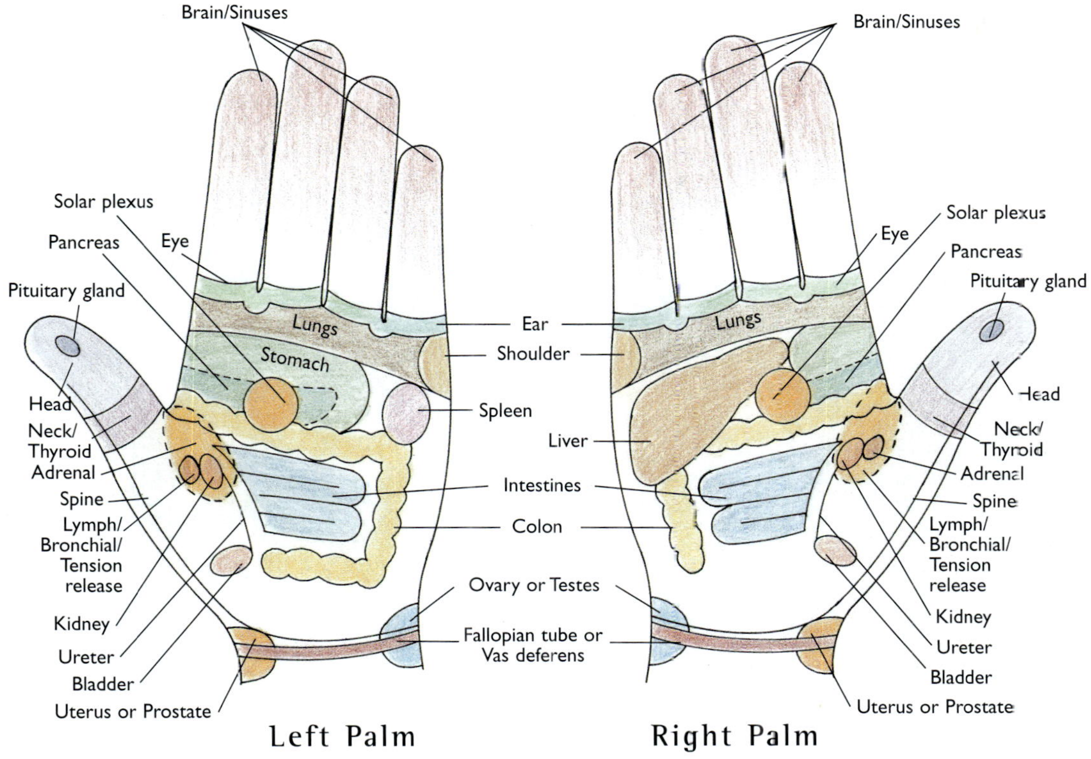

a
abdomen, 28, 61, 74, 84
anxiety, 40, 42–3
arms, 60, 74, 85
aromatherapy, 33–51

b
back, 61, 74
backache, 25–6, 36, 87, 89
baths, aromatherapy, 36
benzoin oil, 49
bergamot oil, 51
bladder, shiatsu, 55
blood pressure, 41
breathing, 43, 66–8, 90
burners, essential oils, 34, 37

c
chamomile essential oil, 49
chest, 61, 74, 83–4
circling, massage strokes, 16
circulatory system, 71
clary sage oil, 51
colds, 92
colic, 41
cramp, 89

d
digestive system, 44, 70, 93
DoIn exercises, 58–61

e
essential oils, 33–51
eucalyptus oil, 50

f
face, 59, 73
feet, 23, 27, 61, 73–95
"fight or flight" response, 40, 54
footbaths, 36

g
gall bladder, 55
geranium oil, 49
gliding, massage strokes, 16
grapefruit oil, 51

h
hands, 60, 95
head, 21, 59, 72–3, 74, 82–3
headaches, 21, 42, 90
heart, 55, 71

i
immune system, 69
indigestion see digestive system
inhalations, steam, 37
insomnia, 47, 90
intestines, 55
invigorating oils, 47

j
jasmine oil, 50
joint problems, 89

k
kidneys, 55
kneading, massage strokes, 17

l
lavender essential oil, 50
legs, 23, 61, 74, 85
lemon oil, 51
liver, 55
lungs, 55, 66–8

m
marjoram essential oil, 50
massage, 13–31, 35, 36, 58–63, 78–9
menstrual pain, 45
meridians, 55
migraine, 42
mood changing, 46–7
muscle problems, 41

n
neck, 20, 24, 58, 74, 82–3, 86
nerve pain, 89
nervous system, 64–5

o
oils, 14–15, 33–51

p
pain, 89
 see also backache; headaches; migraine; toothache
pelvis, 74, 85
peppermint oil, 50
percussion, massage strokes, 17
period pains, aromatherapy, 45
pine oil, 51
potpourri, 37
pre-menstrual problems, 45
pressure, massage strokes, 17
pressure points, 55

r
reflexology, 73–95
relaxation, 62–3
repetitive strain, 87
reproductive problems see women's health
revitalization, 21, 22, 27, 46
rose oil, 51
rosemary essential oil, 50

s
sandalwood oil, 49
scent, 33–51
self-massage, 19–23, 58–61
sensual massage, 30–1
sensual oils, 47
sexuality, 47
shiatsu, 53–73
shock, 43
shoulders, 24, 60, 86
sinus problems, 92
sleep problems, 47, 90
sore throats, 92
spine, 74, 82
spleen, 55
steam inhalations, 37
stomach, 55
stomach upsets, 29, 40–1, 44, 54, 88
strokes, massage, 16–17

t
tension, 20, 25, 72–3, 86
tension headaches, 42
throat, sore, 92
toothache, 89
travel calmers, 44
tsubo, 55

u,w,y
uplifting oils, aromatherapy, 46
women's health, 45, 91
ylang ylang oil, 49

Picture Acknowledgments

Main photography by Don Last.
Additional photography by: Michelle Garrett, Alistair Hughes, Lucy Mason and Debbie Patterson.

Thanks to the following libraries for supplying pictures: Garden & Wildlife Matters: 50TL, TM, BM, BR. The Garden Picture Library: 49BM, BR, TR; 50TR; 51TR, TM.